Scenes from Bourgeois Life proposes that theatre spectatorship has made a significant contribution to the historical development of a distinctive bourgeois sensibility, characterized by the cultivation of distance. In Nicholas Ridout's formulation, this distance is produced and maintained at two different scales. First is the distance of the colonial relation, not just in miles between Jamaica and London, but also the social, economic, and psychological distances involved in that relation. The second is the distance of spectatorship, not only of the modern theatregoer as consumer, but the larger and pervasive disposition to observe, comment, and sit in judgment, which becomes characteristic of the bourgeois relation to the rest of the world. This engagingly written study of history, class, and spectatorship offers compelling proof of "why theatre matters," and demonstrates the importance of examining the question historically.

Scenes from Bourgeois Life

_____

THEATER: THEORY/TEXT/PERFORMANCE

Series Editors: David Krasner, Rebecca Schneider, and Harvey Young

Founding Editor: Enoch Brater

Recent Titles:

Scenes from Bourgeois Life

Nicholas Ridout

University of Michigan Press • Ann Arbor

First paperback conversion 2022
Copyright © 2020 by Nicholas Ridout
All rights reserved

For questions or permissions, please contact um.press.perms@umich.edu

Published in the United States of America by
the University of Michigan Press
Manufactured in the United States of America
Printed on acid-free paper

First published in paperback July 2022

A CIP catalog record for this book is available from the British Library.

ISBN 978-0-472-13200-3 (hardcover : alk. paper)
ISBN 978-0-472-12688-0 (ebook)

ISBN 978-0-472-03920-3 (paper : alk. paper)

for Orlagh

Contents

Digital materials related to this title can be found on the Fulcrum platform via the following citable URL https://doi.org/10.3998/mpub.10181774

Acknowledgments

This book and its author have enjoyed a great deal of hospitality over the past few years. While an employer can hardly be described as hospitable, my colleagues and students at Queen Mary University of London have been generous with their attention and support, and I am very grateful to them all. I have particularly appreciated conversations with Shane Boyle, Faisal Hamadah, Caoimhe Mader McGuinness, Eleanor Massie, Michael McKinnie, Charlotte Young, and Martin Young on subjects related more or less directly to the material of this book.

I discovered the central figure of the book—the Trunk-Maker—while teaching a graduate course at Brown University, and the enthusiasm with which the students in that course shared my fascination with this unexpected discovery did much to sustain me, then and now.

I completed a significant phase of work on this book during a fellowship at the Huntington Library in 2016–17. I am grateful to the Director of Research, Steve Hindle, and to the other fellows at the Huntington, for the opportunity to do that work in a collegial and supportive context. Conversations with John Mee, Tiffany Werth, and J. K. Barret were especially valuable, and the historians among my fellows, especially Steven Hahn, Woody Holton, Bethel Saler, and Margo Todd encouraged me to place a little more faith than I had intended in the historical reality of Trunk-Makers.

In Los Angeles during that year I enjoyed both social and intellectual hospitality from Martin Harries, Daniela Hernández Chong Cuy, Virginia Jackson, Heather Lukes, Molly McGarry, and Alan Page. You were LA. Thank you.

The following year, while I was a Fellow of the International Research Center "Interweaving Performance Cultures," at the Freie Universität in Berlin, the community of directors, fellows, staff, and researchers offered the kind of stimulation and challenge that—along with generous financial support and a beautiful office—made my work a daily pleasure. I thank in particular the Center's director, Erika Fischer-Lichte, as well as Holger Hartung, Torsten Jost, Milos Kosic, Astrid Schenka, Claudia Daseking, and, for his cigar-related response to my talk at the Center's closing conference, Richard Gough.

I have also enjoyed several opportunities to share work in progress, and I am grateful to everyone who made these events possible, and everyone who came to listen and to talk back: Marta Dziewańska, André Lepecki, and Magdalena Lipska at the Museum of Modern Art, Warsaw; Branislav Jakovljević, Kellen Hoxworth, Jisha Menon, and Peggy Phelan at Stanford University; Michelle Liu Carriger and Suk-Young Kim at UCLA; Catherine Cole, Odai Johnson, Scott Magelssen, and Stefka Mihaylova at the University of Washington; Genna Gardini, Sarah Harper, Tatjana Kijaniza, and Vanessa MacAulay, organizers of Quorum at Queen Mary University of London.

It has been a pleasure to develop this project knowing that it was going to be published by the University of Michigan Press, and I am thankful to LeAnn Fields for her faith in it from the beginning. I am also very grateful to the series editors, David Krasner, Rebecca Schneider, and Harvey Young, for hosting it, and to two anonymous readers for their encouragement and questions.

There are, of course, friends without whose conversation over the years this book would not have turned out the way it did. Such contributions are hard to pin down, but their value is beyond measure: Lindsay Goss, Sophie Nield, Louise Owen, Alan Read, Janelle Reinelt, Andrew Starner, thank you.

Martin Harries, Joe Kelleher, Giulia Palladini, and Rebecca Schneider all devoted time and thought to reading parts of this book in draft form and discussing it with me. Each of you also enriched my life by cooking, reading, eating, drinking, smoking (one of you, not me), sailing, going to the theatre, disattending, thinking, and talking with me (even until dawn).

Orlagh Woods was my fellow traveler throughout, opening up a world of possibility. There's no way to thank her enough, but this book is dedicated to her.

Prologues

1. Scenes from Bourgeois Life:[1]
"A Box in the Theatre of the World"[2]

SCENE—Living room in a family home in an English provincial town at some point in the late twentieth century.

"A comfortably and tastefully, but not expensively furnished room."[3]

The layout of the room, its doors and windows, may be assumed or imagined.

Two sets of bookshelves either side of a fireplace hold a complete set of the plays of William Shakespeare, a complete set of the novels of Jane Austen, a volume of Macaulay's History of England,[4] *and "miscellaneous volumes of old plays, poetry . . . all the volumes have the look of having been read and reread."[5]*

On a low table in front of the fireplace there are a few items that look as though they are being read at the moment: a Blue Guide to Northern Italy, *a recent issue of* The Spectator,[6] *a copy of the* National Trust Magazine,[7] *and the Royal Shakespeare Company's Stratford-upon-Avon season brochure.*

There is a television and also a radio, neither of them very prominent and both seemingly switched off. Were either of them switched on, among the programs they might plausibly be broadcasting into this living room are news reports, travel documentaries, recordings or live relays of "classical" music, dramas set in living rooms, and reality shows about buying or building one's own house, cooking, or interior design. Were this the early twenty-first century, television programs about people in living rooms watching television might be added to this repertoire.

Coffee has just been taken. A coffeepot, cups and saucers, spoons, and a sugar bowl have not yet been cleared away.

There is no ashtray, but there could have been.[8]

From another room, nearby, the sound of someone playing the piano: Beethoven's Piano Sonata No. 13 in E-flat major (Op. 27, No. 1).[9]

Notes

1. See the work of Honoré de Balzac, in which the social world of postrevolutionary France is explored across numerous novels that together constitute the *Comédie humaine*, which Balzac organized into categories: *Scènes de la vie privée* (private life), *Scènes de la vie de province* (provincial life), *Scènes de la vie parisienne* (Parisian life), *Scènes de la vie politique* (political life), and so on.

2. "The private individual, who in the office has to deal with realities, needs the domestic interior to sustain him in his illusions. This necessity is all the more pressing since he has no intention of grafting onto his business interests a clear perception of his social function. In the arrangement of his private surroundings, he suppresses both of these concerns. From this derive the phantasmagorias of the interior—which, for the private individual, represents the universe. In the interior, he brings together remote locales and memories of the past. His living room is a box in the theater of the world." Walter Benjamin, "Paris, Capital of the Nineteenth Century," in *The Arcades Project*, translated by Howard Eiland and Kevin McLaughlin (Cambridge, MA and London: The Belknap Press of Harvard University Press, 1999), 14–26, at 19.

"The great novelty of urban life, in fact, does not consist in having thrown the people into the street, but in having raked them up and shut them into offices and houses. It does not consist in having intensified the public dimension, but in having invented the private one—and especially in having transferred the meaning of individual life, and thus also the standard for evaluating what constitutes experience, into this new domain. . . . [B]ourgeois culture is fundamentally a culture of private life, which is reluctant to identify and resolve itself entirely in great collective institutions." Franco Moretti, *Signs Taken for Wonders: On the Sociology of Literary Forms* (London and New York: Verso, 2005), 127.

3. Henrik Ibsen, *A Doll's House*, in *Ibsen: Plays Two*, trans. Michael Meyer (London: Bloomsbury, 2014), 23. Ibsen's "realist" dramas (including *A Doll's House, Hedda Gabler, John Gabriel Borkman*) are widely regarded as critical in establishing what would become a typical feature of twentieth-century bourgeois theatre, a theatre in which people spend their leisure time sitting in the dark watching other people work in the light, and in which—and it is this that Ibsen's drama epitomizes—they grow accustomed to the convention that the stage presents a version of their own living room. In 1886 Eleanor Marx organized a reading of *A Doll's House*, in which she played the role of Nora, with her husband, Edward Aveling, as Torvald and George Bernard Shaw as Krogstad. The reading took place in the living room of Marx's own home at 55 Great Russell Street, London.

4. Thomas Babington Macaulay's *History of England* is one of the prime examples of what has come to be known as "Whig" history. Named after a political party that was established in the late seventeenth century and came to dominate governments in the United Kingdom in the first half of the eighteenth, "Whig" history presents an ideological narrative of British history in which events are understood to constitute a gradual and desirable progress toward an ever more civil, prosperous, and unified nation. It is often associated with similarly optimistic stories in which a virtuous and moderate commercial middle class or bourgeoisie exercises political power to benign social and economic ends. Karl Marx (Eleanor's father) claims that Macaulay "falsified English history in the interests of the Whigs and the bourgeoisie"; Karl Marx, *Capital: A Critique of Political Economy, Volume 1*, trans. Ben Fowkes (Harmondsworth, UK: Penguin, 2004), 384–85, n. 88.

5. Eugene O'Neill, *Long Day's Journey into Night* (New Haven: Yale University Press, 1955), 11. O'Neill's stage directions are more extensive and prescriptive than Ibsen's, and in this case go so far as to specify numerous authors whose books are to be found on the shelves of the Tyrone family's living room.

6. *The Spectator* is a contemporary weekly political magazine. Its most high-profile recent editor has been Boris Johnson (1999–2005), who was later the most prominent Conservative "Leave" campaigner during the 2016 referendum on the UK's membership of the European Union. He was appointed Foreign Secretary in the Conservative government led by Theresa May, and subsequently elected as her successor in 2019, taking office as Prime Minister on July 24, 2019. Its name is borrowed from an earlier publication, a daily newspaper edited and largely written by Joseph Addison and Richard Steele (1710–14). Reissues of material from the original *Spectator*, with its fictional narrator, Mr. Spectator, were staple reading in many educated nineteenth-century British households; Addison, in particular, was adopted in the nineteenth century as a model for moderate politics, elegant and balanced prose, and an admirable (English) mixture of seriousness and levity. Among the authors to write highly appreciative accounts of Addison's work was Thomas Macaulay. In his day, Addison was a prominent Whig, taking senior positions in government, including that of Under-Secretary of State for the South (second in command to the equivalent of the contemporary Foreign Secretary). His biographer, Sir Peter Smithers, was the Conservative MP for Winchester (1950–64), Under-Secretary of State at the Foreign Office (1962–64), and then Secretary General of the Council of Europe (1964–69). It is sometimes suggested that Smithers was a real-life model for Ian Fleming's fictional spy hero, James Bond.

A less appreciative evaluation of Addison and *The Spectator* may be found in a review by the historian J. H. Plumb of Donald F. Bond's 1965 scholarly edition, in which Plumb laments of the prose that "it is as dreary if as smooth as an ocean of tapioca pudding.... [S]ententious platitudes stretch over page after page." J. H. Plumb, "The *Spectator*," in *In the Light of History* (London: Allen Lane, 1972), 53–56, at 54–55; this review was originally published as "Addison's *Spectator*" in *The Spectator* of January 21, 1966. (A fuller version of this critique is reproduced below, in Chapter II, "The Scene with the Spectator.") Plumb's *The Growth of Political Stability in England, 1675–1725* (London: Macmillan, 1967) was a significant contribution to the historical understanding of a period in which this "emerging class" came into being, and his account of the relations between class and political power at this time will be an important resource in the analysis that follows this first exposé.

7. This members' publication includes details of the many "properties" owned by Britain's National Trust for Places of Historic Interest or Natural Beauty and open to visitors. "It is fashionable to admire these extraordinarily numerous houses: the extended manors, the neo-classical mansions, that lie so close in rural Britain. People still pass from village to village, guidebook in hand, to see the next and yet the next example, to look at the stones and the furniture. But stand at any point and look at that land. Look at what those fields, those streams, those woods even today produce. Think it through as labour and see how long and systematic the exploitation and seizure must have been, to rear that many houses, on that scale. See by contrast what any ancient isolated farm, in uncounted generations of labour, has managed to become, by the efforts of any single real family, however prolonged. And then turn and look at what these other 'families,' these systematic owners, have accumulated and arrogantly declared. It isn't only that you know, look-

a

ing at the land and then at the house, how much robbery and fraud there must have been, for so long, to produce that degree of disparity, that barbarous disproportion of scale. . . . What these 'great' houses do is to break the scale. . . . They were chosen for more than the effect from the inside out; where so many admirers, too many of them writers, have stood and shared the view, finding its prospect delightful. They were chosen, also, you now see, for the other effect, from the outside looking in: a visible stamping of power, of displayed wealth and command. . . ." Raymond Williams, *The Country and the City* (New York: Oxford University Press, 1973), 105–6.

8. Tobacco, coffee, sugar, chocolate, and tea, were all colonial products adopted as mass luxuries in modern Britain from the seventeenth century, much of which was "swallowed [or sniffed or smoked] with ease" alongside other "neatly chosen morsels" at the very "tea-table" at which Addisonian "morality" might also be consumed by those members of the "emerging class" learning to live the "middle-class life": "Chocolate made of the best Cracco and Martineco Nuts, . . . 2s. 6d. per pound, all Cracco Nut 3s. per pound. Sold by Rob. Fary Druggist in Grace church-street; where Chocolate-Makers may be furnish'd with all sorts of Coaco [*sic*] Nuts"; *The Spectator*, September 19, 1711. "Bohee-Tea, Coffee Roasted, Chocolate all Nut or with Sugar, Ipococaan-Roots [an emetic found in Costa Rica, Nicaragua, Panama, Colombia, and Brazil], Jesuites-Bark [an antimalarial found in Peru], Sold by Robert Fary Druggist on London-Bridge, with great Encouragement to the Buyer"; *The Daily Courant*, January 24, 1707. *The Daily Courant* was a progovernment daily newspaper. Samuel Buckley, its proprietor and editor at this time, was appointed editor-for-life of *The London Gazette* on the accession of George I in 1714. *The London Gazette* had been the government's official newsletter since its establishment in 1665. Between 1705 and 1707 it was edited by Addison, in his role as Under-Secretary of State for the South, and then, at Addison's urging, by Richard Steele (to help him financially). Buckley would also print and publish *The Spectator*.

9. The piano joined (and perhaps superseded) the portable oil painting as one of the emblematic commodities for the bourgeois subject's self-understanding, especially once the industrial production techniques of the mid-nineteenth century (including the automated manufacture of ivory piano keys—here's another colonial product) had brought the instrument within the economic means of the middle-class household. Like the painting that allowed its owner to feel and imagine him/herself to be the owner of the framed piece of world laid out before his or her eyes by the artist, the piano could produce a feeling of individual command and self-possession. As Dieter Hildebrandt notes, "the piano emerged as the tried and tested universal instrument." It allowed a single player to play all the parts, to make the kind of complex polyphony that would elsewhere require the concerted efforts of many instruments.

At the same time, "the universal instrument emerged as the individual instrument without equal," in that, unlike the organ, upon which all the parts could also be played but which was firmly lodged in the public space of the church, the piano could be possessed privately, either as an item of domestic furniture or, in its concert appearances, as the vehicle for the exhibition of heroic individual virtuosity and power. In this respect, claims Hildebrandt, the piano was not merely symbolic of the high-achieving individualism of the bourgeois revolution in Europe, but it was also an agent in that process—"the true 'instrument' of this musical and social revolution," of which Theodor Adorno had designated Beethoven "the musical prototype." See Dieter Hildebrandt, *Pianoforte: A Social History of the Piano*, trans. Harriet Goodman (London: Hutchison, 1988), 11. For

6 • Scenes from Bourgeois Life

Adorno, Beethoven's music, exploiting the capacity of the pianoforte more thoroughly even than had Haydn and Mozart, embodies in the extensive "development" of its thematic material "the principle of the development as 'doing', accomplishing, something," which he characterizes as "bourgeois bustle." But it is free bustle, and this is what makes Beethoven "the musical prototype of the revolutionary bourgeoisie": his work produces "a music that has escaped from its social tutelage and is esthetically fully autonomous, a servant no longer." See Theodor Adorno, *Beethoven: The Philosophy of Music*, ed. Rolf Tiedemann, trans. Edmund Jephcott (Cambridge: Polity Press, 1998), 37. Pianos are played onstage in *A Doll's House*, *Hedda Gabler*, and *John Gabriel Borkman*, and appear prominently in domestic settings in several of Balzac's novels.

2. To Be a Spectator

A group of people, probably cohabitees of some kind, whether or not they are bound by family relations or some other legal fiction, are gathered, seated, and watching British television. They are looking, together, at something far away. In this particular scene they are watching Series 12, Episode 5 of Channel 4 Television's *Gogglebox*, broadcast on October 12, 2018. In this show selected groups of television viewers—cohabitees of some kind, whether or not they are bound by family relations or some other legal fiction—are filmed as they watch and comment on some of the preceding week's broadcast television. For this episode, the scene within this scene, the selected viewers—described on Channel 4's website, with that ironic tone that had become so characteristic of this channel and of British television as a whole during the second decade of the twenty-first century, as "Britain's sharpest critics"—are shown watching and commenting on the following: an episode of the daytime competitive auction show *Bargain Hunt*, in which Bez from the rock band Happy Mondays is disqualified for getting his sister to bid on items he is trying to sell; the latest installment of the hugely popular *Strictly Come Dancing*; a broadcast of the 1981 comedy horror film *An American Werewolf in London*; an episode of *Celebrity Island with Bear Grylls,* a reality show in which celebrities are abandoned by a popular presenter of survival shows to fend for themselves on a Pacific island, in which a vegetarian is inadvertently responsible for the death of a pig; the new online dating spectacular, *The Circle;* and a TV documentary about the catastrophic quantities of discarded plastic polluting the oceans, entitled *Drowning in Plastic*. They also comment on some political broadcasting, including an interview on the BBC's *Andrew Marr Show* with the leader of the Labour Party, Jeremy Corbyn, and Robert Peston's interview with the (by then) former Foreign Secretary (but not yet Prime Minister), Boris Johnson. The program might be said to have appropriated from the everyday lives of its viewers, into this space of television eating itself (which it always did, of course), that aspect of broadcast television which, in its heyday, made it the staple of much workplace social interaction: the idea that, with just a few channels (or networks) to choose from, one's friends, colleagues and acquaintances could reasonably be expected to have watched the same shows as oneself.

Of course, the spectator's experience of this program also involved commercial messages, including repeated "bumpers" for the program's sponsor—

Gtech (makers of vacuum cleaners, garden tools, and electric bicycles)—and, on this evening, advertisements for, among other products, Maltesers ("The lighter way to enjoy chocolate"), McDonalds, and the cosmetics brand Rimmel ("I think it's important to embrace who you are . . . live the London look"). This is worth commenting upon, for, as we shall see, on the one hand, the entanglement between advertising and the spectatorship with whose history this book is concerned extends back to its earliest years in the first decades of the eighteenth century, while on the other, the contemporary proliferation of occasions (or media) for spectatorship has made the "attention" paid to commercial messages of all kinds a vital (and monetizable) resource. The point is, perhaps, that we (spectators) had been living in an attention economy for about three hundred years before the hegemony of the algorithm.

The irony in Channel 4's description of its lead participants as "Britain's sharpest critics" is complicated. At one level, the term seems to be used to suggest that the "real people" whose nonspecialist commentary appears on television programs are not the kind of people one might ordinarily assume to be the nation's "sharpest critics." But on another level the term seems to recognize that the viewer-participants in question quite regularly offer incisive critiques of the television entertainment they are watching, as it were on behalf of other viewers, including those in the living rooms where others are watching them. In other words, they *are* experts: sharp and incisive in their understanding of the conventions of the television entertainment on offer, and of the social and political issues that arise in the flow of an evening's viewing. They are in fact, expert spectators, just like those connoisseurs of boxing whom Bertolt Brecht imagined might constitute the ideal audience for his new theatre; and because they function dramaturgically as proxies for the other viewers who are watching them, their designation as "Britain's sharpest critics" also makes it clear that all those who watch, even if we are not quite as "sharp" as they are, are also critics.

Clearly what matters most of all in this show is that it is the televised spectators who provide the entertainment. They are the stars. The people responsible for devising and developing for production this program format have clearly recognized that they live in a society in which everyone is a spectator, and in which spectatorship is the main way in which millions of people daily engage with the world around them. It will be my contention throughout this book that this state of affairs represents a continuation and development of conditions of spectatorship that were originally, and which remain today, theatrical, but that have—through various supposedly successor (or supplementary) media, such as film, television, and the diverse platforms accessible online—become more or less pervasive, at least for the bourgeoisie whose spectatorial habits are the subject of this book. It is part of the proposition of this book that, recognizing some historical continuity between the conditions of spectatorship prevailing at the beginning of the eighteenth century and those at the beginning of the twenty-first (when these words were written), is to acknowledge, first, that to talk about television is still to be talking about theatre, and second, that the spectatorship in question, however longstanding and continuous, remains historically contingent. In other words, it is the spectatorship of a specific time and place. The time is capitalism, the place, England.[1] Together they form the stage for these scenes from bourgeois life. The staging of these scenes aims to fashion from this history some conceptual tools for those who live such lives (and, indeed, those who do not), which might be useful for thinking about how contemporary political realities are represented for them.

What holds these scenes together is not what happens onstage, but what happens, as it were, in the auditorium, or to be even more specific, what happens between the two. A subject—a spectator—holds the two together; makes their relation; constitutes the distance between them. By way of a first attempt to describe this subject—who is, after all, the subject of this book—I want to think about a particular passage in Series 12, Episode 5 of *Gogglebox* in relation to a well-known early essay by Stanley Cavell, "The Avoidance of Love: A Reading of *King Lear*."[2] *Gogglebox* will pose the problem; Cavell will attempt to deal with it.

In the passage (or segment) from *Gogglebox* various of the onscreen viewers responded to the screening of a documentary about the plastic pollution of the oceans. In *Drowning in Plastic*, presented by Liz Bonnin, directed by Tom Watt-Smith, and which first aired on BBC One on October 1, 2018, flesh-footed shearwaters were shown being forced to vomit up large quantities of small pieces of plastic, or being cut open to reveal the accumulation of plastic in their stomachs. The onscreen spectators on *Gogglebox* responded with vivid physical shock and horror, recoiling from the image, turning from the screen, holding up their hands as if to push it away: "It's very distressing, even if we're watching it from our armchairs," commented one. "Jesus Christ, look at that," cried another, and, another: "I can't watch, I can't watch." Afterward: "It's really got to me, that." The images were indeed distressing, because they succeeded in dramatizing (one might even say, personalizing) a systemic environmental problem. They contributed to the communication of information about the problem with an affective power that the presentation of data, or even of images of the plastic in the ocean, would not have achieved. The suffering of others—in this case, small and vulnerable seabirds—was what the first set of spectators was given to deal with; the second set, the viewers of the scene within a scene, had to deal with both this suffering and the predicament of the first set. It is in its doubling of the spectatorial situation that *Gogglebox* invites consideration as an example of theatricality in other media. The *theatrical* presentation of suffering, of spectators' incapacity to do anything about it, and their resultant capacity to reflect (and act) upon that incapacity constitute the central problem of Cavell's essay. Although he is not as explicit about this as I have just been, Cavell is also thinking about theatre in relation to television, and, in particular, about the consequences of what has since come to be understood as the first properly televised war: the Vietnam War.

Cavell's essay offers, first of all, an extended reading of Shakespeare's *King Lear*, which, Cavell claims, "is dramatic in a way, or at a depth, foreign to what we have come to expect in a theater" (294). What does he mean by this? How is *King Lear* exceptional? The answer lies in its dramatization of the conditions of theatrical spectatorship. For Cavell, the play itself is concerned with failures of recognition, in which characters fail to see the world clearly because they refuse to let themselves (and their love for others) be seen. It is this refusal of self-exposure that explains what are, for Cavell, otherwise inexplicable moments in the play. Lear himself, for instance, appears unable to allow his love for Cordelia to be seen, even though (or because) his love for her is the most important thing in his life. Edgar delays letting his blinded and suicidal father know who he is, because he is unable fully to acknowledge the love he feels for him. The play's exploration of this kind of "avoidance" and its tragic consequences is an invitation to consider the plight of the theatrical spectator, for whom, as Cavell puts it, the characters onstage "are in our presence" whereas the spectators "are not in their presence" (306). Unable, therefore, to reveal themselves, the spectators find themselves in the same tragic condition experienced by the characters of the play. This condition "literalize[s] the conditions we exact for existence outside—hiddenness, silence, isolation—hence make[s] that existence plain" (307). Confronted with the suffering of others, onstage, spectators can do nothing, except make a full acknowledgement of that suffering. The feeling of helplessness that arises from this state of affairs comes from the spectator's recognition of both "the fact and the true cause of their suffering" (311).

The condition of the spectator, then, is one in which you feel powerless to act, separated from those whose suffering you watch. But it is not simply a matter of recognizing that you are powerless to act (that you can do nothing about Vietnamese villagers, flesh-footed shearwaters, or any of the systems of colonial violence or environmental destruction that they index); rather, it is to understand that the sense of powerlessness is not a necessary component of the real situation, but instead the result of a spectatorial situation that you (as the current incarnation of the historical category of the [bourgeois] spectator) have made for yourself, inserted yourself into. Theatre, then, offers itself as an alibi. In the act of telling you that this suffering should matter, really matter, to you, the theatre also tells you that there is nothing, really nothing you can do about it. And it is in this predicament that the spectator lives. Or, to be a spectator is to live with this experience.

Unless the spectator is watching *King Lear*, it seems. *King Lear*, in Cavell's reading, by making both its own and the world's theatricality "plain" to its spectators, can do what other theatre (which does not make this theatricality its subject) cannot: it arouses a kind of ethical desire to move beyond the condition of being a spectator to which both the theatre and the world—especially the world in which Cavell found himself in 1969, when mass media were dominated by images of neocolonial war—had consigned the citizens of the United States. At this point Cavell takes his argument in a direction that is both peculiar and very familiar. It is peculiar in that he appears to insist upon the need for "tragedy," presented in the text almost as a conscious entity—"it knows something" (321)—as an antidote by means of which both "our status as audience [and] . . . theater must be defeated" (321). But it is of course also familiar, as this is a line of argument he shared with his colleague Michael Fried, who wrote in a now much-debated essay that the imperative for "modernist painting" was that it should "*defeat or suspend theatre.*"[3]

Both Fried and Cavell want to restore the "presentness" that would enable spectators to stop being spectators, to reveal themselves to themselves and to one another, and to achieve, in Fried's term, a kind of "grace"[4]—which, for Cavell, might restore some capacity for political or moral action. For Fried, the answer is modernist painting, whereas for Cavell it is a "tragedy" that is not like any other theatre, unless it is *King Lear*. What might this "tragedy" be? My suggestion is that what Cavell sees in *King Lear*, but nowhere else in the theatre, is in fact something that a great deal of theatre holds, at least in potential: its capacity to compel upon its spectators a recognition of the pain of being the spectator to someone else's suffering (or any other experience, for that matter) simultaneous with the recognition that this experience of spectatorship (and pain) is not inevitable but historically contingent. In other words, both the social, political, or emotional relations represented onstage and the conditions under which spectators are invited to consider them (as entertainment) are the result of specific material and historical conditions, which are alterable. Cavell seems to think this, too, when—addressing the spectator's false choice between "generalized guilt" and "paralysis," on the one hand, and "convert[ing] the disasters and sensations reported to me into topics of conversation, for mutual entertainment," on the other—he writes that "[o]ne function of tragedy would be to show me that this view of the world is itself chosen, and theatrical" (320). Where I differ from Cavell, to the extent that I fully grasp his complex argumentation, is that I think that theatre always contains within it the capacity to undermine or cancel the effects of its own theatricality, by virtue of its capacity to direct spectators' attention to the historicity of the conditions of their own spectatorship. Had Cavell been thinking more about Brecht than about Racine and Ibsen, he might have reached a similar recognition that *King Lear* is exceptional only inasmuch as it is also exemplary.

The argument of the present book is precisely this: that there is indeed a view of the world that has been chosen by and for the bourgeoisie, which places at a spectatorial distance the world in which its own hegemony is the source of suffering, and which has strong affinities and historical connections to the practice of going to the theatre. Far from suggesting that the solution is to be found in tragedy, however, as Cavell does, or in modernist painting, as Fried might, I want to ask whether it might lie instead in attending to the historical circumstances in which such a view of the world came to be "chosen, and theatrical." One preliminary proposal, whose potential and limitations I will tease out in the pages that follow, is that the spectator's powerlessness—whether it be mine, or Cavell's, or that of both the "cast" and audience for *Gogglebox*—is in fact a constituent element of a distinctive spectatorial subjectivity, produced by the defensive self-construction of a colonial bourgeoisie, and that theatre (and the theatrical as it appears in other media) functions as a most effective technology for maintaining it. I will also suggest that, in this respect at least, the theatre often contains the seeds of its own defeat, arising from the ever-present possibility that it will reveal to its spectator-subjects that their lives, as spectators, are a matter of historical contingency rather than tragic inevitability. It is in the space opened by this contingency that the conceptual tools fashioned here will be deployed.

Notes

1. In fact I watched this episode of *Gogglebox* and wrote much of this book in Northern Ireland. This is therefore an opportune moment at which to clarify my use in this book of such terms as England, the United Kingdom (or the UK), Great Britain, and Britain. I will use "England" in two ways. First it will name the nation, with London as its capital city, that, along with Wales, entered into an Act of Union with Scotland in 1707 to form the United Kingdom of Great Britain, which would subsequently, after various colonial episodes, become known by the name given on the passport I hold—United Kingdom of Great Britain and Northern Ireland—and I will use the term "United Kingdom" to refer both to this state and its predecessor from 1707. "England" will also refer to that portion of the present nation-state that is England, rather than Scotland, Wales, Northern Ireland, or any other part of the UK (such as the Isle of Man, Jersey, or Guernsey): in effect, that part of the UK coextensive with the England that preceded the 1707 Act of Union. I will use (Great) Britain to refer to that part of the United Kingdom that is not Northern Ireland, or to the United Kingdom before the partition of Ireland in 1921: this latter usage will designate the imperial state whose formation through colonization was beginning at around the time of the Act of Union. My use of "England" here is therefore a little anomalous, in that here it refers to a space of the cultural imagination that typically involves an England-centric conception of the United Kingdom, based on the current and historical dominance of England within the UK, and the hegemony of what, as we shall soon see, Karl Marx would describe as the "classical form" of capitalist development, and which he (and Engels, who wrote of the "English Working Class") would identify with "England."

2. Stanley Cavell, "The Avoidance of Love: A Reading of *King Lear*," in *Must We Mean What We Say? A Book of Essays*, updated edition (Cambridge: Cambridge University Press, 2015), 246–325. The essay was originally published in 1969, at the time of the Vietnam War, which, as we shall see, is significant. (Subsequent citations to this volume are given parenthetically in the text.)

3. Michael Fried, "Art and Objecthood," in *Art and Objecthood: Essays and Reviews* (Chicago and London: University of Chicago Press, 1998), 148–72, at 160; italics in the original.

4. Ibid., 168.

3. Compassion

A theatre professor is on his way home from a Berlin theatre. On the U-Bahn he finds himself overhearing a conversation between two fellow passengers who have seen the performance he has also just seen. They are doing that thing that people do: comparing their impressions of the show. One of them seems to have been particularly interested by the nonfiction or documentary aspects of the production. His own aesthetic investments appear to be in film, and he comments that he was particularly pleased to witness, in this performance, that it was possible simply and sincerely for the performer to tell her own personal story. His interlocutor is not so sure. He's actually not so sure about his own response, or in his articulation of a response, but he is also not quite sure about how successful the simple and sincere storytelling had been. There was something about the way she told her story, he offers, that was a little bit "acted." The professor did not, of course, intervene in this scene. He only had a few stops to travel before he would get off the train, and in any case, he didn't do that sort of thing. But he found this an interesting uncertainty. It had the slightly odd and unexpected effect of instilling doubt in his own mind as to the sincerity of what he had seen and the extent to which it had been "acted."

He had assumed, from the start of the show—or even before he chose to buy a ticket to see it, since he knew a little about other work of its director, Milo Rau—that the show would be deliberately activating spectatorial uncertainty over the extent to which it represented the truth. He had savored that uncertainty during the course of the performance. Overhearing this conversation made him realize that at least one other spectator had been savoring something very different. What he took to be the film aficionado's certainty that the story had been a sincere presentation of truth made him doubt his own conviction that it had been something else. The anxiety this provoked in him was sufficient to make him go online when he got home to check some biographical information about the storyteller herself, which confirmed him in his earlier certainty that the production had, as he had thought, been playing in a corridor of uncertainty as regards its apparent truth-claims. The story told by the actress Ursina Lardi, in Milo Rau's *Mitleid: Die Geschichte des Maschinengewehrs* (*Compassion: The History of the Machine Gun*), ostensibly about herself, clearly included significant fabrication or appropriation of other people's experiences. In particular, the traumatic and self-loathing narrative in which "she" was forced by perpetrators of genocide to urinate on a Rwandan woman she knew personally before the woman in question was murdered, seems unlikely to have been a narrative from Lardi's own life, as there is no indication that she spent significant periods of time in Rwanda at the time of the genocide, which took place when she appears to have been either training as a teacher in Switzerland, on an internship in Bolivia, or enrolled at the Hochschule für Schauspielkunst Ernst-Busch in Berlin. The good thing about this, from the professor's point of view, was not so much that his own theatre-spectatorial expertise was confirmed, vindicating him in his bourgeois professionalism, while the film aficionado was revealed as naïve in his conviction that what he heard was entirely sincere, but rather that it restored to his own experience a certain kind of distance between himself and the Rwandan genocide. This was a distance that the performance had simultaneously established, bridged, and made available for contemplation. What the film aficionado's interlocutor had identified as the "acted" quality of Lardi's performance had something to do with the complexity of the experience.

Let me explain. *Mitleid* (*Compassion*) is a production that was created by Milo Rau at the Schaubühne in Berlin in 2016. Staged there in an arena-style configuration of part of its adaptable stage and auditorium space, on a stage piled with everyday detritus (abandoned plastic chairs, tires, electrical goods), it is a show for two performers, both of whom present monologues. The opening monologue is from Consolate Sipérius, who sits at a table stage right with a table microphone, a laptop, and a video camera. She speaks to camera, and her image is projected onto the center of the rear wall of the stage. She introduces herself and tells the story of her parents' murders in the Burundi genocide and her own adoption by a Belgian couple. She substantiates her story by displaying to the camera documents such as her passport and her adoption papers. She talks about growing up in an almost exclusively white environment. She reveals that she is now an actress. This monologue is short, no more than ten minutes, maybe less. She remains onstage as Ursina Lardi enters. Lardi is white, blonde, older than Sipérius (having been born, as online research revealed, in 1970). Her appearance, dress, and manner seem designed to suggest a cultured, fairly well-to-do European bourgeoise of the present day. Like Sipérius, she makes no allusion to the idea that she is playing anyone other than herself here. Indeed she makes it fairly clear that it is intended that the audience should understand her to be herself: she talks about traveling with "the director" of this production (whom she does not name) for research in the Mediterranean into the lives and deaths of migrants trying to reach southern Europe from the wars and economic catastrophes of Iraq, Syria, and Lebanon. She offers some opinions about the limitations of humanitarian NGOs and some cynical observations about contemporary theatre's attempts to address issues of political representation, noting that this show is part of the current fashion for theatre about refugees.

It is, I think, precisely at this point in the show (fairly early on, that is) that the question of her acting started to require some spectatorial attention. By contrast with the "simple" sincerity of Sipérius's self-presentation, there is something, as the spectator on the U-Bahn noted, "acted" about Lardi's. Are spectators expected to take (only) at face value her cynical remarks about the production in which she is currently appearing? There is an Ursina Lardi here: her name is in the program, and many of the audience are likely to have seen her before. (She appeared in four productions at the Schaubühne during the 2017–18 season in which the performance discussed here was presented, including Rau's most recent contribution to the repertoire, *Lenin*, in which she played the title role.) But there may also be an "Ursina Lardi": a slightly repellent character whom one is tempted to associate with former liberals who have recently sought security in that toxic brand of basic bourgeois racism that likes to advertise itself as realistic, hard-headed, and just a little bit iconoclastic. It is in the emergence of this persona and its slight difference from what Ursina Lardi might be imagined to be like that acting makes itself visible. Or, perhaps it is the other way round: there is something in her manner that suggests that something is being "put on" or "played," and that is what permits the emergence of the persona.

That Lardi follows Sipérius onto the stage also shapes the way in which Lardi is received, but the effect of the comparison is far from unambiguous. Sipérius's self-authentication—through the relative intimacy of her address to camera, and through the presentation of her official documents (assuming these are accepted as genuine by an audience momentarily hailed as some kind of official body)—initially serves to authenticate Lardi, too, as it establishes as a convention that the women who appear here do indeed appear as themselves. Lardi's discussion of her own role in the preparation of the production, supplemented with photographic evidence of her presence on research visits supposedly undertaken as part of that process, also works to consolidate the convention that she is speaking as herself. Lardi's video image appears where Sipérius's did, on the large screen center stage. Also, to begin with, she speaks from a lectern, as though she were a speaker at a conference of some kind, rather than a performer in a theatre. But although all these choices seem to work in favor of accepting Lardi at face value, the longer Lardi is onstage the more her mode of self-presentation comes to contrast with Sipérius's. As her persona—and the acting that seems to make it visible—starts to take over, the doubt it generates retrospectively contaminates the earlier authentication devices, opening up some slightly unnerving questions about the theatricality of ostensibly nontheatrical representations. Why accept that the photographs Lardi shows are of what she says they are, and not, for example, some entirely different trip, undertaken with people who have nothing to do with this production? Why, for that matter, accept as real the documents displayed earlier by Sipérius? The whole edifice of authenticity is crumbling. This is what happens when you put things onstage. Contamination. Did they not say they were actresses? What had he been thinking? Well, actually, this is exactly the sort of thing he had been anticipating; to be caught up in precisely these kind of questions.

The difference between the effects generated by Sipérius and those produced by Lardi may have something to do with different ways of using the camera. Sipérius's performance seems to have been calculated, in terms of tone and address, to generate the intimate effect of a personal disclosure directed to the camera. She does not look at the audience (*this* audience), she looks only into the camera (which she herself operates). The feeling that she is addressing *this* audience comes from the position of the screen rather from the position of either Sipérius or the camera. Or, rather, it comes from the conventions associated with a particular configuration of speaker–camera–screen–viewer relations, in which the elements are organized so as to make the onscreen speaker addressing the viewer directly the primary aim of this configuration. This configuration is familiar to most spectators, in the theatre or elsewhere, from television, and it continues to exercise a powerful "reality effect," even though most spectators would probably, if asked, express at least some uncertainty about the reality of what they see presented on television. Lardi's performance—in addition to being picked up as video—is addressed directly to the audience in the room, with its mediation via camera and screen organized as a secondary effect of its primary address. She speaks to the audience, and the audience sees and hears her doing so. The audience also sees her doing so, in close-up, onscreen. It is as though these two ways of watching her result in two performances, or, perhaps more precisely, allow an audience to see the performance for what it is, something that has been made for this particular setup, calculated for the effects it will have in this room—this room that is a theatre. Toggling between Lardi onstage and Lardi on-screen is to consider how a performance is produced rather than simply to attend to what is being said—to acknowledge how Ursina Lardi is producing "Ursina Lardi." This is not the television *dispositif* at all, although the question of television is clearly in the air.

The story Lardi tells of the production team's research in the Mediterranean appears, above all, to be the story of an attempt to get as close as possible to a reality previously seen only at a distance—in other words, a television reality. This story involves, in its most obvious move, traveling to Bodrum in southwestern Turkey to observe just how close the city's thousands of tourists are to the beach where the dead body of a three-year-old Syrian boy, Alan Kurdi, was found and photographed by Nilüfer Demir in September 2015. As though the problem with the photograph, which circulated so rapidly across multiple media platforms, had been that it somehow failed to get close enough to something you could call real. As though you'd get any closer to that kind of real by spending time in Bodrum among the tourists, going out to sea to look at where the boat the boy had been on had capsized, or, as in another moment in Lardi's story, showing up at migrant centers to observe that the young men she encountered there wore the same kind of clothes as young men in Europe. The theatre professor thinks that this sort of authenticity seeking is as limited as Brecht famously found the photograph of a IG Farben factory to be in its capacity to reveal the reality of the chemical company. In other words, neither the location (I am as close as I can be) nor the image (I am at a distance) have any particular claim on the truth. Milo Rau—almost certainly far from innocent of Brecht's observations on photographic realism—seems to be inviting the audience for *Compassion* into a position of relative immunity, in which moral and political judgment (and its attendant feelings) are suspended in the face of epistemic doubt.

The final part of Lardi's monologue pushes back against the comparative comfort in the face of suffering that this epistemic doubt might otherwise underwrite. Needless to say, it is this part that can most readily be identified as not having been derived from Lardi's own experience, since it concerns the story of "her" years in Rwanda at the time of the genocide, which, as the reader will remember, were not in fact her years at all. If not actually fictional, these days in the life of an NGO worker are presumably other people's experiences, gathered through a research process and synthesized as an autobiographical narrative to be presented by "Ursina Lardi." This means, of course, that it is going to be all acting from here on in. The theatre professor might say that it has been that way from the start. In any case, what Lardi acts now is the confused and traumatized recollections of a young woman who has been working as a teacher for an NGO, alternately grappling with the contradictions of her position (in a refugee camp she finds herself teaching men who were among the perpetrators of the genocide) and trying to keep her distance from the lives and deaths among which she is living (drowning out the sounds of mass murder by turning up her classical music really loud). Eventually she moves from narration to enactment, completing her transition from presentational theatre to fully embodied drama. She recounts a dream in which, on the verge of her return home, she is forced by a group of soldiers to urinate on a woman—formerly employed as her maid—whom they are, as she knows only too well, about to kill. She acts it out. Not without a certain theatrical self-reflexivity—about which more in a moment. She squats onstage—in her elegant blue dress—and urinates, commenting, as she prepares to do so, that she has never done this in public before.

This is a complicated moment. First of all, it is the moment at which the logic of acting is fulfilled most completely: the actual or imagined event of the script is represented in front of the audience, in action. But the action performed is one of those actions that are not routinely performed onstage: this is no simulation, it carries a certain charge of "realness" that is often held to puncture the membrane of dramatic illusion. Furthermore, Lardi's observation (casual but embarrassed) that she has not done "this" in public before, draws attention to the "realness" of the action by insisting upon the realness of the theatrical situation (I am doing this here and now in the theatre) rather than (or as well as) the reality of the action that it represents (which was, in any case, "only" a dream). In directing spectatorial attention in this way, Lardi (or, rather, the production) makes the action serve a disturbing double function. It is an invitation for spectators to imagine, with the intensity that enactment is supposed to induce more powerfully than mere narration, the moral ugliness of the moment being represented. But at the same time, the reference to the actual embarrassment of the performer of the action potentially serves to confuse whatever feelings a spectator may have about the act they are being invited to imagine with the feelings (of embarrassment) they may also be experiencing at watching a woman urinate in public. If these two feelings are somehow the same—interchangeable, indistinguishable from one another—what is the "compassion" that the bourgeois spectator might feel for the victims of genocide, beyond a feeling of awkwardness arising from having something they don't like—public urination or the fact of genocide—brought to their attention; the embarrassment of a comfortable distance momentarily bridged? This problem is by no means alleviated by the recognition that Lardi is, of course, "only" acting when she says that she has never done this in public before. This is theatre, after all, and she has done it repeatedly (as if for the first time) in theatres from Belfast to Colombo. *Compassion* is about genocide, about Africa, about migration, about the white European bourgeoisie and their political complicity with it all. In this respect it seems to articulate, through Lardi and "Lardi," some kind of conclusion: "We are all assholes." But in being about these things it is also, and not just for the theatre professor, about itself, about the proximities and distances of theatre, and about those distances and proximities in relation to those of other representational media.

There is a problem with all this. It's a problem that besets this entire project, and, indeed, might be said to confront all work in theatre and performance studies that tries to have something to say about spectators and what it is they experience in the theatre. After all, the film aficionado, as the reader will remember, seems to have been immune to the "acting" effect and the uncertainty it induced in the theatre professor. He may therefore be imagined to have experienced a distinctly different event from that described by the theatre professor: one in which a woman not only told the story of her own helplessness in the face of genocide, but also in which she reenacted in public her own obscene forced humiliation of another human being. An event of this kind is likely to leave this reenactment and the sense of its earlier historical reality as a much more powerful residue in the memory of a spectator than the rather more conceptual questions about representation and media that seem to have endured for the theatre professor. One might say that the film aficionado just didn't get it. But that would simply be to privilege one experience of an event over another, or to suggest, even, that specialist professional expertise somehow makes for better spectators. Neither of these can really be justified. In this particular instance, it might make more sense to conclude that the case is not proven, and to leave it at that. But the problem has wider ramifications. After all, the theatre professor need not be taken as representative or typical of bourgeois theatregoers. He may, for example, be "reading too much into it," as students have been known to complain when faced with theatre professors. But is this not, in fact, another way of describing precisely the subjectivity attributed by this project to the bourgeoisie in general; the critical-contemplative observation that always does a little more than taking this at face value (even if it is rarely able to move beyond the limitations of its own class-historical position)? Would it make sense, then, to suggest that the theatre professor is merely an intensified or specialized version of the bourgeois spectator? And then, of course, to notice that the theatre professor may be trying, over the course of this book—or, if we think of him as a kind of allegorical figure for, say, the humanities, over the course of the history of humanities research as a professional practice— to universalize his own subjectivity? He might still be insisting upon the repeated exclusion of other subjectivities, be they those of film aficionados, women, people of color, proletarians, or whomsoever?

He will have to live with that.

1 • An Essay Regarding the Bourgeoisie

This book asks, among other things, how theatre professors came to be. Where did they come from, and what was it that made them who they are? In other words, what were their conditions of production and, finally, is there anything that can be done to change them? The preliminary answer to these questions is that they were produced as a function of a transformation that took place in English life at a specific historical moment. They—or rather, perhaps, their various immediate and necessary antecedents—were produced as bourgeois subjects in the context of an emergent capitalist culture some time after the "Glorious Revolution" of 1688 (of which, more later). They came into their own as spectators of that culture, and they were formed, as subjects, at least in part, through their spectatorship. This book will devote many of its pages to considering the activities of just one exemplary figure, who will be made to stand for all the other spectators like him; for all the theatre professors, of course, but also for all the other bourgeois subjects produced through their participation in a culture that solicited their continual spectatorship. An early instantiation of this culture is often referred to now as the "bourgeois public sphere."[1] The exemplary figure—an inhabitant of this "sphere"—is commonly known as Mr. Spectator, and he was produced, in textual form, as the central character in a long-running serial fiction called *The Spectator*, edited and largely written by Joseph Addison and Richard Steele, between 1711 and 1712 (and, again, without Steele, in 1714). He will be the star, therefore, of the scene that follows this essay. This essay explores what it means to say, as I will, repeatedly, that this character is bourgeois, in order, later, to suggest, through some further scenes, how he (like his contemporary successor, the theatre professor) might be mobilized today as an ideal figure for a distinctive bourgeois subjectivity, and also, perhaps, how he might be demobilized.

Bourgeois

The word bourgeois, whether as noun or adjective, has often been intended, and received, as an insult. There was a time when this insult would have been directed at its target from a position of assumed social superiority, *de haut en bas*, referring, usually, to the pretensions of an *arriviste* who dismally fails to master the social performances required of a real gentleman. In theatre, the classic instance of such a figure is Monsieur Jourdain in Molière's *Le Bourgeois Gentilhomme*. No doubt this usage still persists today in the corners of the modern world still inhabited by remnant aristocrats, but it has been largely if not entirely superseded by a usage that captures what appear at first to be a very different set of attitudes, in which the bourgeois is to be despised for characteristics, behaviors, and values that are supposed in some way to represent the bourgeoisie's sense of superiority: an insult directed *de bas en haut*, as it were. It is worth pausing for a moment, however, to consider that this more recent and contemptuous usage is as often heard on the lips of the bourgeoisie as it is from those who identify as members of the working class. In other words, to condemn someone else as bourgeois may be a very bourgeois thing to do. This may always have been the case. After all, Molière was not a member of the nobility, even though his play was first presented at the court of Louis XIV. As an insult, then, the term "bourgeois" is clearly not a precise term of either political theory or sociology. Instead, it might be considered as an act of *disidentification:* a means by which a subject resists or repudiates the terms by which they are named by the institutions and the social order in and through which they live.[2] Although I may be, technically speaking, bourgeois, I don't behave in a bourgeois manner. I decry bourgeois taste. I defy bourgeois morality. To show that I do so, I use the term as an insult.

This disidentification seems to work in two ways. One involves a relatively elite distaste for both the aesthetics and the morality of the "mere" or ordinary or perhaps "petty" or "petite" bourgeoisie: a preference for kitsch over the avant-garde, for example, or commitment to "conventional" family arrangements. This need have no particularly political content. The other expresses a slightly more politicized position, in which bourgeois life and culture is condemned for its own elitism and, perhaps most particularly, for its self-satisfied and exclusionary possession of property and hegemonic social position. Both positions are common among left-wing or in other ways dissident children of bourgeois parents, who will typically castigate their parents for their bourgeois values and privileges while also constantly examining their own behavior and attitudes for signs of residual contamination. The bourgeois can be either staid, boring, unadventurous, lacking in refinement, obsessed with comfort and probably a little right-wing, or a little posh, snooty, champagne-quaffing, opera-fancying, insufficiently "down-to-earth" and either naively or self-interestedly liberal in social and political matters, depending on who is doing the insulting.

In British English, these uses of bourgeois are more or less exchangeable with disparaging uses of the term "middle class." In American English this usage is not available, since the term "middle class" has acquired a rather different and ostensibly affirmative value (referring to all the "ordinary" people to whom the speaker wishes to appeal—for votes, typically). There is also, in the USA, a term I take to be a derivation of bourgeois—"bougie"—used most often to describe the aesthetic dimensions of either homes or cafés and restaurants, and which, like the term "bourgeois" itself, suggests that there is also a well-established cultural habit, among Americans and other English-speakers, of thinking of the bourgeoisie as people who are a little more French than they ought to be.

This use of the French term in non-French speech has a distinguished history. For it can also be observed in the work of the nineteenth-century writer who has probably done the most to establish the term, both as a category of political analysis and as a term of abuse. In the standard English translation of the celebrated first volume of Karl Marx's *Das Kapital* (*Capital: A Critique of Political Economy*), the word "bourgeois" appears frequently, and serves to translate two different words in the German text: "bourgeois" and "bürgerlich."[3] The German word "bürgerlich" appears more frequently than the French word "bourgeois" in Marx's German: there are sixty-three occurrences of "bürgerlich" and thirty-eight of "bourgeois" and its cognate terms ("bourgeois" appears twelve times as a noun, once as an adjective, and seven times as part of a compound noun; "bourgeoisie" appears eighteen times). Nearly half of the appearances of the French word "bourgeois" and its cognates (eighteen) are in footnotes, and nine of these are instances of self-citation (most often from the *Communist Manifesto*). It is as though the French term is part of a running commentary, maintained by Marx alongside his principal text as a supplement to its main purpose, which is the sober analysis of the social and economic system to which he gives the name "capitalism."

While "bürgerlich" in Marx's text is regularly used as a term to describe works of political economy (the main theoretical target of Marx's critique), the word "bourgeois" is not used for this purpose, with one exception: an anonymous political economist, author of an "Essay on Trade and Commerce we have often quoted already," is described as the "most fanatical representative of the eighteenth-century industrial bourgeoisie," with the French word "Bourgeoisie" used in the original.[4] "Bourgeois" and "bourgeoisie," then, are typically used, in *Capital*, in polemical contexts, often with the intention to insult and also with an ear to comic effect. Those of us interested in thinking about the English bourgeoisie of the eighteenth century (readers of Addison, for example) might pay particular attention to the fact that Edmund Burke is condemned by Marx as a "durch und durch ordinärer [thoroughly ordinary] Bourgeois" (Chapter Twenty-Four), and that the historian Thomas Macaulay is described as having "falsified English history in the interests of the Whigs and the bourgeoisie" (Chapter Eight).[5] Fans of French politics will note the use of the term "roi bourgeois" ("bourgeois king") to refer to Louis Philippe.[6] In other words, the use of the French term is all about attitude: it conveys the writer's attitude to the person designated as "bourgeois." A quick survey of the compound nouns is also revealing: Marx writes in *Capital* of a bourgeois standpoint, a bourgeois interest, a bourgeois epoch, a bourgeois writer, a bourgeois doctrinaire, a bourgeois instinct, and a bourgeois class. Like its uses as an insult, these compounds almost always imply an attitude, or, one might even say, communicate an attitude about an attitude. The bourgeois in question has an attitude (a standpoint, a class, a text he or she has written, an instinct), and Marx's use of the French term on each occasion indicates his attitude to a bourgeois attitude. It is his own act of disidentification. It is beside the point, but like all supplements, perhaps, it is also very much the point.

The Capitalist Bourgeoisie

Probably the single most influential text for the dissemination of the term "bourgeoisie," however—as a political category, as a derogatory description, and also as a French import into another language—is an earlier Marxist text, which, as we have seen, Marx himself cites in *Capital*. This is, of course, the *The Communist Manifesto* (*Manifest der Kommunistischen Partei*) of

1848, which he coauthored with Friedrich Engels.[7] In Chapter Three of this text, the authors describe their own historical moment as the "bourgeois epoch," one in which class struggle—which, they have already maintained, constitutes the history of all hitherto existing societies—has now been simplified into a confrontation between two opposing camps:

> Our epoch, the epoch of the bourgeoisie, possesses, however, this distinct feature: it has simplified class antagonisms. Society as a whole is more and more splitting up into two great hostile camps, into two great classes directly facing each other: Bourgeoisie and Proletariat.[8]

At stake in this struggle, in their account of historical change, is ownership of the means of production. At its simplest, then, for Marx and Engels, the bourgeoisie is the class that owns the means of production, and the proletariat is the class that does the actual production.

Two important points deserve emphasis here. First, the bourgeoisie is not a "middle" class, sitting, as it were, between a ruling or upper class and a subaltern or lower class. Class, at least in this historical moment, is not a question of stratification, but a relation of conflict. This conflict, according to Marx and Engels's logic here, will only intensify, with a progressive polarization into these two antagonistic camps. The term "middle class" in English derives from a rather different understanding of class structure and social relations, and does not imply either the necessity or inevitability of class conflict. It might tend, instead, to foster an understanding of social relations in which progress toward social harmony is achieved by the emergence and eventual rise of a "middle class" capable of mediating or moderating class conflict between the classes it imagines as above it and beneath it. The political aspirations associated with such logic might be best summed up by the hopeful suggestion that "we are all middle class now," attributed by journalists either to the impeccably "bourgeois" leader of the Labour Party, Tony Blair, or to his much more plausibly working-class deputy, John Prescott.[9] They are aspirations for the successful administration of capitalism by a benign and managerial Third Way.

Second, the bourgeoisie described here by Marx and Engels is not a transhistorical category: the "bourgeoisie" here is the bourgeoisie in and of capitalism. It is to be distinguished from earlier social formations or classes, such as the urban merchants and traders of the European Middle Ages.

Although these bourgeois merchants were involved in the process that led, according to Marx, to the development of a fully fledged capitalism, or bourgeois society, it is their historical successors alone who, as owners of the means of production in this novel social and economic system, are being described here.

This second point is important: the precapitalist bourgeoisie created neither capitalism nor the capitalist bourgeoisie. Or to put it in a more properly dialectical way—and in recognition of Marx's own celebrated claim, in *The Eighteenth Brumaire of Louis Bonaparte* that "[m]en make their own history, but . . . they do not make it under circumstances chosen by themselves, but under circumstances directly encountered, given and transmitted from the past"[10]—the precapitalist bourgeoisie contributed to the making of capitalism, and were simultaneously made into the bourgeoisie, as we know them in Marx, by the development of capitalism. It is this understanding of historical causality that lies behind such propositions as Max Weber's, that the origin of the bourgeois class and the origin of capitalistic organization of labor are "closely connected . . . but is not quite the same thing. For the bourgeois as a class existed prior to the development of the peculiar modern form of capitalism, though, it is true, only in the Western hemisphere."[11] It may be found in Ellen Meiksins Wood's insistence that "there is no necessary identification of *bourgeois* . . . with *capitalist*," or in Cedric Robinson's argument that the bourgeois merchants of eleventh- and twelfth-century Europe, whose economic networks were shattered by the devastations of the Black Death, are not to be understood as the same class who started the expansion of primitive accumulation beyond European shores in the sixteenth century.[12] There can be a bourgeoisie without capitalism, it seems, but no capitalism without a bourgeoisie. It is the bourgeoisie with capitalism that concerns me here, since capitalism is where we are.

For Marx and Engels, then, the bourgeoisie is one of two antagonistic classes in capitalism, and it is defined in terms of its struggle to maintain ownership of the means of production, from which it derives its economic and social position. In this struggle, it is opposed by the proletariat, and this is a specific historical configuration. A third crucial point now follows. The bourgeoisie described by Marx and Engels in *The Communist Manifesto* has been the single most revolutionary or transformative class in history. At the same time it is also the most destructive of human capacity and potential. This double aspect is most vividly expressed in the most celebrated passage of

The Communist Manifesto, in which Marx and Engels affirm the following of the bourgeoisie:

> It has been the first to show what man's activity can bring about. It has accomplished wonders far surpassing Egyptian pyramids, Roman aqueducts, and Gothic cathedrals; it has conducted expeditions that put in the shade all former Exoduses of nations and crusades.... Constant revolutionizing of production, uninterrupted disturbance of all social conditions, everlasting uncertainty and agitation distinguish the bourgeois epoch from all earlier ones. All fixed, fast-frozen relations, with their train of ancient and venerable prejudices and opinions, are swept away, all new-formed ones become antiquated before they can ossify. All that is solid melts into air, all that is holy is profaned, and man is at last compelled to face with sober senses, his real conditions of life, and his relations with his kind.[13]

This potential for revolutionary creativity that is also a source of life-denying oppression is crucial for the understanding of "bourgeois life" that I am trying to reach in this book, and that is captured in so many instances of bourgeois cultural production. This is an ambivalence that does not come from being stuck in the middle, but arises, I suggest instead, from the intuition that everything that the bourgeoisie values and enjoys—and perhaps especially its most cherished cultural achievements, some of which might even be found in a theatre—are both produced and threatened by an underlying political struggle.

There is a further complication. Marx and Engels, writing in the middle of the nineteenth century, seem to present a vision of a world of absolute polarization, in which the development of capitalism leads to the formation of "two great classes directly facing each other," a process from which no one is exempt: either you are or are becoming the bourgeoisie, or you suffer proletarianization. Viewed from a twenty-first-century perspective this reads as a crude simplification of the class composition of capitalist society, especially in its suggestion that ownership of the means of production is the defining characteristic of the bourgeoisie. This would seem to make the bourgeoisie a very small class, indeed. For are there not now millions of people who might, however grudgingly, accept that they are bourgeois, but who do not own any means of production at all? What about all the teachers, doctors, lawyers, accountants, software engineers, game designers, and theatre professors who work for fees and wages? What is their place in the schematic history outlined in Marx and Engels's polemic? Does their existence testify to a deep flaw in the Marxist account of class struggle?

Not necessarily. What Marx and Engels claim, it turns out, is that in the establishment of their dominant position within capitalism—or, as Marx and Engels call it in recognition of that dominance, "modern bourgeois society"—the bourgeoisie has not simply created the proletariat, but has also co-opted in support of its own interests most of those who might once have worked according to different logics. In other words, as part of its ruthless transformation of the world and the profanation of all that was once sacred, it has desanctified the professions, making "the physician, the lawyer, the priest, the poet, the man of science into its paid wage-labourers."[14] What this means is that alongside the industrial masses of the proletariat, who, for Marx and Engels, possess the capacity to identify their own class interests distinct from and in direct opposition to those of the bourgeoisie, there is also produced a large body of people whose own economic interests at least appear to coincide with those of the bourgeoisie proper, and who also come to share with the bourgeoisie proper their dominant view of the world and social and economic relations. The point is not simply that the modern world is divided into those who own or do not own the means of production, it is rather that the modern world is dominated by those who own the means of production and who have also acquired, through their capacity to employ "the priest, the poet, the man of science," the means for producing the ideological materials that secure their hegemony. In other words, the desanctified professions have become the well-paid producers of bourgeois communications and culture (from advertising to performance art), and it is they, above all, therefore, who are responsible for the emergence of a distinctively bourgeois culture.

This is the process described by Immanuel Wallerstein, who notes an increasing lack of clarity, since the mid-nineteenth century, over precisely to whom the term "bourgeois" should properly be applied.[15] He attributes this lack of clarity to a series of historical developments that are not fully accounted for or anticipated in Marx's (and Engels's) accounts (even if, as we have just seen, at least one of them is anticipated as early as the *Manifesto*). These include *aristocratization*, the process whereby the bourgeoisie marries into or otherwise acquires assets and attributes from the aristocratic landowning class, from whom they are supposedly seizing power, but with whom they are also seeking a socioeconomic coalition; and the related failure of the bourgeoisie fully to establish a bourgeois state (to which he sees Britain as an exception). He also notes the process whereby ownership becomes separated from control of the means of production, giving rise to the emergence of what he calls a "new middle class," using this term somewhat interchangeably with "bourgeoisie": "In English we tend to avoid the term 'bourgeois,' preferring in general the locution 'middle class' (or classes)."[16] This "new middle class" may be most readily observed in the advanced capitalist societies, such as the United States, where Barbara Ehrenreich and John Ehrenreich have named it the "professional-managerial class," but Wallerstein also draws attention to a version of the same social formation in many "Third World" countries, where a cadre of civil servants with money makes many African states into what Frantz Fanon called "dictatorships of the bourgeoisie."[17]

Although this bourgeoisie is salaried—it lives off what it earns rather than off what it owns—it is still, Wallerstein insists, to be distinguished from the proletariat. One very obvious way: "The bourgeois I am describing . . . lives much, much better."[18] Why does this not make Wallerstein's bourgeois a rich proletarian? Because "somehow this bourgeois, product of bourgeoisification, obtains the surplus-value created by that proletarian, product of proletarianization. So if it is not control of the means of production, there must still be something this bourgeois controls which that proletarian does not." That something, Wallerstein proposes, is "human capital," acquired through education.[19] So, although the bourgeois of the twentieth century bears no resemblance either to the medieval precapitalist merchant or to the paradigmatic nineteenth-century figure conjured by Marx, "it is nonetheless true that the bourgeois as receiver of surplus-value is the central actor of the capitalist drama."[20] In this sense, then, this salaried bourgeoisie is as bourgeois as the bourgeoisie proper, if not more so. While the bourgeoisie proper (the owners of the means of production) may indeed be paying for everything that is produced in the theatre of the world, it is this wider bourgeoisie who are really making the scenes that comprise their bourgeois life. These producers of the scenes from bourgeois life are also its principal actors and spectators, and their ambivalence and disidentification is the subjectivity whose history (and whose hedonism) I am seeking to trace here, first of all, by attending to what has been called "the transition to capitalism."[21] How did England get to 1711 the way it did, in order to produce consumers of culture—such as Mr. Spectator and the theatre professors—as its ideal bourgeois subjects?

The "Transition to Capitalism"

Let me put paid, from the beginning, to the idea that the transition was accomplished by the bourgeoisie: that they brought their own life into being. They did not bring into being the historical circumstances that made them what they were. One way to retain clarity on this important point is to insist upon maintaining the distinction we have already articulated between the precapitalist bourgeoisie and the capitalist bourgeoisie. They are not the same people: not the same thing at all. The confusion, as I have already suggested, comes from the use of the term "bourgeois" to refer to legally privileged town dwellers in precapitalist Europe. Because Marx later adopted the term to refer to one of the two antagonistic classes in capitalism (and these are the people with whom I am concerned), there has been a tendency casually to conflate the two. This is followed, more damagingly, perhaps, by the stealthy (or unconscious) habit of introducing causality into what was really only ever a casual connection. It is therefore imagined that capitalism was something that these town dwellers—among whom, of course, there were merchants who look very much like our later idea of what a capitalist bourgeois might look like—succeeded in making for themselves. It is then assumed that they did so in order to advance their own economic interests, by breaking the shackles of a precapitalist mode of production with its fixed social order based upon the power of the landowners and nobility. This conflation of one bourgeoisie with another is made easier because the capitalism of the nineteenth century—the mode of production and attendant social system that Marx describes—appears to be dominated by an urban interest, and because its most obviously dynamic productive forces are those of industry rather than of agriculture. With this confusion and conflation at work it becomes possible to imagine a process of historical development in which medieval merchants in the towns of Europe slowly build a society based on attitudes and values already in existence in the fifteenth century and that enables them either to enjoy or to be offended, according to taste, by the realist dramas of Henrik Ibsen by the end of the nineteenth.

It is in response to Adam Smith's account of this process, to which Smith gives the name "previous accumulation," that Marx offers his account of "ursprüngliche Akkumulation" in volume 1 of *Capital*.[22] In Smith's account the simultaneous presence, in capitalism, of a group of people with sufficient resources to employ other people and the people available to be so employed, is explained by a prior process in which those with the inclination to do so accumulate wealth, while those without such an inclination prefer simply to exchange their labor power for a wage. The bourgeoisie, in this version of the prehistory of capitalism, are simply those more naturally endowed with the qualities of a bourgeois (they are dynamic, hard-working, and creative). This is why, in so much of the "common sense" talked about the virtues of capitalism, these qualities are routinely attributed to the bourgeoisie (or to the middle classes, or to "businesspeople"), while the same ideology tends to attribute failures of imagination and laziness to the working class. Clearly this attribution is entirely circular and self-justificatory. The bourgeoise become the bourgeoisie in capitalism because they always already were the bourgeoisie, fully equipped with bourgeois attributes. Their accumulation of wealth was simply the inevitable outcome of human nature. Marx's account, by contrast, emphasizes the violence involved in this historical process, which, far from being natural, as in Smith, is even in fact illegal, according to the society in which it takes place. For Marx, the primary historical example is England, whose historical development takes what he calls "the classical form." My interest in the English example arises not from any belief that it took a "classical form"; there have been and still are, after all, so many different transitions to capitalism that it seems highly contentious to designate any specific example as "classical" and all others as somehow derivative or abnormal.[23] I am interested in the account of the English transition because it is an English account of spectatorship that I am working my way toward in this essay.

For Marx, "ursprüngliche Akkumulation" is actually a process of violent expropriation. He retains the term "Akkumulation," however, presumably in order to sustain in the reader's mind the contrast between his and Smith's account, even though the use of "accumulation" tends to support a naturalizing account of the process he describes, rather than its violence and illegality, which is what he seeks to emphasize. Indeed, as the title of Part Eight of *Capital* in which the relevant chapters appear, indicates, Marx's use of Smith's terminology is already at a distance from Smith's own use of it: here it is referred to as "sogenannte ursprüngliche Akkumulation" (so-called original accumulation). As Rosalind Morris observes in an extensive critical consideration of Marx's analysis (and its subsequent development and revision by Rosa Luxemburg, Kalyan Sanyal, and David Harvey), its designation as "so-called" is part of a wider complex of translation and occlusion associated with the term. This includes the retention in the standard English translation by Ben Fowkes (inherited from the English version by Samuel Moore and Edward Aveling, published in 1886) of the term "primitive" for "ursprünglich," for which she suggests a better translation might be "originary." Although this does not carry with it the violent connotations of "primitive"— which are, in any case, dependent upon a distinctly racist conflation of non-European "primitive" people with violence—it is, she suggests, preferable to both Smith's "previous" and Fowkes's suggestion that, were it not for the convention established by Aveling and Moore, he would have preferred to use "original." Morris prefers "originary" because this suggests an ongoing capacity to originate, rather than a single point of origin that may be located in the past. As subsequent readings of Marx (such as those by Luxemburg et al., and also, as we shall see, by Silvia Federici) have frequently argued, locating this process of accumulation safely in the past is to ignore the fact that it continues in the present as a constantly self-renewing logical moment in capitalism's reproduction. In thinking about the term as it appears in the standard English text, it might be better to think of it as a process of so-called primitive and/or so-called original so-called accumulation.[24]

Stripped of these complications, the history of violent expropriation offered by Marx as his account of the "origin of capitalism" is fairly straightforward.[25] As Morris notes, it is also rather more unilinear and teleological than her own preference for "originary" (and the subsequent theorizations she records) would make it, not least because Marx presents it as a "prehistory of capitalism," rather than as a process that is part and parcel of capitalism's ongoing historical development. Marx's story goes like this. It starts in the countryside, toward the end of the fifteenth century. Landowners, seeking to generate additional income from their holdings, start to dissolve key aspects of the feudal system. They don't do this systematically, in order to transform their society by reorganizing its mode of production. Instead, they are acting in response to the social and economic situation in which they find themselves, making their history, not, as Marx would say, "under circumstances chosen by themselves, but under circumstances directly encountered, given and transmitted from the past."[26] The immediate historical circumstance for their action, in Marx's account, is that these noble landowners, who have already seen their resources depleted by the costs of European wars, identify wool production as a far more lucrative use of land than arable farming, and ride roughshod over feudal entitlements to seize as much land as they can for sheep runs. Peasants who have been tenant farmers on their land are dispossessed and thereby "divorced" from the means by which they produce their subsistence. Common lands, to which the same peasants, as well as others, also have rights of use, are also seized and enclosed by the noble landowners. At the same time all kinds of other servants and retainers are released from their traditional occupations and relations, and are also forced to find other ways of making their living. It is through this process—which constitutes a rupture with longstanding social convention and legal forms—that the two key conditions necessary for the development of a capitalist mode of production are met: the simultaneous existence of a group of people who possess only their labor power (the dispossessed peasants and retainers) and another group with the resources to employ them (the landowners). In effect, dispossessed peasants are thrown off the land they had once farmed as tenants, which is seized and enclosed by the landowners, who then hire the former tenant farmers as landless or "free" wage laborers. So, while the former peasants now labor for a wage, rather than to produce their own subsistence, the landowners start to function as capitalists, managing production with a view to surplus-value rather than the satisfaction of basic needs.[27]

This inaugurates the distinction upon which Marx has insisted earlier in *Capital*, between two different kinds of economy. The first is one in which commodity exchange is designed to satisfy reciprocal needs, which Marx expresses in the formula C-M-C, where a commodity (C) that you don't need is sold for a sum of money (M) in order to acquire another commodity (C) that you do need. The second is one in which the same process of commodity exchange is designed to permit the accumulation of money: M-C-M′, rather than the satisfaction of need through the purchase of specific commodities. The second formula describes how commodity exchange works in a capitalist mode of production. The trick or "secret" lies in the production of M′ (more money) where there was once only M. How does this process produce more money than there was before the exchange? By means of the exploitation inherent in the new wage relation, is Marx's response. The employer pays the worker M in return for the commodity C that is their labor, but is able to sell the (expropriated) product of that labor for more than the worker was paid to produce it. This happens over and over again and becomes the basis for a completely new mode of production, which is, as a totality, oriented toward the maximization of M (and its concentration in the hands of the owners of the means of production—at this stage, land), rather than the production of the appropriate quantities and distribution of C (at this stage, food, clothing, tools, etc.).

Marx's account of this English history of capitalism's agrarian origins emphasizes that what began as an illegal process—and which successive state bodies sought, from time to time, to check or reverse—was eventually accelerated and intensified once the state decided to take part, first, after Henry VIII's rupture with Rome (1536), by means of the expropriation of Church lands and property, and later, after the Stuart Restoration (1660), by the systematic distribution of Crown lands to the new landed capitalist class, the latest in a series of acts of privatization commonly referred to as "enclosure." Marx's story of this transition takes the "Glorious Revolution" of 1688 as a crucial moment at which a new state formation consolidated the transformation of the mode of production in a new political settlement. This would lay the foundations for the distinctive English (or British) capitalism that would be (or, because of the order in which he organizes *Capital*'s text, has already been) the principal object of his critique:

> The "glorious Revolution" brought into power, along with William of Orange, the landlord and capitalist profit-grubbers. They inaugurated the new era by practising on a colossal scale the thefts of state lands which had hitherto been managed more modestly. These estates were given away, sold at ridiculous prices, or even annexed to private estates by direct seizure. All this happened without the slightest observation of legal etiquette. The Crown lands thus fraudulently appropriated, together with the stolen Church estates, in so far as were not lost again during the republican revolution, form the basis of the present princely domains of the English oligarchy. The bourgeois capitalists favoured the operation with the intention, among other things, of converting the land into a merely commercial commodity, extending the area of large-scale agricultural production, and increasing the supply of free and rightless proletarians driven from their land. Apart from this, the new landed aristocracy was the natural ally of the new bankocracy, of newly hatched high finance, and of the large manufacturers, at that time dependent on protective duties.[28]

The private property that was first secured by means of successive acts of violent expropriation of feudal, common, Church, and even state property will from now on be appropriately protected by a new legal and political order in England. The violence will come to be forgotten, as private property itself gradually becomes the most natural thing in the world, and the basis not just for an enduring legal order but also for both formal philosophical thought and the arguably even more significant dimension of common sense. Private property ceases to be understood as the outcome of a historical process (such as that described by Marx) and comes to be understood, inasmuch as it is even thought about, as just the way things are in the world—things belong to people, and people naturally want to have things that belong to them, rather than, say, hold things in common.

The political promise of the commons has been a prominent theme in much recent political theory, especially among writers associated with or inspired by the autonomist or post-Operaist tradition.[29] Among these, Silvia Federici has been one of the most influential figures. Her articulation of the commons as a space for the instantiation of non- or anticapitalist political practices arises out of her own history of the transition to capitalism, which involves a significant revision of the story told by Marx in *Capital*. In *Caliban and the Witch*, Federici argues that Marx's history is inadequate because it focuses exclusively on the production achieved by means of wage labor, and therefore fails to take any account of the enormous amount of reproductive labor without which this production—to which, alone, value is ascribed in capitalism—would be impossible.[30] By reproduction Federici names all the work that does not contribute directly to the generation of value for exchange and does not therefore ordinarily attract a wage: in particular she insists upon the work normally done by women, often in the form of housework—hard, essential, and largely unremunerated. Her theorization of reproduction points toward the anticapitalist potential of the political organization of those whose work falls into this category, as an alternative to the conventional Marxist emphasis on the political power of the organized male industrial proletariat.[31] Federici's theorization also relies upon her revision of Marx's history, in that her account of the transition recognizes that the new mode of production depended not just upon the creation of a proletariat comprised of wage laborers (predominantly men) but, most significantly of all, upon "the destruction of the power of women which, in Europe as in America, was achieved through the extermination of the 'witches.'"[32] The systematic "degradation" of women during the extended period of the transition was facilitated by the separation of the workplace from the household and the monetization of the economy. These developments meant that women became increasingly dependent upon men, whose wages were used to purchase as commodities those necessities of life that were once produced by the household for subsistence. At the same time they consigned women to the reproductive labor functions of maintaining the household to enable wage earners to work, and giving birth to and caring for their children, who would in turn become vital participants in both the productive and reproductive workforces of the future.

It also meant, for both proletarian and bourgeois women, that as the institutions of the state were reorganized in line with the demands of capitalist production, state officials became increasingly interested in controlling and managing procreation. In the case of the proletariat, capital's interests lay primarily in making sure that there was a viable supply of labor power (numerous and healthy enough to generate the surplus-value necessary for growth and profits). In the case of the bourgeoisie, capital's interests were to guarantee the transmission of wealth from generation to generation, which necessitated comprehensive legal clarity regarding paternity (a fictional relationship that had to be elevated over the material relationship between women and children). The consolidation of the restricted family (of parents and their children) as the standard household under capitalism thus enabled both the social division of labor (between production for wages and reproduction for no wages) and the social control of women's bodies in the service of capital.

The witch-hunts of the sixteenth and seventeenth centuries were a violent consequence of these logics: their clear purposes were to deprive women of the political power associated with economic position while simultaneously taking control of sexual reproduction out of the hands of women and into the power of (eventually) state-appointed male professionals. This last process was also an instance of the relegation of women to the "wrong" side of an emergent division between intellectual and manual labor. This was not because men were not doing manual labor, of course, but rather because the new category of intellectual labor was organized in such a way as to exclude women. It involved, for example, the reorganization and recategorization of what we would now think of as spiritual, medical, and pharmaceutical knowledge and expertise, that had once been possessed and exercised by women (as healers, counsellors, midwives), into a new array of medical "professions." The medical professions were established alongside other bourgeois professions involving intellectual labor, sanctioned by state institutions and largely if not exclusively filled by men. Thus the consignment of women to the "private" sphere of the home progressively disqualified them from participation in the "public" sphere of intellectual life. This will turn out to be significant for the character of the public sphere, in which the spectators who are the topic of this book (the theatre professors, the bourgeois subjects) did their spectating and developed their distinctive ways of thinking about the world.

In most versions of the story of the transition, whether or not they approve of the bourgeoisie and the capitalism with which they are associated, the bourgeois is usually presented as the active, creative (or destructive) hero of the narrative: the agent whose initiative produces the world we now inhabit.[33] It is the bourgeois who drives the people from the land and herds them into the freedom of waged labor, who builds the networks of increasingly long-distance trade, and who develops the technologies of industrial production, first in agriculture and then in manufacturing. The bourgeoisie seize, they forge, they spread. Others respond: complaining, complying, contesting, and resisting. The bourgeoisie does capitalism to them, and sometimes they fight back. But another kind of story is also possible, in which the bourgeoisie may indeed create itself—though not, to return again to Marx's famous proposition, in circumstances of its own choosing. In this story the bourgeoisie is made by the circumstances in which it finds itself, circumstances that, as we have seen in both the histories offered by Marx and by Federici, involve the vital presence of an array of people against whom they must struggle, often violently, to define and differentiate themselves.

It might make more sense to say instead that the bourgeoisie comes to historical consciousness of its own existence, at least in part, as a defensive reaction to the existence and activities of a complex, differentiated, and very numerous body of men and women, of many different cultural backgrounds— the "many-headed Hydra" of sailors, the enslaved, indigenous rebels, laborers, and radical activists presented by Peter Linebaugh and Marcus Rediker in their history of anticapitalist resistance in the space of Europe's Atlantic colonization.[34] In Linebaugh and Rediker's story it is the bourgeoisie who fight back and, in the process, emerge into a sense of themselves as a class. It is this that makes the bourgeois Marx's "central actor of the capitalist drama."

Unless, of course, that drama is viewed on a different stage, from a different perspective, entirely: that of the global proletariat who might lay claim to being the real if unintentional "producers" of this capitalist world, and the motive force for the production of the bourgeoisie as a class. From the perspective, that is, of Caliban and the witch.

My concern in this book, therefore, is not with the bourgeoisie as a specimen that can be understood and examined (under some kind of empirical microscope), but with the bourgeoisie as a phenomenon that moves, takes shape, and exists in relation to others. In other words, this is not a study of a sociological category, or of a class viewed as the outcome of a process of classification through which it might be determined, upon the application of a set of objective criteria, whether any particular historical individual might be correctly identified as bourgeois. It is, instead, a study of a relationship and a struggle: the relationship to the "rest of the world" and the political struggle out of which the bourgeoisie came into existence. It is a relationship characterized, above all, by the production of distance. Bourgeois distance is both the necessary precondition for the bourgeoisie to come to know itself as a class, and also the deliberate, if not always conscious means for the maintenance of that class and its own economic, social, and psychic well-being. Two kinds of distance concern me here. The first is the distance of the colonial relation. This means, of course, the literal distance between Jamaica and London, for example, but also all the social, economic, and psychological distances involved in that relation. The second is the distance of spectatorship. In many of the specific instances dealt with in this book, this is the spectatorship of the modern theatregoer as consumer; but it involves a far more pervasive disposition to observe, to comment, and to sit (in judgment), which becomes, I will argue, characteristic of the bourgeois relation to the (rest of the) world, and which may also variously be understood as objectivity, reason, science, or even just common sense. To think of these distances in relation to one another is the project of this book as I attempt to take the measure of bourgeois life and its many self-representations.

Doing such thinking and writing about distances involves the ongoing production or reproduction of one further distance—critical distance. In one sense this is simply a dimension of the second distance: the distance the critic (or theatre professor) requires in order to make a judgment of an object, an action, or a state of affairs. There is nothing exceptional about this. It is in fact more or less built into what remains of bourgeois education in Europe and North America, readily observed across a vast range of texts and utterances, from the philosophical project of "critique" (the modern philosophical tradition generally seen as having been inaugurated by Immanuel Kant), in which people are enjoined to inquire rigorously into the very conditions of possibility of the world they inhabit and their own understanding of it, to the homilies of twenty-first-century liberal defenders of unlimited "free" speech in the universities, who insist that students' capacity to "think for themselves" is best nurtured by exposure to fascist hate speech on their campuses. But it is also a distance that can open up within the critic, the distance which that critic—such as, for example, the present author—chooses to mark out between a subjectivity apparently given by circumstances of class, race, and gender (which may include the condition, for instance, of being to all intents and purposes a bourgeois), and a subjectivity that might wish to make of itself something different (a revolutionary subject, for example).

Possessive Individualism and the Sexual Contract

But what does any of this have to do with Mr. Spectator, or, for that matter, the theatre professor? I mean, a little setting of the scene is fine, but is it really necessary to summarize the historical development of capitalism to understand what a theatre professor is? My response, predictably, would be Yes, of course it is. You can only see things (spectate) from where you are (most of the time). And where you are now is a time and a place in which you are in possession both of yourself and of your personal property. Me, myself, and my stuff. Unless you don't have any stuff, which means, unfortunately, that you are lacking in self, in which case, it's probably time you got yourself some stuff. This is how it goes in capitalism. There is a philosophical term for this commonsense (and as we shall see in due course, bourgeois) idea of the relationship among me, my self, and my stuff. It's "possessive individualism." This term—used by C. B. Macpherson in his study of seventeenth-century English political theory—expresses an essentially liberal understanding of what it is to be a person, in relation to other persons. Macpherson—writing in the 1950s and 1960s, for a book eventually published in 1962—discusses three key political theorists, Thomas Hobbes, James Harrington, and John Locke, as well a range of work by mid-seventeenth-century English Levellers (John Lilburne, Richard Overton, William Petty, Thomas Rainborough, and others). It is his analysis of Locke that has proven to be most influential, and which will be especially helpful for the present attempt to articulate the relationship between the historical development of capitalism and the figure of the spectator.[35] Locke was writing and publishing at precisely the moment at which the capitalist relations of production whose development Marx describes is establishing its political hegemony through the effective capture from 1688 of the English state by the "landlord" and "capitalist" appropriators. His work gives lasting philosophical legitimacy to a conception of the self—the possessive individual—that was gradually coming to be accepted as common sense.[36] It is this sense of the self that will underpin the emergence of the figure of the critic in subsequent decades, including the exemplary figure who will take to the stage (or rather, take his seat in the auditorium) in the next chapter—Addison and Steele's Mr. Spectator, who first addressed his public in 1711, and thereafter became a persistent model for bourgeois critical sensibility and practice even unto the present day, for theatre professors, among others. Locke, then, offers a bridge between the political and economic transformation described by Marx and the spectator as ideal bourgeois self who is the real subject of this book.

The crucial passages in Locke's *Second Treatise* are in his chapter on property. All "men" (this is Locke's language: the question of women and property is clearly a problem from the start, and I shall return to it shortly) are by nature free and equal, and their lives, their persons, and their possessions are all their own property. No one, he proposes—not even a sovereign power— may infringe upon a man's right to this property. A man may, however, increase his own property by means of labor. For any substance in which you mix your labor becomes your property. This is particularly important as far as land is concerned. Here Locke's relatively abstract and ahistorical political theory starts to suggest some direct and properly historical connection to the story of enclosures in England as recounted by Marx. For Locke, it is possible and, indeed, rational (in a dual sense of moral and expedient) that you should accumulate land as long as three key conditions are met: that your accumulation of land doesn't deprive others of the chance to accumulate land for themselves that is "enough, and as good"; that you don't allow any of the land you have accumulated to "spoil" or go to waste; and that you make the land you accumulate your own by working it yourself.[37] In a situation where land is finite, this would seem to place limits upon any individual man's scope for accumulation. I shall leave to one side, for the time being, the question of how these ideas are related to the appropriation of "new" lands in the American colonies, on which Locke had his own definite and enthusiastic views. However, even without invoking what David Harvey has called the "spatial fix" of colonial expansion, those limits may be exceeded under specific historical circumstances.[38] These circumstances involve the use of money: because a landowner who possesses more land than he can actually make use of himself, thereby risking that land going to waste, can avoid the land going to waste by storing its value in money (which is imperishable, never spoils). He may do this because, as his property, it is alienable. Because the accumulation and appropriation of otherwise unworked land increases the overall productivity of the available land, it creates opportunities for those without land of their own to make their living by working someone else's land. Which, in turn, reveals that the third limitation may effectively be ignored, since it is understood, in Locke's argument, that having your "servant" work your land is the same thing as working it yourself, at least insofar as property rights are concerned. Thus Locke's supposedly abstract account of how property works turns out to describe fairly accurately the actual historical conditions of English agrarian capitalism. The land is progressively appropriated and put to productive use, and those without land (property) of their own work the land for a wage, allowing the landowners to convert the fruits of their servants' labor into money, which they can then use as capital for the acquisition of more land or other means of production. Locke does not present this, however, as an account of economic relations in his own historical moment, but rather as a state of affairs that is entirely natural, and that can be produced purely by virtue of rational agreements—contracts—between individuals, and does not even require the formation of civil society or government institutions. Marx's account of this entirely unnatural set of property relations emphasizes the contrary: it was eventually by means of their effective capture of the institutions and instruments of government that the "landlord and capitalist" appropriators were able, in England, to intensify and consolidate their appropriation. In England a person in possession of some property (who will be white and male) will eventually be able to vote, and by virtue of the same underlying (philosophical, ideological) common-sense assumptions, to enslave and own other people.. This state of affairs will seem natural (at least to some people, and at least for some time): indeed, the right freely to possess one's own property was frequently advanced as an argument against the abolition of slavery.[39]

For the purposes of understanding the relationship between emergent capitalism and the self understood in terms of property, the key consequence of this state of affairs is, Macpherson claims, that "the man without property in things loses that full proprietorship of his own person which was the basis of his equal natural rights." Furthermore, the man without property who is, as a result, a member of the laboring classes, and lives "hand to mouth," lacks the time or the capacity to look up from the daily tasks of ensuring his own subsistence and to consider higher things.[40] Only those with property, it may be concluded, possess either the capacity or the inclination for participation in political life. They alone can enter into contracts—or, for that matter, participate fully in arts and literature. Under the historical circumstances described by Marx and by Locke, only certain kinds of people will ever become theatre professors: people with property.

This person in possession of property will also, in keeping with the commonsense acceptance of this state of affairs as natural, come to see all sorts of attributes of their self in terms of the possession of property. In speaking of houses, wives, furniture, the enslaved, children, land, paintings, they will refer to them with possessive pronouns ("my" or "mine), and others will reciprocate with "your," "yours," "their," and "theirs." This relationship between the self and those things that properly belong to it will also be extended, without anyone stopping to ask about what sort of possession might really be involved, to such things as experiences, attitudes, perspectives, and opinions. To have or to possess an opinion is an aspect of your participation in the social world. Like property, opinions also turn out to be alienable, in a particularly interesting way: while remaining yours, you can also put them out into the market. They may be acquired by participation (as a consumer, as a spectator, as a reader), accumulated, and then sold, either by means of an imaginary contract—for example, when your capacity to offer your opinion is the ticket of entry to a certain kind of public discourse—or, crucially, as economic sectors of leisure consumption and entertainment become increasingly significant from the early eighteenth century onward, by means of actual commodity exchange, in which you find you can earn money by selling opinion. You have the capacity to make something of yourself, in other words, out of the language you produce.[41]

This individual in question will be, as already indicated, a man, even if he will have been encouraged by the logic of the social contract in which he is engaged to think of himself without gender, or at the very least as someone the expression of whose thoughts and feelings, however determined or constrained by the limited perspective of a single, gendered (classed and racialized) individual, can legitimately offer himself as representative of the thoughts and feelings of people in general, including women. It is to the consequences of what Carole Pateman calls a "deep silence" on this aspect of the civil society (or bourgeois life), supposedly inaugurated by the social contract of liberalism (of which Locke is the most prominent philosophical advocate in English), that Pateman addresses her critique in *The Sexual Contract*.[42] Pateman's critique of liberalism (which applies equally to certain strands of liberal feminism as well as to many Marxist analyses) is that our understanding of the social contract as the enabling fictional origin of modern civil society omits its sexual dimension, and thus fails to see that patriarchy, as the subordination of women to men, is fundamental to the structure of that society, as well as to the nature of the individual in whom liberalism places its faith. In this respect her line of argument parallels Federici's critique of Marx and Marxism in *Caliban and the Witch*. Both Pateman and Federici insist that gender is incidental neither to the establishment of the capitalist mode of production nor to the production of the bourgeois subject. Indeed, one possible implication of their arguments is that gender as we understand it under capitalism is in fact a category produced in the establishment of the capitalist mode of production and by means of the modes of thought, such as Locke's, that the bourgeoisie have selected to assist them in understanding themselves. I shall return to consider this idea about the historical contingency of gender difference under capitalism more fully in the following chapter.

Far from inaugurating the historical movement by which women struggled to undo at least some of the structures of patriarchy (as much liberal thought would suggest), Locke's liberal conception of "possessive individuals" entering freely into contracts with one another to form a civil society together actually inaugurates a new form of patriarchy. In this "modern patriarchy," Pateman argues, the subordination of women to men is not based, as it had been in a prior "classic patriarchy," on religious arguments about the God-given status of men and women (derived, for example, from the story of Adam and Eve in the Book of Genesis), but rather on considerations of biological capacity. Gender difference becomes ontological rather than relational, and the only individuals considered capable of making contracts turn out to be the very same individuals who, as it happens, have started to contract themselves out as "free" laborers in the increasingly wage-labor-dominated economy of the new capitalism. These men—whose wages established them as the heads of households, upon whom women and children, who do not earn wages, thus become materially dependent—also enter into marriage contracts with women that enshrine this relation of dependency, and that go so far as effectively to deny married women any independent legal existence: under the common-law doctrine of coverture, married men and women are considered a single person, and it is the man who is that person.[43] The paradox inherent in this contractual understanding of the gendered individual (as with many such legal fictions, such as, for example, the US Declaration of Independence) is that it is unclear on what basis the woman supposed to be party to this contract possessed the capacity in the first place to enter into a contract.[44] Notwithstanding this technical complication, it is clear, from Pateman's account, that in this "modern" patriarchy, gender is understood in terms of differential capacities to act autonomously, to enter into contracts, to own property, to earn a wage, and to be represented in law. This is the "sexual contract."

The civil society that is constituted on the basis of this fictional contract is one in which a public sphere is entangled with and dependent upon a private sphere (neither of which are natural, of course), and wherein the public sphere is the one in which men predominate, while women are consigned to the private sphere, where, of course, they organize their work and subjectivities on terms that make them subordinate to men, and enable, by means of their subordinate reproduction of the means of life, the formation of the public sphere. Since it is primarily in the public sphere that practices of spectatorship take place, at least in the eighteenth century, and in which bourgeois subjectivity is produced and tested through relations with others, the subjectivity of the bourgeois spectator whose production I examine here is a subjectivity normally attributed to men, and associated with male characteristics and behaviors. It is the subjectivity of the individual. "The capacities that enable men but not women to be 'workers' are the same masculine capacities required to be an 'individual,' a husband and head of a family. The story of the sexual contract thus begins with the construction of the individual."[45] The individual is male. Where Federici's writing in *Caliban and the*

Witch emphasizes the violent suppression experienced by proletarian women, Pateman's contribution in *The Sexual Contract* is significant here for the light it sheds on the way the same historical developments are experienced—in many cases with less obvious violence—by women of the bourgeoisie. Although their class position may have given them a range of advantages and opportunities not available to proletarian women (or indeed proletarian men), it did not in any way protect them from the epistemological violence of being denied the capacity to be individuals and to participate, even as spectators, in the public sphere.

What was it like to be one of these people who understood themselves as being in possession of their selves and of their stuff; to be an individual, in other words? There's no room here for even a modest attempt to summarize the enormous range of ways in which bourgeois subjectivity has been produced, experienced, analyzed, historicized, and theorized over the hundreds of years during which people of this subjectivity have simultaneously ransacked the globe and agonized over the consequences of that ransacking. The scope of the present essay, which is more modest, saves me from having to do that work here. What I want to attempt, instead of such a survey, is to draw out those aspects of this subjectivity that will be most helpful to me in thinking about the specific feature of bourgeois life with which this essay is primarily concerned—to which I will give here the shorthand term "spectatorship"—and, indeed, that very special subcategory of bourgeois spectatorship called going to the theatre. What is it like, we might then ask, to be one of these people who understand themselves as being in possession of their selves and of their stuff, and to go to the theatre? What these people enjoy, I have suggested, is the capacity for producing critical distance. This capacity is, of course, as I have also suggested, historically contingent. But the subjects characterized by the capacity to produce for themselves this distance frequently assume that it is in fact the result, not of their own historical situation, but of some natural disposition of the world, which is, they imagine, ordered into the "me" and the "not-me," the here and the there, the subject and its objects. This capacity for producing and reproducing distance will be put to work in all sorts of bourgeois professional and managerial occupations, including by theatre professors, who are, of course, just one subset of a entire class of bourgeois philosophers.

Bourgeois Philosophy

The bourgeois achievement of critical distance, then, whatever its positive values (and in a world in which corporate media seek to dominate mass consciousness, these are not readily rejected *tout court*), is historically contingent. It ought not to be elevated to the status of a universal or transhistorical imperative. The objectivity, the reason, the science, or even just the common sense that are often unconsciously recognized and celebrated as the hallmarks of modern bourgeois sensibility (and its triumph over unreason, religion, superstition, and the lack of individual autonomy that attends such residues of the irrational) must also be historicized. In other words, they must be understood as partial rather than total rational accounts of the world, as accounts that come from a particular historical moment, and from a particular social and economic position within that historical moment. In this sense, then, these values are the values of a bourgeois philosophy. This is the influential argument developed by György (Georg) Lukács in *History and Class Consciousness*. Lukács's book (first published in 1923) is of particular importance for my project because it inaugurates a turn within Marxist thought toward considerations of culture and, obviously, consciousness. It offers a way of thinking about cultural production and the subjectivities of cultural consumers, effectively launching in the process a rich strand in Marxist thought in which questions of mediation and culture are of the utmost significance, and to which I will devote some further thoughts in Chapter IV below. In other words, Lukács's work—like that of those who both followed and contested his thought (such as Walter Benjamin, Theodor Adorno, and Bertolt Brecht, to name just three of his contemporaries whose work is most germane to the present project)—is concerned, as am I, with questions about how people feel and think about their relations to one another and to the world in which they find themselves.

By considering modern philosophy—and specifically the dominant figure of Kant—as bourgeois philosophy, Lukács associates its achievements (which, for him, are, of course, considerable) with what he argues is its fundamental blindness. Although Kant's philosophy (and that which follows it, including, inevitably, Hegel's) is "critical," in that it recognizes that there are limits upon its capacity to know the world "in itself," it is only able to be "critical" in this way by failing to question one of its own fundamental assumptions, or, in other words, by failing to recognize that the limits upon its capacity to know the world "in itself" are historical rather than ontological in character. These are limits that other people, in different historical circumstances, or with a different (class) relation to the same historical circumstances, might not share, or that they might be able to transcend. For Lukács, writing in 1923, those other people are going to be the proletariat. Bourgeois philosophy, however, according to Lukács, cannot see this, and consequently comes to understand the world in which it finds itself, and which it seeks to explain, as a fixed rational system rather than a constantly shifting and historically contingent complex of human relations. It fixes, or, to use the term that Lukács himself made central to this kind of thinking, it *reifies* these human relations. In so doing it makes itself—and with it the bourgeois subject more generally—into the passive observer (or even sometimes the victim) of an ostensibly rational system. Although this is in fact a system of the bourgeoisie's own making (in the Marxist account that Lukács follows), the typical bourgeois subject comes to experience and understand it as a natural and immutable structure entirely beyond its capacity for action or intervention:

> It cannot be our task to investigate the question of priority or the historical and causal order of succession between the "laws of nature" and capitalism. (The author of these lines has, however, no wish to conceal his view that the development of capitalist economics takes precedence.) What is important is to recognize clearly that all human relations (viewed as the objects of social activity) assume increasingly the objective forms of the abstract elements of the conceptual systems of natural science and of the abstract substrata of the laws of nature. And also, the subject of this "action" likewise assumes increasingly the attitude of the pure observer of these—artificially abstract—processes, the attitude of the experimenter.[46]

The bourgeois subject, according to Lukács, even in its most philosophically sophisticated incarnations, learns to become the passive and complaisant observer of the system it actually created. It may be worth noting that Lukács first presented ideas about the process of reification that is central to *History and Class Consciousness* in his 1911 *A modern dráma fejlődésének története* [A history of the development of modern drama], during the research for which he had read Marx's *Capital* for the first time in 1908.[47] So, to translate Lukács's idea into my own lexicon by way of this hint that there may be a connection between drama, or theatre, and reification as an experience of the world, I might say that this subject—the bourgeois subject—is defined by its spectatorial relation to a world of its own making. The bourgeoisie made the scene, but they think they are simply there to watch it play out.

Equally ambitious and far-reaching in its attempt to understand the subjectivity I am concerned with here is Alfred Sohn-Rethel's theorization of the "real abstraction." Sohn-Rethel, a much less prolific or well-known writer than Lukács (or, for that matter, Adorno, Benjamin, and other figures associated, as he was, with the Frankfurt School) was engaged in a complementary intellectual project, and had been among the circle of Marxist intellectuals who had been in regular conversation with one another in southern Italy in the early 1920s (where, via his friend Ernst Bloch, he had met Adorno, Benjamin, and Siegfried Kracauer). His major work, which was not published until 1970, was a book entitled *Intellectual and Manual Labour*, and subtitled, crucially, *A Critique of Epistemology*.[48] For Sohn-Rethel's aim was no less than to do for modern philosophy (in other words, philosophy since Kant) what Marx had done for political economy: to reveal the historicity that its claims to a transcendent universality had obscured. In other words, through a critique of epistemology—the practice of thinking about how we know what we know—he sought to show that the entire conceptual foundations upon which we (we "moderns," that is) have built our understanding of the world in which we live is historically contingent. It is the result of of material realities and human activities, not the product of purely mental processes of so-called rational thought. The most significant and, for Sohn-Rethel, foundational material reality of human action upon which our modern conceptual apparatus has been constructed is the practice of commodity exchange. This, argues Sohn-Rethel, is the human action that makes abstract thought itself possible, and its centrality to human life under capitalism is what makes abstract thought the dominant, seemingly natural, and largely unchallenged means we have available to us for understanding the world. Modern science, from Galileo onward, he claims, is made possible by this capacity for abstraction, and maintains its epistemological hegemony (as the only proper way to think about nature, for example) because of our failure to recognize the underlying abstraction as something that is historically produced (by humans in specific circumstances). Instead, the results of this abstract way of thinking are taken as given truths, as being themselves a part of the world or nature as it is, rather than as just one of a series of historical attempts to understand, explain, or control it. This is what he calls "bourgeois science," and the concluding sections of his book are concerned, as is Lukács in his efforts to develop a new philosophy grounded in proletarian class consciousness, with the construction of a new epistemology and a postbourgeois science in the context of a socialism in which commodity exchange is no longer the dominant logic of social and economic life. That is an epistemology whose historical moment is yet to come. The task here is to understand the implications of Sohn-Rethel's "real abstraction" for an understanding of bourgeois subjectivity in the present historical moment (of capitalist modernity).[49]

In commodity exchange two things change hands. These are usually two entirely real material things, each with their own distinctive properties of size, weight, texture, taste, smell, and so forth. In order for them to change hands as commodities, however, these qualities have to be momentarily set aside, in order for a relation of equivalence to be established between them. Their value must be established, and established in relation to one another. This operation of assigning and agreeing value, so that the two things may be exchanged, is, Sohn-Rethel argues—following, of course, Marx's analysis of the commodity in the opening chapters of *Capital*—a process of abstraction. Something that is not a physical or material property of either of the things involved in the exchange must be conjured into existence in the minds of the people exchanging them. This something—value—is an abstraction, but it is also real: it makes the exchange happen. This is not always readily apparent to the people making the exchange, however, so the existence of this "real abstraction" does not impinge in any significant way upon their consciousness: it has no effect, one might say, upon their epistemology. The exchange happens, and no one stops to think very much about how it happens. However, at a certain historical moment and at a specific historical location, the practice of commodity exchange intensifies to such an extent that it becomes useful to develop a new technology to make each transaction easier. That technology is money, and, specifically, the development of coins. The time and place, according to Sohn-Rethel, are the sixth century BCE in Miletus, a Greek Mediterranean port city (and Athenian colony) that had become the region's busiest and most important center for trade (or, as we have called it so far, commodity exchange).[50] The use of coins to facilitate commodity exchange (trade) brings the real abstraction to conscious attention for the first time. For here is an object that actually embodies the rather paradoxical nature of what is going on—the process through which material objects may move around (change hands) on the basis of a seemingly imaginary (immaterial) property alone (their value). The coin itself, made of silver, is meaningful and functional not for its properties as a silver object, but because it serves as a material representation of the value around which the exchange is taking place. This reality—the coin—is something that can be grasped, and whose paradoxical quality can be puzzled over. Once the paradoxical nature of the coin is grasped—the fact that it is a material object with a value that bears no relation to its physical properties—it becomes possible to realize that this is true of all commodities. The coin is not, in fact, a uniquely paradoxical thing; it is simply the most obviously commodity-like of commodities. From this recognition the abstraction that is at work throughout commodity exchange becomes available to thought, and can be used as the basis, Sohn-Rethel argues, for the development of those conceptual practices, such as mathematics and logic, upon which the entire tradition of Western thought depends. Sohn-Rethel attributes the groundbreaking philosophical work of Pythagoras, for example, to this historical development. This is the philosophical epistemology of which his project suggests itself as a critique.

But this account of Sohn-Rethel's book seems to attend only to his subtitle. What does this have to do with his apparently higher-level interest, signaled in his title, in the distinction between intellectual and manual labor? And what, indeed, does a process with imagined historical origins in a Greek colony over 2,500 years ago have to do with the specific historical circumstances in which the "bourgeois science" or bourgeois epistemology for which we are trying to account is actually to be found?

The answers lie in Sohn-Rethel's identification of the differentiation between intellectual and manual labor as one of the primary social consequences of an increasingly pervasive exchange abstraction. Following Marx's history of the emergence of capitalism, and with it a distinctively capitalist bourgeoisie, Sohn-Rethel argues that commodity exchange, for many centuries simply part of an ensemble of social and economic practices, establishes itself as the predominant figure for all social relations. Not only is the economy organized on this basis—upon production for exchange rather than production for use by the producer—but all relations between people come to be understood in terms suggested by commodity exchange. Moreover, as I have argued in my discussion of Marx's historical analysis, the beneficiaries of this process—the bourgeoisie—become who they are by means of their capacity not to produce the things, but to manage the processes of their production and their exchange. To those who calculate and plan, rather than to those who labor and make, fall the profits of this economic system. In other words, the capacity for abstract thought becomes a matter of class. The bourgeois, increasingly involved in those "intellectual" labors essential to the economy—accountancy, banking, management, design, advertising, and so on—comes to understand the world of things (including nature) as separated from their own being and consciousness; as a scene, in other words, to be observed, commented upon, and acted upon only indirectly, through the command and control of the physical activities or manual labor of others.

This epistemology places the knowing subject—the intellectual laborer in the broadest sense of the term, the bourgeois—in front of a scene. The scene presents itself to its spectator as something that has been made by someone else (by God or, as bourgeois science would ever more persuasively insist, by Nature). You do not intervene in the scene, except by techniques of observation, contemplation, and reflection. As Sohn-Rethel notes, modern science places "nature" under its microscope (or within any of the myriad observational and computational technologies at its disposal), derives its understanding of nature from its reading of the instruments, and records its findings in abstract terms, in mathematical or other specialist scripts. My claim throughout this book is that the practice of theatre spectatorship during the historical period under consideration comes to participate as fully as scientific inquiry in this epistemology (of abstraction and reification). In the theatre the bourgeois subject continues to learn what has been learned from the "scientific" contemplation of the world. The "world" onstage is a world made by someone else, into which only a fool (a peasant, perhaps) would try to intervene. The proper response, if there is to be a response at all, is to pass judgment upon the world, not to seek to change it. "The philosophers have only *interpreted* the world in various ways; the point, however, is to *change* it."[51] To accede properly to full (bourgeois) subjectivity in the theatre is to recognize and abide by this separation of oneself from the "world" of the stage—to become, as it were, a theatre professor. To fail to recognize or abide by this separation might involve a very different kind of "critical" activity and might make for a very different kind of theatre professor. It is the tension between these two modes of critical activity, and the role of this tension in the production of bourgeois subjectivity, that concerns me in the scenes that follow.

Notes

1. The term is taken from the influential early work of Jürgen Habermas, *The Structural Transformation of the Public Sphere: An Enquiry into a Category of Bourgeois Society*, trans. Thomas Burger (with Frederick Lawrence) (Cambridge, MA: MIT Press, 1991). It was originally published in German, in 1962, with the title *Strukturwandel der Öffentlichkeit: Untersuchungen zu einer Kategorie der bürgerlichen Gesellschaft*. The term "public sphere" is a translation (by Burger and Lawrence) of the German *Öffentlichkeit*, which carries no sense of a space with a particular shape, but indicates, rather, the condition of being in the open or public. Further discussion of Habermas and the implications of his work for critical and historical understanding of publicness, spectatorship, and bourgeois subjectivity will follow in the next chapter, "The Scene with the Spectator."

2. Here I am drawing, almost unconsciously, on Louis Althusser's influential account of the process by which subjects are produced, in his essay "Ideology and Ideological State Apparatuses (Notes towards an Investigation)," in *Lenin and Philosophy and Other Essays*, trans. Ben Brewster (New York: Monthly Review Press, 2001), 85–126. The most famous passage of this essay is what Althusser describes as "my little theoretical theatre," and what the present book might want to call a "scene" in which the process of becoming a subject involves responding (reiteratively) to the "hail" of an ideological state apparatus. This ideological state apparatus is embodied in Althusser's "scene" by a policeman who calls out, "Hey, you there," in response to which an individual—and "nine times out of ten it is the right one" (118)—will turn around. Thus a concrete individual is hailed as a concrete subject—one who is known and, as it were, named, by the ideology of the state. Two aspects of Althusser's "little theoretical theatre" will bear further elaboration. The first is his choice of theatre as the institution that supplies the metaphor for this account of the production of subjects in and through ideology. The second is his observation that this process functions effectively "nine times out of ten." I am grateful to Martin Harries for pointing out that this means a surprisingly large number of such hails actually fail. Not only does someone not intended by the hail turn around, but, presumably, while this is happening, someone else, for whom the hail was in fact intended, does not turn around. It is the latter subject who is performing an act of disidentification. I shall return to the implications of this theatrical disidentification in my own next scene, in Chapter II.

3. Karl Marx, *Capital: A Critique of Political Economy, Volume 1*, trans. Ben Fowkes (Harmondsworth, UK: Penguin Books, 2004).

4. Marx, *Capital*, 685, n. 4. See also Karl Marx, *Das Kapital: Kritik der Politischen Oekonomie, Erster Band* (Hamburg: Otto Meissner, 1872), 566, n. 33.

5. Marx, *Das Kapital*, 790, n. 248; Marx, *Capital*, 384–85, n. 88.

6. Marx, *Das Kapital*, 279, n. 133; Marx, *Capital*, 390, n. 99.

7. Karl Marx and Friedrich Engels, *The Communist Manifesto*, trans. Samuel Moore (Harmondsworth, UK: Penguin Books, 1967).

8. Ibid., 80.

9. This claim is frequently attributed to John Prescott. See, for example, Judith Woods, "We're All Middle Class Now, Darling," *The Telegraph,* January 22, 2010. But Prescott insists that it was not he, but Blair, who said it. See Prescott on Twitter, September 10, 2013, after the BBC journalist Emily Maitlis had repeated the familiar attribution: https://twitter.com/johnprescott/status/377569071752949760.

Owen Jones credits them both, in "We're Not All Middle Class Now: Owen Jones on Class in Cameron's Britain," *New Statesman*, May 29, 2014. Online at https://www.newstatesman.com/culture/2014/05/we-re-not-all-middle-class-now-owen-jones-class-cameron-s-britain (accessed August 18, 2019).

10. Karl Marx, *The Eighteenth Brumaire of Louis Bonaparte* (New York: International Publishers, 1963), 15.

11. Max Weber, *The Protestant Ethic and the Spirit of Capitalism*, trans. Talcott Parsons (Mineola, NY: Dover Publications, 2003), 24.

12. Ellen Meiksins Wood, *The Origin of Capitalism: A Longer View* (London and New York: Verso, 2002), 63; Cedric Robinson, *Black Marxism: The Making of the Black Radical Tradition* (Chapel Hill: University of North Carolina Press, 2003), 13–17.

13. Marx and Engels, *Communist Manifesto*, 83.

14. Ibid., 82.

15. Immanuel Wallerstein, "The Bourgeois(ie) as Concept and Reality," *New Left Review* 167, no. 1 (1988): 91–106.

16. Ibid., 96, 91.

17. See Barbara Ehrenreich and John Ehrenreich, "The Professional-Managerial Class," in *Between Labor and Capital*, ed. Pat Walker (Boston: South End Press, 1979), 5–45; and Wallerstein, "Bourgeois(ie)," 97, using a term from Frantz Fanon, *The Wretched of the Earth* (New York: Grove Press, 1964), 121–63.

18. Wallerstein, "Bourgeois(ie)," 104.

19. Ibid., 105.

20. Ibid., 106.

21. The widespread use of this term usually signals an engagement with historical research and writing in English in the mid-twentieth century—often referred to as "the transition debate"—that sought to enrich, complicate, and in some instances contextualize the account offered by Marx in *Capital*. Much of this debate, which was conducted in socialist journals such as *Science & Society*, is collected in Rodney Hilton, ed., *The Transition from Feudalism to Capitalism* (London: Verso, 1978).

22. Adam Smith, *An Inquiry into the Nature and Causes of The Wealth of Nations*, 2 vols., edited by Edwin Cannan (Chicago: University of Chicago Press, 1977). See also Marx, *Das Kapital*, 742.

23. For an important critique of those positions that assume a European history is the model against which other histories and other encounters with capitalist modernity are to be measured, see Dipesh Chakrabarty, *Provincializing Europe: Postcolonial Thought and Historical Difference* (Princeton and Oxford: Princeton University Press, 2008). For an analysis of the political and cultural functions of the idea of the "classical" itself, see Salvatore Settis, *The Future of the "Classical,"* trans. Allan Cameron (Cambridge: Polity Press, 2006).

24. Rosalind C. Morris, "*Ursprüngliche Akkumulation:* The Secret of an Originary Mistranslation," *Boundary 2* 43, no. 3 (2016): 29–77.

25. There is, of course, within the Marxist tradition alone, and focusing primarily on the English experience, an extensive literature on this transition, upon whose detailed insights I draw here fairly promiscuously. Key texts in this literature include Maurice Dobb, *Studies in the Development of Capitalism* (New York: International Publishers, 1947); Paul M. Sweezy and Maurice Dobb, "The Transition from Feudalism to Capitalism," *Science & Society* 14, no. 2, (1950): 134–67; Hilton, ed., *Transition from Feudalism to Capitalism*; Robert Brenner, "Agrarian Class Structure and Economic Development in Pre-industrial Europe," *Past & Present* 70, no. 1 (1976): 30–75; T[revor] H[enry] Aston

and C[harles] H. E. Philpin, eds., *The Brenner Debate: Agrarian Class Structure and Economic Development in Pre-industrial Europe* (Cambridge: Cambridge University Press, 1987); Wood, *Origin of Capitalism*; Henry Heller, *The Birth of Capitalism: A 21st-Century Perspective* (London: Pluto Press, 2011).

26. Marx, *Eighteenth Brumaire*, 15.

27. The key passage for this history is Marx, "The Expropriation of the Agricultural Population from the Land," *Capital*, 877–95.

28. Ibid., 884–85.

29. In addition to Federici, see, for example, Michael Hardt and Antonio Negri, *Commonwealth* (Cambridge, MA: Harvard University Press, 2009); and Cesare Casarino and Antonio Negri, *In Praise of the Common: A Conversation of Philosophy and Politics* (Minneapolis: University of Minnesota Press, 2008).

30. Silvia Federici, *Caliban and the Witch: Women, the Body and Primitive Accumulation* (New York: Autonomedia, 2004).

31. In a contemporary political context this anticapitalist proletariat might include industrial and agricultural laborers, care workers (many of whom, in Europe and North America, are migrants), as well as all kinds of other precarious, contract, and unwaged workers.

32. Federici, *Caliban and the Witch*, 63; for such "degradation" during the transition, 61–131. The conjunction of "Caliban," as a figure for all the laborers in the production facilities of the capitalist colonial "West," with "the Witch," as a figure for women and their knowledge of the world, indicates the character of this potential political alliance. (In *The Tempest*, act I, scene 2], "the foul witch Sycorax" was, of course, Caliban's mother.)

33. Such narratives are, of course, prevalent in those texts that celebrate the virtues of capitalism, among which a series of related books by Deirdre McCloskey have been some of the most successful. See, for example, Deirdre McCloskey, *The Bourgeois Virtues: Ethics for an Age of Commerce* (Chicago: University of Chicago Press, 2006) and *Bourgeois Equality: How Ideas, Not Capital or Institutions, Enriched the World* (Chicago: University of Chicago Press, 2016).

34. Peter Linebaugh and Marcus Rediker, *The Many-Headed Hydra: Sailors, Slaves, Commoners, and the Hidden History of the Revolutionary Atlantic* (London and New York: Verso, 2003).

35. C. B. Macpherson, *The Political Theory of Possessive Individualism: Hobbes to Locke* (Oxford: Clarendon, 1962). See also Neal Wood, *The Politics of John Locke's Philosophy: A Social Study of "An Essay Concerning Human Understanding"* (Berkeley and Los Angeles: University of California Press, 1983) and *John Locke and Agrarian Capitalism* (Berkeley and Los Angeles: University of California Press, 1984).

36. John Locke, *Two Treatises of Government*, ed. Peter Laslett (Cambridge: Cambridge University Press, 1960).

37. Ibid., *Second Treatise*, "Of Property," esp. 290–1, §§32–34.

38. David Harvey, *The Limits to Capital* (Oxford: Blackwell, 1982), 415.

39. See, inter alia, David Brion Davis, *The Problem of Slavery in the Age of Revolution, 1770–1823* (Oxford: Oxford University Press, 1999).

40. Macpherson, *Political Theory*, 230–31.

41. This capacity to make your self through your use of language is explored at length in Stephen Greenblatt, *Renaissance Self-Fashioning: From More to Shakespeare* (Chicago: University of Chicago Press, 1980).

42. Carole Pateman, *The Sexual Contract* (Cambridge: Polity Press, 1988).

43. Ibid., 37, 90–100.

44. I am thinking here of Derrida's essay on the US Declaration, in which he explores the founding contradiction of a document that no one who signed it had, at the time of signing it, the authority to do so, but which they conferred, as it were, upon themselves in the act of signing. See Jacques Derrida, "Declarations of Independence," *New Political Science* 7, no. 1: 7–15.

45. Pateman, *Sexual Contract*, 38.

46. Georg Lukács, *History and Class Consciousness: Studies in Marxist Dialectics*, trans. Rodney Livingstone (Cambridge, MA: MIT Press, 1972), 131.

47. See Michael Löwy, *Georg Lukács: From Romanticism to Bolshevism*, trans. Patrick Camiller (London: New Left Books, 1979), 97, 122. An English translation of a part of this book, written by Lukács in Hungarian, was published as George Lukács and Lee Baxandall, "The Sociology of Modern Drama," *Tulane Drama Review* 9, no. 4 (1965): 146–70.

48. Alfred Sohn-Rethel, *Intellectual and Manual Labour: A Critique of Epistemology*, trans. Martin Sohn-Rethel (London: Macmillan, 1978). Its original publication, in German, was *Geistige und körperliche Arbeit: Zur Theorie der gesellschaftliche Synthesis* (Frankfurt-am-Main: Suhrkamp, 1970).

49. Ibid., 135 ("bourgeois science"), 20 ("real abstraction").

50. The capture of Miletus by the Persians in 494 BCE provided the subject for an early Greek tragedy, Phrynichus' *The Capture of Miletus*, and Athens' subsequent military campaign to reverse Persia's territorial gains is the source for one of the earliest extant tragedies, Aeschylus' *The Persians*. Sohn-Rethel's claim that Miletus was the location for the first production and use of coins betrays a Eurocentric focus, which, as I will argue in the final chapter of this book, is typical of the Western Marxist tradition in which he worked. Similar claims might legitimately be made for the production and use of coins in both India and China.

51. Karl Marx, "Theses on Feuerbach," in Karl Marx and Friedrich Engels, *The German Ideology: Part One, with Selections from Parts Two and Three*, ed. C. J. Arthur (London: Lawrence and Wishart, 1970), 121–23, at 123.

II • The Scene with *The Spectator*

The most obvious location for this opening scene from bourgeois life would be a coffeehouse. The scene might be set with an evocative description of the bustling establishment and the sociable sound of its patrons' conversation. If the narrative conventions of filmed drama were observed, this establishing shot might be followed by a close-up of a man reading from a single printed sheet, bearing, conveniently, a date. It is Thursday, November 29, 1711. The single printed sheet is today's edition (No. 235) of *The Spectator*, a publication that appeared in London, six days a week, between March 1711 and December 1712.[1] Today's paper is a fairly typical one, consisting of a single prose text, preceded by a Latin epigraph, and followed by a series of short advertisements, the first of which, because this is the theatre season, gives details of the play and cast for this evening at the Theatre Royal, Drury Lane. The reader will perhaps make a mental note that tonight's entertainment will include a performance of George Etherege's *The Man of Mode; or, Sir Fopling Flutter*, with Colley Cibber as Sir Fopling Flutter, and Robert Wilks (comanager, with Cibber and George Doggett, of the Theatre Royal) as the notorious "rake" Dorimant. In May that year an earlier edition of *The Spectator* had carried a critical evaluation of *The Man of Mode*, acknowledging it to be one of "our most applauded Plays," but warning that even though it might be truthful in what it shows of "Nature," it presents "Nature in its utmost Corruption and Degeneracy."[2]

During the London theatre season, such notices of the evening's theatre at both the Theatre Royal, Drury Lane and the Queen's Theatre, Haymarket (which during this period offered programs of opera) appeared in each edition, as the first advertisement to appear beneath the "authored" essay. This is a fairly clear indication that there was a significant overlap between the readership of *The Spectator* and the audiences at these two patent theatres. Such notices did not appear from the very beginning of the publication of *The Spectator*, however. Through the first week of its publication the only advertisements were for books, often religious and philosophical (No. 16 announced the sale of the sixth edition of John Locke's *Essay Concerning Human Understanding*, for example). Only with No. 10 were these joined by notices advertising silk gowns (including some new Venetian examples "to be seen next Wednesday"), a five-room house "to be Lett" in Sutton, some "Plain Spanish Snuff," and consignments of French claret, Villa Nova Barcelona red wine, and Mountain White. The first advertisement for a theatrical performance appeared on March 16, in No. 14, and drew readers' attention to the news that "*On the first of* April *will be performed at the Playhouse in the* Haymaaket [sic] *an Opera call'd* The Cruelty of Atreus. N.B. *The scene wherein* Thyestes *eats his own Children will be performed by the famous Mr.* Psalmanazar, *lately arrived from* Formosa : *the whole Supper being set to Kettledrums.*" Readers will have noted the date of the forthcoming performance, and some of them may also have known that Psalmanazar was the name chosen by a French con-man who had arrived in London, posing as a Formosan who had been abducted by Jesuits, and who had published a fake historical and geographical description of Formosa, including a made-up language. He had confessed to his imposture in 1706.

Issue No. 13 (March 15) features a sequel to an earlier commentary (in No. 5) on the supposed use of real birds in the "modern Opera" at the Haymarket, which tackles the recent rumors that for performances with Nicolini as Hydaspes (in *Idaspe*, by Mancini) the Haymarket will be "supplied with Lions at the publick Expence, during the whole Session." Mr. Spectator determines to go and see for himself, "whether this pretended Lion is really the Savage he appears to be, or only a Counterfeit." He tells a story of coming across a very polite lion backstage, and his discovery that there have been various people playing the lion: a "Candle-snuffer" (who was too furious); a tailor (the lion who was polite to him backstage and was considered sheepish); and "the Acting Lion at present," an anonymous country gentleman who plays the role for fun. He refutes the scurrilous rumor that Nicolini and the Lion have been seen sitting and smoking together, claiming that this only happens after their combat, when, according to the "Rules of the *Drama*" the lion may be considered dead. In the subsequent issue (with the notice for *The Cruelty of Atreus*), the story of the lion is pursued further with a reflection upon the decline in public taste in entertainment in recent years; moreover,

The Spectator has received a letter written by the lion, "*From my Den in the Hay-Market, March 15,*" complaining about having being misrepresented in the previous issue and revealing that he is not playing the role for fun, but, having fallen on hard times, is doing it for the money.

That these early editions of *The Spectator* contained a fantasy about people playing animals at the opera, includes made-up letters from animal impersonators—as well as a fictional advertisement for an opera that featured a performance by a man who had become famous as an impostor who invented a language—might be taken as a hint that the worlds of commerce and theatre, in which *The Spectator* participates, albeit perhaps ambivalently, share with the paper itself an interest in make-believe and impersonation. It also suggests that the authors of *The Spectator* could be reasonably confident, pretty much from the outset, that their readers would be sufficiently in the know (about recent public life, about performance, and about advertisements and letters) to appreciate such jokes. The sense that authors and readers shared a familiar social and media space is particularly well illustrated by an advertisement in No. 22, requesting assistance in the case of a lost lieutenant's commission belonging to a Mr. Tully, and offering a reward of four guineas for whoever brings it to John's Coffeehouse, no questions asked.

Another theatrical fantasy is offered in No. 31 (April 5), in the form of an account of a "Projector" who regales Mr. Spectator with his idea for a performance that brings together in a single place, from multiple different London locations, all the city's strange and diverse entertainments in an opera to be called *The Expedition of Alexander the Great*. It is envisaged that this production will be of particular value to "Ladies," who would not normally be expected to travel to the various out-of-the-way corners of the city in which such entertainments are usually to be found. Performers will include monkeys, lions, and famous actors riding elephants and camels. It will be performed in Greek, on the grounds that fewer people in the London audience will understand this than understand Italian, the use of which, in operas at the Haymarket, *The Spectator* has already ridiculed (No. 18), and this will enhance their enjoyment of the performance. The choice of performance language will necessitate the importing of native-speaking Greeks from "our Factor at *Smyrna*," because this makes more sense than teaching the only people in England who can speak Greek—people in the universities—how to sing. Mr. Spectator manages to evade the Projector and his proposal that he invest in this spectacular imperial entertainment by financing the employment of an organist from Switzerland. Like the Psalmanazar fantasy, the presentation of the *Alexander* project relies upon a readership that can be relied upon to recognize and potentially share a perspective that simultaneously admires and mocks deluded financial speculation as well as both elite and popular entertainment, and sees them as recognizable features of a social world underwritten by the movement of goods, people, and services.

I emphasize the ludic quality of some of these early editions here because they illustrate the extent to which *The Spectator* participates enthusiastically, with both delight and dismay, in the everyday nonsense of the commercial media and leisure sector of which it is also supposedly a critic. This emphasis, particularly on impersonation, also allows the reader of today to avoid attributing views expressed by figures and characters invented for the pages of *The Spectator* to its authors. It works against the grain of an influential strand in *Spectator* criticism, which has tended to take the essays by *The Spectator*'s editors, Joseph Addison and Richard Steele, on moral and aesthetic subjects as the primary significance or even the purpose of the publication, and presents it accordingly as a far less playful and far more stable text than I think it really is. It is worth noting, also, that the standard scholarly edition of *The Spectator* does not include the advertisements, thus abstracting the "essays" from the social and media environment in which they first appeared and making it a much more "literary" and less commercial and journalistic undertaking than it really was.[3]

The author of each issue's principal text is identified only by a single letter: in the case of the November 29, 1711 essay—the "today" of our scene—that letter is C; in the case of the attack on *The Man of Mode*, R. Most readers, however, would have known that *The Spectator* was the work of two principal author-editors, Addison and Steele, and many may also have been aware that the letter C indicated that Addison was the author of today's text. Both authors wrote in character, either as Mr. Spectator or as various other members of his social circle—or, on occasion, as the imaginary authors of letters supposedly sent to the editors by readers of the paper. On the day of the present scene, then, Joseph Addison, writing as Mr. Spectator but "signing" as C, offers readers a report on his recent investigation of a theatrical phenomenon. Mr. Spectator has heard reports that the "upper Gallery of the Playhouse" is now frequented by a figure known only as "the *Trunk-Maker in the Upper-Gallery*," who "expresses his Approbation" of the finest moments of performances "by a loud Knock upon the Benches, or the Wainscot, which may be heard over the whole Theatre." Mr. Spectator has decided to find out for himself who this mysterious figure might be, and finds that he is "a large black Man, whom no body knows."[4]

The scene of a coffeehouse reader gives way to a scene within a scene, a scene of theatre spectatorship. At the center of this scene within a scene stands a figure I had not expected to encounter. This book is my attempt to make something of that encounter. What might this figure of "a large black Man, whom no body knows" have to say about this and other scenes from bourgeois life? What, first of all, can be made of the appearance of this particular spectator in a text written by a Mr. Spectator in a periodical named *The Spectator*? One claim of this book, which I hope to substantiate as my scenes unfold—partly in light of *The Spectator*'s contemporary success and subsequent canonization in English literary culture—is that the act of spectating had a special role in the emergence of bourgeois life as such, and that *The Spectator* was one of the ways in which participants in that new form of life started to become aware of themselves living it. If this is the case, the question remains and becomes, if anything, more pressing: what is "a large black Man, whom no body knows," doing here? After all, even though he appears here briefly, in this scene, he cannot be recognized by, nor can he recognize himself in, any emergent bourgeois life, since "no body" knows who he is. The Trunk-Maker appears, then, only to be made to disappear. Unlike Addison and Steele, he has left almost no trace in the history of either theatre or literature. But he is there, still, in Addison's text, in the London coffeehouse on November 29, 1711, and here, again, in mine. He will return, soon. First, as always, historicize. How did this scene happen? What were the historical conditions of its possibility, of the appearance, on the scene, of the Trunk-Maker? To establish these conditions will involve lingering awhile on the scene with *The Spectator* first.

The Spectator as "Literature"

The Trunk-Maker and Mr. Spectator appear as figures, or perhaps even as characters, on the pages of a journal that eventually came to be regarded as a highly influential contribution to a new kind of culture in England, or in the larger political entity of which it had just become a part by means of the Act of Union of 1707: the United Kingdom of Great Britain. For although it was by no means the first publication of its kind, *The Spectator* occupies an unusually central position in many subsequent understandings of its historical moment. Of its two editors, it is Addison who seems most fully to represent *The Spectator* and the values with which it has come to be associated, and since he was the author of the Trunk-Maker essay, his role and subsequent influence will be emphasized in the account offered here (although some aspects of his relationship with Steele will turn out to be important). The values associated with Addison and *The Spectator* are, I will argue, among the values that the bourgeoisie of England (and of Great Britain) have claimed—entirely tendentiously, of course—as their own. Why and how does *The Spectator* occupy this position? To answer the question about the appearance of the Trunk-Maker within the pages of *The Spectator* requires attention to the historical significance of *The Spectator* itself, in order to develop in full the relationship between the appearance of the Trunk-Maker upon a scene from the bourgeois life that is the subject of this book. That is the task of the present chapter. In the following one, "The Scene with the Trunk-Maker," I will take up a range of questions about the figure of the Trunk-Maker, his identity, and his cultural and political significance.

Let *The Spectator* appear first, then, and with the first issue of the new periodical, Mr. Spectator himself.[5] On March 1, 1711, the reader in the imaginary coffeehouse of this scene (from bourgeois life) will have read "Prefatory Discourses" in which the supposed author of the "following Writings" introduced himself and his "History." He does this, he claims, because he understands that readers rarely enjoy what they are reading unless they know something of the character of the author: whether, first of all, he is "a black or a fair Man"; whether he is "mild or cholerick"; and whether or not he is married. In none of these "Particulars" does the text that follows offer any information. Instead, the reader learns, first, that the author was born into property, the "Hereditary Estate" of his family having been passed, intact, from generation to generation for six hundred years. He was a serious child who rejected noisy toys and, at university, devoted himself to study while maintaining almost complete silence. After the death of his father he toured Europe, saw everything there was to be seen, including an excursion to Egypt to "take the measure of a Pyramid," and returned to his native country where he has been ever since, a constant but silent observer in "most publick Places." "Thus I live in the World," he writes," rather as a Spectator of Mankind, than as one of the Species"; or, in a description that emphasizes not just the fictional but the dramatic character of this "Character": "I have acted in all the parts of my Life as a Looker-on, which is the Character I intend to preserve in this Paper." He will not disclose his name or his age, or where he lives, as this information being made public would expose him to "the greatest Pain I can suffer": interactions with other people. The daily writing and publication to which this character commits himself here will compensate for the social loss that would otherwise be incurred by a man in possession of "so many useful Discoveries" choosing to remain silent.

The character being created here moves in society but does not participate. He is recognized everywhere, but while his face is familiar (even though the reader remains ignorant as to whether he is "black or . . . fair") his name remains unknown. This condition is appropriate for the kind of spectatorship he claims to practice: it renders him immune from the passions and interests that would otherwise threaten his impartiality. It means that he enjoys the "high Satisfaction of beholding all Nature with an unprejudic'd Eye; and having nothing to do with Mens Passions or Interests, I can with the greater Sagacity consider their Talents, Manners, Failings, and Merits." The supposedly impartial judgment of this propertied, learned, and well-traveled "Spectator" is placed at the service—as he will explain to the growing body of readers who are following his writing by No. 10, published on March 12, 1711—of "the Fraternity of Spectators who live in the World without having any thing to do in it," that is, of "every one that considers the World as a Theatre, and desires to form a right Judgment of those who are the Actors on it." The theatre spectator is here proposed as the ideal form of a wider category (or class, perhaps) of people (since they are members of a "Fraternity," we may assume they are men) whose way of life (or, one might say, whose position in relation to the means of production and reproduction) leaves them at leisure to look at the world around them as a source of entertainment, rather than as a set of relationships in which they must participate in order to survive.

The number of people enjoying a life of this kind in the London of 1711 was probably fairly small. It is, nonetheless, possible not only to imagine such people but also to propose such a life as a kind of ideal, to which, despite its "trivial Disadvantages" (No. 4, March 5), those who do have to earn a living might aspire. Even the hardworking man of commerce will have enjoyed fleeting or even regular glimpses of what such a life might be like in a society in which a distinctively capitalist distinction between the spheres of work and leisure was beginning to take hold. The very act of reading *The Spectator* was to participate in the emergent sphere of leisure, characterized by commercial entertainment (such as the theatre) and the consumption of the new (colonial) economy's newly affordable luxuries (such as coffee and tea). You go to the theatre, you drink your drinks, you read the paper: this is how you make your scenes from bourgeois life. It is a form of participation in social life that some observers would not recognize as participation at all.[6] And it is this form of nonparticipatory participation that, according to a long-established "classical" tradition—to be revived, quite self-consciously, in this new "Augustan" Age—qualifies this gentlemen of leisure to consider questions of aesthetic and political significance In other words, in order to become a critic one must be spared the necessity of work. This is Plato's Guardian remade by an emergent bourgeoisie as the property qualification. It is, also, as I have suggested in Chapter I, "An Essay Regarding the Bourgeoisie," the logical consequence of the "possessive individualism" of John Locke's contractual understanding of society.

Ellen Meiksins Wood and Neal Wood track this idea that only those with the leisure to do so should consider political questions, from Socrates, through Plato, to the work of Plato's student, Aristotle: "If the knowledge necessary for virtue depends upon leisure and constant enquiry and self-examination, it is quite outside the resources of the common man; and not only because he lacks leisure time, but because in a more fundamental sense he is bound in body and spirit to the world of material necessity by the need to earn his livelihood, while knowledge implies liberation from the world of appearances and necessity."[7] This account of virtue finds its full political expression in Plato's speculative states. In *The Republic*, for example, Plato proposes that the educational program for the Guardians of the state should be reserved for those "freed from all forms of manual work" so that they may attend to the "provision of freedom for our state."[8] As Wood and Wood note, the term used here by Plato for "freedom" is "eleutheria," which also carries the connotation of "gentlemanliness."[9] This educational program depends, then, upon a social division of labor, not simply between different modes of labor (manual or intellectual) but between those who labor and those who do not, who "live in the World without having any thing to do in it." "It is difficult, then," write Wood and Wood, "to avoid the conclusion that the essential condition for the existence of the virtuous or philosophic few is the ensured existence of a class of men whose livelihood does not depend on their own labour or trade and who can command the labour of others to supply their needs and wants."[10] Aristotle carries forward this conception of the relationship between class and government in his own *Politics*, where, "in his incomplete description of the ideally best polis—reminiscent of Plato's Magnesia of *The Laws*—Aristotle proposes the exclusion of artisans, shopkeepers, farm labourers, and all wage-earners from citizenship on the grounds that such occupations are 'ignoble and inimical to goodness.'"[11]

The eighteenth-century incarnation of this ideal citizen and possessive individual is an impartial and dispassionate critic who, because he does not have to defend his own material interests (these are all, happily, already taken care of) may stand above political faction, and may be imagined, too, to be without any commercial interest in the transmission of his opinions. For several subsequent generations it is Addison (rather than Steele) who comes to represent this ideal most effectively. For his eulogists, such as his near-contemporary Samuel Johnson and the nineteenth-century colonial administrator and historian Lord Macaulay, he embodied a combination of admirable personal qualities, political achievements, literary style, and social and moral influence. He possessed integrity, balance, modesty, pragmatism. Although well-read, he was neither pedantic nor unworldly. This cultural status appears to have been established very early, as though by the time of his death (and his burial in Westminster Abbey) in 1719, Addison had already been selected by his contemporaries as the founder of the culture posterity would credit them with having established. In a consideration of Addison's influence as a "culture hero" for eighteenth-century Britain, Lawrence E. Klein writes that "Addison was, in one important model of British self-perception, a kind of cultural legislator: he was a founder of polite culture, of an age in which 'taste' was a key word across discursive fields and in the lives of many participants in cultural life."[12]

For Johnson, he is the model for anyone wishing to write well in English: "whoever wishes to attain an English style, familiar but not coarse, and elegant but not ostentatious, must give his days and nights to the volumes of Addison."[13] Both Johnson and Macaulay consider Addison's literary and personal "style" in relation to what they regard as the overheated factionalism of his era's politics, and claim for Addison the capacity to stand above it (despite the fact that, as we shall see, he was at the time strongly associated with the Whig interest). Johnson observes that both *The Tatler* (Steele's publication, 1709–11, to which Addison was a major contributor) and *The Spectator* were published at a time when two parties, loud, restless, and violent, each with plausible declarations, and each perhaps without any distinct termination of its views, were agitating the nation; to minds heated with political contest they supplied cooler and more inoffensive reflections; and it is said by Addison, in a subsequent work, that they had a perceptible influence upon the conversation of that time, and taught the frolick and the gay to unite merriment with decency; an effect which they can never wholly lose, while they continue to be among the first books by which both sexes are initiated in the elegances of knowledge.[14]

Macaulay follows suit, commenting that

faction itself could not deny that Addison had, through all changes of fortune, been strictly faithful to his early opinions, and to his early friends; that his integrity was without stain; that his whole deportment indicated a fine sense of the becoming; that, in the utmost heat of controversy, his zeal was tempered by a regard for truth, humanity, and social decorum; that no outrage could ever provoke him to retaliation unworthy of a Christian and a gentleman; and that his only faults were a too sensitive delicacy, and a modesty which amounted to bashfulness.[15]

Matthew Arnold would largely endorse these views, in his edition of *The Six Chief Lives from Johnson's "Lives of the Poets,"* in which he included Johnson's essay on Addison, alongside those on Milton, Dryden, Swift, Pope, and Gray, and did so because "whenever I have had occasion to use Johnson's Lives of the Poets, the thought has struck me how admirable a *point de repère*, or fixed centre of the sort described above [a natural center to which the disoriented can always return], these lives might be made to furnish for the student of English literature."[16] For Arnold, a "critic" of both literature and culture, who thought that the study of literature (for children as well as for adults) was an essential part of education, English literature was a vital element in a struggle against the Philistinism into which he feared his bourgeois contemporaries were lapsing, at the risk of impending anarchy. Addison was therefore an important cultural resource in a specifically "English" project of cultural consolidation and renewal.

These texts clearly identify a collection of virtues which the English (co-lonial) bourgeoisie, once established in their political and economic domi-nation, liked to attribute to themselves and to cultivate in their sons, includ-ing those who, like Macaulay (and Addison before him) would take responsibility for colonial administration and so-called liberal education (Arnold). These virtues are raised above the sphere of the political by their inclusion in the field of literature, which is imagined, like Addison himself, to transcend the petty considerations of politics and to offer inspiration and comfort of a universal character to all its readers. This conception of litera-ture (or "Literature") would be strongly contested, *at some point in the late twentieth century*, by a range of politically engaged critics of literature and the way it had been taught, the publication of whose work, particularly in the mid-1980s when I studied literature at university, had a significant role in the orientation of my own critical thought.[17] Such critics argued that this con-ception of Literature contributed to the formation of the "liberal humanis[t]" conception of the subject that Catherine Belsey rejected for what she de-scribed as the "conservatism" of its implication of an unchanging, ahistorical essential human nature.[18] It is what Terry Eagleton describes as a "moral technology" for the "production of human subjects" designed "for quite spe-cific purposes of social control."[19] Alan Sinfield, in an essay in *Political Shake-speare*, shows how the teaching of Shakespeare as "the keystone which guar-antees the ultimate stability and rightness of the category 'Literature'" encouraged students in postwar British secondary education to accommo-date themselves to the values appropriate to their future participation in "the new petty bourgeoisie working in finance, advertising, the civil service, teaching, the health service, the social services and clerical occupations": a late twentieth-century version, perhaps, of the ideal citizen.[20] Students who succeed in examinations that test their knowledge and understanding of Shakespeare are those, Sinfield argues, who effectively reproduce accounts of the plays that emphasize the "purposeful individual" and the "neutrality of culture" as timeless and universal sources of value and meaning. Such sub-jects will, among other things, be "trained at giving opinions—within certain prescribed limits."[21] They will be critics, but only up to a point: they will not, on the whole, extend their critique to the institutions through which they are acquiring the practice of critique.

My own very mild experience of the coercive nature of the way knowl-edge and appreciation of the work of Shakespeare was examined in British schools toward the end of the period discussed by Sinfield had involved doing exceptionally badly in a "mock" O-level examination (itself a scene from bourgeois life) in which I failed to treat with due seriousness the essay prompt's proposition that the title character of *Henry V* was, as the act II Prologue put it, "the mirror of all Christian kings." As a white male bourgeois subject with considerable inherited cultural capital, my brief lapse was very limited in its consequences: Sinfield's essay suggests that subjects without such structural advantages would have encountered such friction much more frequently and damagingly. I subsequently managed to find ways of moderating my critique to align myself compliantly with what Sinfield describes as the "progressivist" variant of a conservative conception of the function of both literature and education: that it should awaken and nurture the creativity of the autonomous and purposeful individual.[22] This progressivist emphasis on autonomy and creativity arguably makes it a more effective "moral technology," by virtue of its capacity to remain largely invisible. In order for Shakespeare's work, and for Literature in general, to contribute effectively to this ideological and pedagogical project, it must be taught, whether by progressives or conservatives, Sinfield argues, without any meaningful connection being made between the literary text and the conditions of either its social and economic production or reception. Some efforts had been made, at the time Sinfield wrote his essay, to introduce just such considerations—primarily by inviting students to think about their responses to plays in relation to the structural conditions of their own reception of them (race, gender, educational institutions). The cultural materialist project to which Sinfield's work was a contribution sought to combine this kind of attention with attention to the conditions of textual (and theatrical) production. My debt to this work, encountered as a student, should be clear throughout the present book.

Joseph Roach, in an article that makes explicit use of Eagleton's term "the ideology of the aesthetic,"[23] as well as to more Foucault-oriented new historicism, makes a case for considering theatre, especially during the eighteenth century, as a particularly significant moral technology: "One of the goals of bourgeois aesthetics is to make the historically produced seem natural, universal, and timeless. I would add that a principal instrument for the aestheticization of daily social life, for the micropolitical inculcation of the ideology of the aesthetic in the eighteenth century, was the theatre."[24] This claim amplifies an argument advanced by Michael Hays, for whom "the new dominant order [he is referring to capitalism] found, in the italianate theater, the medium through which to visually and verbally project its experience into the rest of the world and thereby to deny the complex collective structure of which it was really part."[25] In this account, appropriate thinking and behavior is inculcated by a textual and scenographic realization of a world in which the part the bourgeois spectator may have played, and is still playing, in its construction, is hidden: the world onstage appears quite separate from the spectator, available for observation but not for participation. Roach adds to this fairly conventional (and, as we have seen in the preceding "An Essay Regarding the Bourgeoisie," Lukácsian) emphasis on the ideological work of the visual and the textual, a distinctively performance-focused attention to the entanglements of vision and the body in such practices as dance notation and acting manuals. He makes the connection between choreography and social discipline, first by reference to Napoleon's decision to take a *corps de ballet* on his 1798 military campaign to conquer Egypt, and subsequently through a reading of Joseph Addison's satirical fantasy, published in *The Spectator* No. 102 (June 27, 1711), in which he imagines a program that trains women in the correct use of fans using the language and techniques of a military academy. Roach's point, made across a range of scenes from bourgeois life, is that theatre possesses techniques that inscribe ideology into everyday bodily practices. He also reveals, through the example of Addison's text, in particular, that those concerned with the moral technologies of both literature and theatre knew full well that this was the case. Addison's satirical piece only makes sense if there is an assumption that author and reader share an understanding of such corporeal training, and a recognition that there is some real social basis for the comically plausible scenario presented.

Roach is right, of course, to draw attention to the significance of theatre for the production of the right kind of (bourgeois) citizens from its spectators, and he makes a persuasive case for extending the analysis of Literature offered by Eagleton and Sinfield into other areas of aesthetic experience. That we learn how to do things and be the people we are through the repetition of bodily performances is now much more widely accepted than it was when Roach wrote his essay, and has been the subject of extensive critical work (much of it by feminists and scholars of race) since the late 1980s. Judith Butler's *Gender Trouble* (1990), Saidiya Hartman's *Scenes of Subjection* (1997), Daphne Brooks's *Bodies in Dissent* (2006), Robin Bernstein's *Racial Innocence* (2011), and Kyla Wazana Tompkins's *Racial Indigestion* (2012) come to mind as major contributions to this literature.[26] All of these have helped me think about the processes of subject formation I am considering here. Roach, perhaps because he begins with the arresting historical conjuncture of ballet and the military, seems to present the "moral technology" or Althusser's "ideological state apparatus" as highly effective in its production of the right kind of subject.[27] Similar impressions have also been created through readings of Foucault (especially *Discipline and Punish*), where the "ideal" model institution (the prison) suggests a capacity for total control that not all such technologies might possess. Eagleton's essay and, to a lesser extent, Sinfield's seem to assume, perhaps for rhetorical reasons, that the production of subjects by Literature and its institutional uses is similarly efficient. They leave little room for the possibility that the technology or apparatus might sometimes malfunction. The possibility that it might malfunction, or be interrupted or diverted, immediately raises questions about agency in relation to ideological processes of subject formation, which have been a source of continuing and fruitful debate—in response to Foucault and Butler, of course, but also throughout the body of work to which I have pointed here.

In my earlier discussion of the bourgeoisie, I alluded briefly to the possibility of such technological (ideological) malfunctions when I observed (in a note, admittedly) that, in the famous "little theoretical theatre" devised by Louis Althusser to represent the process by which subjects are produced, things can always go wrong. The individual hailed as a subject in this theatre, by what Althusser calls the "ideological state apparatus" (embodied by a policeman), does not always respond as anticipated to the officer who calls out, "Hey, you there." Nine times out of ten, Althusser notes, the intended individual turns around, but therefore once in every ten either the wrong individual turns, or no one turns. In both variations on this one-in-ten malfunction, we may assume that there is an individual to whom the hail was in fact addressed, but who, for some reason, either fails to hear it or chooses not to respond. Furthermore, the individual who hears and responds on one occasion may, during other productions staged in Althusser's "theoretical theatre," fail to hear or choose not to respond. Each and every concrete individual has the capacity and the potential to disidentify. This is why those accounts of the way theatre works such as that offered by Michael Hays are insufficiently attentive to the possibility that, in using the technology of the "italianate theater" to "project" its experience of life onto the rest of the world—and, in the process, cement its own preferred (ideological) picture of that world—the "dominant order" is taking up an apparatus with unpredictable effects. It is not just that some specific concrete individuals, perhaps with track records of disidentification, might not get the message, but that there is an additional risk that any individuals hailed as subjects in such a theatre may notice what is going on, recognize it for what it is (an attempt at the production of appropriate subjects), and thereby acquire fresh capacities for seeing and understanding precisely what ideology's naturalizations are designed to hide. Roach's example of Addison's satirical image of a fan-use training program is in fact one such case: Addison not only recognizes the process of subject production at work, but possesses the resources to produce a comic version of that process that will, in turn, alert readers to the presence of such processes. It is not simply that in order to get Addison's joke readers must know that corporeal training takes place, and that its aim is subject production; they must also grasp the idea that it is possible, as it were, to get behind the scenes of such processes. The fact that Addison and his readers can share this joke demonstrates that the process has already gone wrong.

"'Dressage,' in short, does not always work," writes Carrie Noland, in *Agency and Embodiment*.[28] Drawing, for this particular insight, on the work of Marcel Mauss, Noland's book on "the corporeal performance of gestures" is particularly suggestive and productive, I think, because she affirms simultaneously that "gestural performances secure belief systems in a way that no recitation of myth, no chant, alone, can," and that "the sensations experienced by the body that bears the social meaning are not always experienced in the same way by each individual body."[29] It is in the latter discrepancy that a space for agency opens up, and in which the faulty reproduction of social norms or the deviant formation of subjectivity becomes imaginable, or, as Noland herself puts it, "the performance of acquired social practices—involving kinesthetic feedback—may create forms of resistance that no inscription can entirely fix."[30] Consider then, a theatrical performance. Perhaps, for the sake of the present discussion, it could be a performance of a play by Shakespeare. Consider it not simply as the visual and verbal transmission of a work of Literature, but also as the reception of that material, in the form of an evening's entertainment, by people with bodies, who attend a specific building, designed, perhaps, for this specific purpose, and who engage there in an ensemble of social, physical, intellectual, and affective activities that we could plausibly call an "acquired social practice." Of course, this event might very well function, and may even have been intended, by some person or institution, as a kind of "moral technology" for the production of human subjects who will do and live as they are told, in accordance with dominant social norms and in support of the class interests of the bourgeoisie. But there will always be something else going on. For a start, as I have already hinted at the very beginning of this chapter, theatre is in fact a somewhat dubious "moral technology." Richard Steele's objection in the pages of *The Spectator* to George Etherege's *The Man of Mode* (performances of which the journal advertises, of course) is just one example of a famous and long-standing moral unease over theatre's capacity to encourage feelings and attitudes that defy a dominant moral order. As a moral technology theatre might be faulty because it performs the wrong kind of ideological work. In other words, the tech is working, but it has been misprogrammed. My argument—in concert, I think, with Noland's, and with specific reference to theatre in the characteristic modern form that is emerging at the beginning of the eighteenth century—is (and has been, in the past) that the technology itself has a tendency to failure: whatever you try to do with it, something else will frequently be produced. Worse than that, it is actually these "side effects" that constitute one of the most appealing features of this particular entertainment technology.[31] In inviting you to enjoy the most lifelike representation of another human being, the theatre often risks reminding you that the process of representation is imperfect and on the verge of some kind of rather embarrassing death. Subjects under production who glimpse or intuit that they are being produced tend to become recalcitrant.

With this theatrical problem in mind, let's get back to Addison. Addison, I've observed, was once assigned a special place in retrospective accounts of the formation of English (colonial) culture and in the production of the bourgeois subjects whose role it would be to reproduce that culture and the social and economic arrangements upon which it was based. I have shown how subsequent critics of this culture have understood this to have been an ideological process in which education, literature, and theatre functioned as technologies for social control and the presentation of historically contingent class relations as natural and universal. But I have also suggested, with specific reference to the social practice of going to the theatre, that these technologies or ideological apparatuses cannot be relied upon to work properly on all of the people all of the time. (If they could, Terry Eagleton would presumably not have been possible.) What I want to do now is observe a (theatrical) discrepancy at the very heart of the process by which Addison (as the impartial Spectator of social life) is produced as the ideal form of the bourgeois subject. To put it simply, this ideal figure is produced by conflating Joseph Addison with the character he plays in the pages of *The Spectator*, by assuming that everything Mr. Spectator claims for himself may be attributed to Addison, and, finally, by failing to recognize the deadly presence of irony in the opening "self"-description.

The effect of reading the opening text with the possibility of irony in mind is to realize that Mr. Spectator has social deficiencies that, far from qualifying him to perform the role he claims for himself, actually render him, in some respects, at least, remarkably ill-equipped to do so. He proposes himself as a knowledgeable commentator on social life, while offering as the basis for the quality of such commentary the revelation that he actually has no social life of his own. The position of the spectator who does not participate is therefore simultaneously endorsed and undermined. In order to comment on the life of his fellow humans, Mr. Spectator has to separate himself from the "Species" altogether. Might it not be the case that, rather than a reliable mouthpiece for their own views and opinions, Addison and Steele concocted, for the entertainment of their readers as much as for their edification, a fictional character who may have shared many of those views and opinions, but from whom both authors could always place themselves at a distance. Mr. Spectator, we might conclude, may have taken a narrower view of the moral, aesthetic, and social phenomena on which he commented than did his authors, and that the object of subsequent eulogies was not Addison at all, but Mr. Spectator. Who was it, really, who objected to *The Man of Mode*? When the twentieth-century historian of eighteenth-century English culture, J. H. Plumb, deplored Joseph Addison's writing as the expression of a bourgeois culture he detested, he, too, may have been missing the point of the impersonation, while also identifying a truth that an ironic reading would also encourage:

> [I]t is as dreary if as smooth as an ocean of tapioca pudding. . . .
> [S]ententious platitudes stretch over page after page. Although the
> prose runs as sweetly as toothpaste, the matter is awful in its banal-
> ity. . . . [R]ather like a schoolmaster Addison inserts a little knowledge
> in the pulp . . . a few neatly chosen morsels of learning, that could be
> swallowed with ease by the most self-distrusting readers. . . . But the

real boredom lies, for the present age, in the *Spectator*'s all pervading, arch, cosy morality, a tea-table morality which is less of the heart than of manners. . . . [I]t was a morality for those who had arrived and could look forward to a *place* in Heaven. . . . [F]or an emerging class such precepts helped to provide social cohesion, to give the air of truth to attitudes to which it was necessary to pay lip-service, if nothing more. . . . This, at least, was how the middle-class life should be lived, even if it rarely was so in practice.[32]

Even Plumb appears to detect the possibility that a theatrical insincerity—which we have learned to call, after the Greek word for actor, hypocrisy—may be in play here. Perhaps it is irony rather than platitudes, hypocrisy rather than a complacent moral integrity, that should be considered the most significant contribution made by *The Spectator* to the production of scenes from bourgeois life. But it is too soon to say. A little further and fuller historicization may help.

The Spectator in History

The culture in which *The Spectator* participated has subsequently come to be understood in multiple ways. It was a culture shaped by the political settlement of 1688, generally referred to as the "Glorious Revolution" (by Marx, among others, as we have seen) in which the Dutch William of Orange was maneuvered onto the English throne to replace the deposed Stuart monarch, James II, in order to guarantee a Protestant succession, and to fashion a new understanding of the respective rights and responsibilities of the sovereign and a parliament in which the interests of the expanding merchant elite found their political representation. William was succeeded onto the throne by Anne, daughter of the previously deposed James II but considered staunchly supportive of the 1688 settlement and the approach to government established by William. It was during Anne's reign, in 1707, that the Act of Union between England and Scotland created the United Kingdom. Crucial underlying developments of this period involved the combination of financialization and colonial expansion, epitomized by the foundation of the Bank of England (1694) and the accelerated exploitation of newly acquired territories in North America and the Caribbean. In 1713, at the conclusion of a lengthy European war with positive outcomes for the new United Kingdom, British traders and plantation owners gained major new advantages over their French competitors and were granted, under the terms of the Treaty of Utrecht, a thirty-year monopoly over the slave trade to Spanish colonies.[33]

So in the colonial metropolis—London—a merchant elite is consolidating its political power, and deriving substantial new revenues from colonial production that is increasingly sustained by slave labor. The economy of this metropolis, and the country in which it is increasingly dominant, is changing. The development of new financial instruments, including maritime insurance and bills of exchange, is part of a process in which an increasingly abstract market is coming to dominate urban life, and is effecting a gradual separation of labor from other aspects of everyday life. In other words, more and more people are getting used to producing for exchange rather than for subsistence. One of the consequences of this is that the category of leisure, involving a set of activities distinct from work, is starting to apply across a far wider social spectrum than ever before. And as part of this new dimension of daily life, the consumption of mass luxury commodities, including, crucially, some key colonial products such as coffee, sugar, chocolate, and tobacco, is becoming one of the ways in which that leisure time is organized and articulated. And reading newspapers like *The Spectator*, either in the coffeehouse or at home, over tea, perhaps, is part of this new culture of consumption.[34]

Participants in this culture of consumption—including of course such active movers and shakers within it as Addison and Steele—will have been fully aware of its economic underpinnings. Both enslaved and free people of color were visible presences in London at the time. The travel diary of a German bibliophile, Zacharias von Uffenbach, records a visit to London in 1710, during which he made a trip to Hockley-in-the-Hole, where he saw an Englishman fight a Moor with swords, and notes, as a result, that "there are, in fact, such a quantity of Moors of both sexes in England that I have never seen so many before."[35] The American colonies, especially those of the Caribbean "West Indies," had been the subject of numerous cultural representations of the kind consumed by members of the emerging merchant culture, from the travel narratives of Richard Ligon (*A True and Exact History of the Island of Barbadoes*, 1657) and Hans Sloane (who would go on to found the British Museum; *A Voyage to the Islands Madera, Barbados, Nieves, S. Christophers and Jamaica*, 1707), to numerous plays in which encounters between Europeans and a variety of American people were dramatized. Two of the most performed plays of this period were *The Enchanted Island,* John Dryden and William D'Avenant's musical adaptation of Shakespeare's *The Tempest,* and Thomas Southerne's adaptation of Aphra Behn's novella *Oroonoko.*

And of course, Steele and Addison themselves were not just well-informed but actively involved. Steele inherited Barbados plantations from his wife, and therefore also found himself a slave owner. We know this thanks to the records of financial transactions with Addison, who loaned Steele £400 in 1704 and a further £1000 in 1706, against which Steele mortgaged his plantations. Addison had served in senior positions in the government, including, most relevantly for the present discussion, as Under-Secretary to the Secretary of State for the South (the equivalent of today's UK Foreign Secretary or US Secretary of State), and in that role, as his biographer (and former Tory MP and possible model for James Bond) Sir Peter Smithers notes, would therefore have had administrative responsibility for the American and Caribbean "plantations."[36] As writers they turned to colonial topics on numerous occasions. Steele was responsible for elaborating and popularizing a story first told briefly in Ligon's *True and Exact History,* when in *The Spectator* of March 13, 1711 (No. 11), he published the story of Inkle and Yarico, in which a feckless young British slave trader sells into slavery the Native American woman who had earlier loved him and saved him from captivity. Addison wrote twice about the 1710 visit to London of the so-called Indian Kings, and also about the "Mohock" phenomenon, in which a club of wealthy young men, adopting the name of the Native American nation, apparently attacked fellow citizens on the streets of London for the hell of it.[37] I shall have more to say about these texts in due course. Both Addison and Steele, then, are visibly reflecting upon the real and imaginary interconnectedness of their colonial metropolis with the plantations and peoples of the Caribbean and North America, an interconnectedness to which they are themselves contributing.

I have so far hesitated to use a key term to name this culture. I have not mentioned the bourgeoisie for a while. There is, of course, extensive and politically charged debate as to whether the culture I have been describing here is evidence of the emergence and even the hegemony of a distinctive new class, one that we might choose to call either the middle class or the bourgeoisie. Some historians of this moment in English culture and society—Peter Earle, for example, author of *The Making of the English Mid-*

dle Class—seem confident in identifying this as the rise of the middle class. E. P. Thompson, however, insists in his earlier *The Making of the English Working Class* (which title Earle adapts for his own work) that, although there is clear evidence of new patterns of sociality that might indicate a new class formation, this is of limited significance, at least in political terms, since political power is not passing to a middle class at all, but remains firmly in control of an alliance between the landowning aristocracy and a financial and merchant elite.[38] Distinctively middle-class or bourgeois values are not, he claims, achieving any kind of hegemony at this time. Thompson's position illustrates one of the problems with the term "middle class": its stratificatory logic does not allow—as the term "bourgeois" does—for the understanding that the financial and merchant elite (including real owners of means of production) are among those to whom hegemony is passing. Indeed, one might say that the term "middle class" is intrinsically depoliticizing, in that it is conceptually difficult to imagine that those in the "middle" are actually on top. Dror Wahrman is like many scholars of the period now who prefer to hedge their positions, and to use a term from the period itself, referring to those people we might wish to claim for the new bourgeoisie or middle class simply as "the middling sort," an expression, it seems, first used by Daniel Defoe.[39] Broader accounts of the emergence of the bourgeoisie and the development of a distinctively capitalist economic and social system, however, such as those of the political historians Ellen Meiksins Wood and Robert Brenner, or the German social historian Jürgen Kocka, are more ready to identify the culture taking shape at this time as at least protobourgeois.[40] And there's no doubt, if we recall the cultural centrality accorded to *The Spectator* itself and the values it was supposed to embody (balance, politeness, moderation, learned wit) for later British letters and culture, that the bourgeoisie of the nineteenth century wanted to see themselves reflected in this earlier, Augustan Age. Might it be said, then, that while there may be no fully fledged bourgeoisie in full possession of political hegemony at this time, we are, at the very least, looking at the moment that the fully fledged European bourgeoisie or English middle class have subsequently come to nominate or adopt as their own preferred point of origin? In other words, that in selecting the urbane, coffee-drinking, wine-purchasing, newspaper-reading, and theatregoing elite of early eighteenth-century London as their preferred, even ideal antecedents, the fully fledged bourgeoisie of the nineteenth and later centuries has done us all the favor of identifying

themselves decisively with the slave-owning, financializing elites of the colonial metropolis I am describing here.

Certainly Jürgen Habermas saw no difficulty in thinking of this culture as
bourgeois.[41] Habermas's conception of the bourgeois public sphere, which
rests upon an analysis of precisely this culture, has been influential and, like
all influential ideas, widely debated and contested. Here I wish simply to outline what I see as its core propositions, and to indicate the significance of the
relationship between the public sphere and the economic transformation
that made it possible, in order, then, to say something about how this relationship might be manifested in the theatre and for theatre spectatorship.
The public sphere, argues Habermas, is where public opinion is formed: this
opinion might be formed over political or moral questions, and also—and
this connection is important—over questions of aesthetics, and, by extension, judgments as to the quality of entertainment and other commodities of
the emergent consumer society Habermas describes. It constitutes an area of
social life that is governed neither by the state nor by commercial or business
interests, although it is by no means autonomous in relation to either, and to
which access is theoretically guaranteed to everyone, based on the assumption of at least a temporary equality among them. Participants in the public
sphere are assumed to be speaking in their own person rather than on behalf
of others, or of particular interests (either political or economic). The value
of the contributions they make is judged without reference to assumptions
about their social status. Opinion is formed through the free and equal exchange of ideas, in acts of communication that are, ideally, rational, and that,
in practice, also depend upon a shared language, often sustained by the publication and circulation of printed matter. Thus the *locus classicus* of the public sphere, at least in England, where it finds perhaps its exemplary expression, is the coffeehouse, where social exchange dedicated to the pursuit
neither of politics nor of business (but that might touch frequently upon
both) takes place amid daily luxury consumption and the circulation of
newspapers. Much of the subsequent critique of Habermas's work addresses
the exclusions implicit in making the coffeehouse (with its almost entirely
male clientele, for example) the model for the public sphere.[42]

The idea that the public sphere as it came into being in the early eighteenth century might serve as a model for the development and, indeed, re-
vival of public discourse for late twentieth-century social democracy arises
from what follows Habermas's description of its initial emergence. For in

Part II of *The Structural Transformation of the Public Sphere*, Habermas describes its transformation into the false public spheres of later modernity, in which all allegedly public discourse is either controlled by the state authorities, or, in the supposedly "democratic" societies, irredeemably contaminated by, and subject to, rival political and commercial interests. Here public opinion is no longer the product of two-way rational communicative exchanges between equal and autonomous subjects, but rather the aggregation of data derived from the essentially one-way operations of marketing and market research or its political branches, such as opinion polls and focus groups.

But the model itself, as Habermas is careful to show, is far from being free from economic and political considerations. Indeed, the public sphere itself becomes possible only as a result of processes of economic and political transformation. It was commercial interests—in particular, those that derived their wealth from the exponential expansion in long-distance trade—that first acquired the political power to challenge state and court monopolies over public representation, and that developed technologies, such as the newspaper, upon the basis of which this new sphere for the constitution of a public could be constructed. In a revealingly abbreviated summary of this process, Habermas refers to the central significance of "the *traffic in commodities and news* created by early capitalist long-distance trade."[43] Although it is perhaps an accident of the translation of Habermas's German into English, it is hard (for me, at least) not to hear in this phrase an allusion, not just to the expropriative colonialism that is the basis (the incentive and then the foundation) of the long-distance trade in question, but also to the "traffic" in one particular commodity central to that trade and the expropriation upon which it is based: the enslaved person. For now let us just register that the "free" exchange of opinion in the bourgeois public sphere is dependent (in Habermas's own view) upon acts of "originary" accumulation in which not only are new commodities (such as coffee) brought to a growing consumer market, but in which the labor of "unfree" enslaved subjects is "exchanged" in a violent and often deadly trade. It is not simply that a key element in the social activities that came to constitute the bourgeois public sphere—conversations conducted around the drinking of coffee, often flavored with sugar—are stimulated by consumption of a product of colonial expropriation (which is itself interesting enough), but that the very social and economic conditions for the emergence of such sociality, and the sphere in which it takes place, are the result of developments in the English economy directly attributable to the growth of its colonial possessions and expropriations. There is no longer any purely "English" economy at this time, if indeed there ever was. Without slavery—and, in particular, the modern form of plantation slavery—there would have been no bourgeois public sphere.

It is sometimes suggested that the theatre itself instantiates this public sphere; that the airing of issues of shared concern in the public space of the theatre is part of the operations of the public sphere. This belief is most often expressed in relation to performances of plays with immediate and straightforward contemporary political subject matter, such as, for example, the "verbatim" tribunal plays staged at London's Tricycle Theatre from 1994, or work such as Anna Deveare-Smith's *Fires in the Mirror* and *Twilight: Los Angeles, 1992*. Implicit in the idea that such productions activate the public sphere is a conviction that such theatre will get closer to truth and justice than the formal mechanisms provided by the state, which are subject to a range of institutional biases and constraints through the operations of vested interests, from which the theatre, by contrast, might believe itself to be free. The idea that the theatre might be a public sphere also surfaces metaphorically when the public sphere is described as a theatre, as in some influential commentary on Habermas's work itself, by Nancy Fraser, for example, who describes the public sphere as "a theater in modern societies in which political participation is enacted through the medium of talk."[44] Both Fraser's metaphorical use of theatre and the idea that the theatre can function as a part or an instance of the public sphere rest upon a momentary forgetting of one of theatre's most striking characteristics: that the "talk" is all one-way. The modern theatre does not, typically, encourage or even usually permit, participation. That, it might even be said, is precisely its point. Participation by the public is in fact an exception, sometimes even an aberration, and when it happens it is usually felt worth remarking upon, or even elevating into a principle by which a particular theatre might wish to distinguish its own practice from the norm. As a metaphor for the public sphere the theatre, then, is inadequate, suggesting not an exchange of views and ideas between equal participants, but rather a situation in which one group of people sit in silence while another, usually smaller group, moves about and speaks. As Christopher Balme notes in a recent book, the theatrical public sphere is not to be found inside the theatre; the public sphere should not be confused with a public space.[45] How, then, to account for the persistent association of the theatre with the public sphere?

One explanation may lie with the practice of criticism. As Terry Eagleton has shown, the modern conception of the critic—someone who speaks or writes to pass judgment upon the actions, productions, performances of others—is established in and through the constitution of the public sphere.[46] It is in the coffeehouses and periodical publications of early eighteenth-century London, argues Eagleton, that the figure of the critic took shape. Early and influential examples of this figure were, of course, Joseph Addison and Richard Steele of *The Spectator*, a newspaper whose central conceit and title, as we have seen, is the existence of a particular kind of observer of modern life: the spectator who circulates reports and analysis of what he has observed; the man about town who sees everything, but does not take part, opening his mouth only to report on what he has seen—either in the comfort of his club, or, now, as Addison writes in the inaugural edition of *The Spectator*, within the pages of the newspaper:

> I have passed my latter Years in this City, where I am frequently seen in most publick Places, tho' there are not above half a dozen of my select Friends that know me; of whom my next Paper shall give a more particular Account. There is no place of general Resort wherein I do not often make my appearance; sometimes I am seen thrusting my Head into a Round of Politicians at *Will's* and listning with great Attention to the Narratives that are made in those little Circular Audiences. Sometimes I smoak a Pipe at *Child's*; and, while I seem attentive to nothing but the *Post-Man*, over-hear the Conversation of every Table in the Room. I appear on *Sunday* nights at *St. James's* Coffee House, and sometimes join the little Committee of Politicks in the Inner-Room, as one who comes there to hear and improve. My Face is likewise very well known at the *Grecian*, the *Cocoa-Tree*, and in the Theaters both of *Drury Lane* and the *Hay-Market*. I have been taken for a Merchant upon the *Exchange* for above these ten Years, and sometimes pass for a *Jew* in the Assembly of Stock-Jobbers at *Jonathan's*. In short, where-ever I see a Cluster of People, I always mix with them, tho' I never open my Lips but in my own Club.

This figure of the critic develops over time, Eagleton argues, into a number of social functions, including, by the late nineteenth century, the humanities scholar or professional critic (including the theatre professor), housed within and paid by the university as a teacher and researcher, who, in accordance with a tradition (or, as Eagleton would say, an ideology) of disinterestedness, is supposed to exercise an educated and refined judgment on his or her subject, without reference to his or her own material interests or political commitments. As Addison's introductory text indicates, the theatre is one of the places where the spectator or critic is to be found. Indeed, as Marcie Frank argues, the practice of criticism that Eagleton identifies with the public sphere of the early eighteenth century may in fact have begun in the theatre, and somewhat earlier (in the late seventeenth century) than has been assumed in accounts such as Eagleton's.[47] From the 1660s onward, theatre, she suggests, was where the practice of criticism first came to identify itself as such and to make itself visible as a distinctive public practice. The theatre was the site of the critical discourse of the period between 1660 and 1714 in multiple senses: theatrical texts were frequently the subject of criticism, offering analytical pretexts in the form of prologues, epilogues, letters of dedication, and prefatory essays. Although the materials appended to seventeenth-century plays were most often directed at an audience of social superiors, at potential or actual patrons, criticism itself became a platform for public discourse, its very proximity to the stage marking a critic's social position between the court and the theatre, between an older model of literary production dominated by court sponsorship and patronage and one increasingly oriented toward a consuming public.

If the theatre comes to be imagined as part of, or even an exemplary manifestation of, the public sphere, then, it is because it is in the closest proximity to the theatre that the practice of criticism—in which anyone who wishes to be involved in the public sphere might expect to take part—first emerges as a practice in its own right. It is also worth noting that in Frank's account it does so in relation to precisely the shift in economic and political power between the court and new commercial interests that Habermas identified. The public sphere as a set of practices rather than as a particular space or place comes into being first as a set of conversational and written exchanges in and around the theatre, at a time when the theatre is taking its place among those experiences now available to an emergent consumer public. The figure of the critic, whose history is written by Eagleton, is, first of all, the figure of the theatre spectator, and only thereafter, and by a kind of analogy, *The Spectator* of the modern world and its pleasures.

Both Habermas and Eagleton, with varying degrees of approval and derogation, associate Addison and Steele with the public sphere as described by Habermas. Others have tried to suggest that the theatre might be included within this bourgeois public sphere. I have shown already that the theatre maybe didn't and doesn't function in the way these metaphorizers have suggested, because it does not in fact promote the kind of dialogic reciprocity upon which the public sphere concept depends. Others have gone further, right to the source, as it were, to suggest that, far from encouraging this kind of dialogic reciprocity, *The Spectator* contains and limits it: that while the public sphere may indeed be bourgeois, it is not, in fact, or was not, the public sphere for which Habermas was looking. At least not in *The Spectator*.

Such recent contributions to the critical literature on *The Spectator* have qualified and complicated the kind of claims underwritten by Habermas and extended by Eagleton. Brian Cowan, for instance, argues that, far from endorsing the mode of open political conversation and debate that Habermas identifies as characteristic of bourgeois "publicness," the "*Spectator* project" seeks rather to "tame it and make it anodyne."[48] Anthony Pollock emphasizes the significance of the "spectatorial" rather than the "conversational" mode of the project (a conceptual development that, he suggests, may be inferred from the titles of *The Tatler* and *The Spectator*), to argue that the nonparticipation of Mr. Spectator himself in the social world that he offers up for the consideration of his readers seeks to cultivate in them a "neutral" stance, one more inclined to a withdrawal toward private aesthetic contemplation of the social world than active participation in its disputes and divisions.[49] Cowan sees the "*Spectator* project" as part of an effort to "make the cultural politics of Augustan Britain safe for a Whig oligarchy" by exemplifying a model of civil discourse that avoids partisan politics and public debate, rather than encouraging it, even in a contained form, as Habermas's account suggests.[50] In other words, if the coffeehouse is the site for open political contestation, *The Spectator*, although widely read in the coffeehouses, is firmly and clearly opposed to such politics and the social practices with which it is associated. This project, as described by Cowan, is, of course, perfectly ideological in precisely the sense that Eagleton would claim it to be: it presents as settled common sense a position that is in fact the outcome of class struggle in both the political and the cultural domains. Pollock's analysis complements Cowan's in presenting the figure of the "neutral" spectator as "a perfect model for culture-consumers," far preferable, in the eyes of Mr. Spectator, to all the many versions of the politically engaged partisans of the coffeehouse world.[51]

The figure that emerges from these two persuasive accounts is a spectator—an ideal bourgeois subject, even—whose freedom to consume and to enjoy cultural production more generally is dependent upon one's capacity to act and present oneself as an entirely neutral observer of the world in which one lives, and to deny (to oneself as much as to others) any relation between that consumption and the political processes by which one is enabled to enjoy it. Scenes from bourgeois life, in the world promoted in the pages of *The Spectator*, are simultaneously scenes where aesthetic contemplation and commodity consumption (at the theatre and elsewhere) are promoted, and scenes in which class relations and the colonial relation are repressed. The subject whose production they encourage is one who learns, like those subjects Alan Sinfield describes being produced by examinations in Literature, to be critical only within certain limits, and to leave the structures (of consumption, examination, and subject production) entirely unchallenged. But amid all this promotion of consumption and repression of class relations, there is, as I have suggested, ample scope (even a one-in-ten chance, perhaps) that things will go wrong in the theatre of subject production, and that other kinds of subjectivity might accidentally be produced.

The Spectator as Subject

Alan Sinfield probably had specific individuals in mind. Rather than ideal subjects, he may well have been thinking of living, breathing subjects who, having passed their examinations in Literature, had now arrived on campus to start studying for degrees in English at university departments such as his as the University of Sussex; or subjects like myself, arriving at the university where I was to study (and where I would read things by Alan Sinfield); or like those with whom I work on a regular basis at Queen Mary University of London, where I currently teach. When we encounter these student-subjects it is always clear that, whatever they may share in terms of class background or educational formation, they differ from one another in one significant way, at least as far as this project is concerned, and in which the subjects assembled in the coffeehouse, with which this scene opened, presumably did not. Unlike the customers in the coffeehouse, who would usually have all been men, it is likely that the majority of subjects we (Alan Sinfield and I) are thinking of now will identify as women.

It is time, then, to ask about the Mr. in Mr. Spectator, and to return the question of gender to the story of bourgeois subject formation and the public sphere. Was the subject in question a male subject? To what extent were women excluded from the bourgeois public sphere, and to what extent might such an exclusion have prohibited or inhibited the production of a nonmale bourgeois subject? Silvia Federici modified Marx's account of the transition to capitalism by means of primitive accumulation, to show how women were systematically "degraded" in the new economy of wage labor and commodity production. This historical account can usefully be complemented by Carole Pateman's demonstration that, far from bringing patriarchy to an end, the social transformations wrought by capitalism facilitated a shift from a "classical" patriarchy based on God-given status to a "modern" patriarchy grounded in the fiction of the social contract. Under the terms of this modern patriarchy, women were regarded as dependent upon men, who alone possessed the vital attributes of choice and agency that allowed them to enter into contracts and thereby play a full and active role in public life, which would have included forming and expressing the opinions appropriate to a spectator.[52] Both these analyses would suggest that women, at least in this relatively early phase of capitalist development, would have been structurally positioned outside the bourgeois public sphere (in a new and supposedly complementary private sphere) and would not have occupied a subject position equivalent to that of their male counterparts. They would not, in other words, have qualified fully as spectators, let alone as theatre professors.

Yet, as extensive scholarship over recent decades has very clearly shown, earlier accounts of eighteenth-century cultural production in England, which featured a canon of almost exclusively male producers, were simply incorrect. This canon had, of course, been produced and distributed by men, who had for several centuries been occupying most if not all of the key positions in the cultural and educational institutions through which bourgeois subjects managed and evaluated cultural production (universities, newspapers, journals, publishing houses). That this should have been the case in the twentieth century, in spite of the social and political advances achieved by the feminist movement, suggests that the situation could not have been very different in the eighteenth. This was indeed the case. Even fewer women occupied influential positions in such institutions (or ideological state apparatuses), notwithstanding the now well-known contributions to the culture of the time made by numerous female playwrights, essayists, philosophers, actresses, journalists, scholars, and novelists. It is this reality of female contributions that poses a conceptual problem. How to account for this apparent contradiction between the consignment of women to the private sphere and the presence of so many women contributors to the public sphere? In *The Gender of Freedom*, Elizabeth Maddock Dillon argues that the modern conception of gender is the product of precisely this construction of the public–private distinction, which is, in itself, the result of capitalism's separation of the workplace from the household.[53] It is in this sense, then, above all, that the figure of the bourgeois spectator-as-critic emerges as male, in relation to the simultaneous production of an otherwise-gendered subject who does not possess the requisite capacities for participation in the public sphere, and who is, in other words, produced as a different kind of subject, or a subject liable to disidentify with the ideal forms of subjecthood on offer. For Dillon, who wants to complicate the arguments offered by Pateman, "far from being written out of social contract theory, women are written in, albeit in a problematic fashion."[54] Women are written in as custodians of a private or domestic sphere, while those who inhabit (and contribute to the development of) the public sphere are understood to be responsible, also, for preserving the privacy of the private sphere (a responsibility that can readily be interpreted as requiring the active exclusion of women from the public sphere). As Dillon puts it, "the privacy of women's bodies and labor must be continually produced in order for the autonomous liberal male to emerge, on a daily basis even, into his public sphere identity."[55] No bourgeois public sphere, then, without women's reproductive labor. This dependency is not simply material (the public man must eat and pass on his wealth to his sons) but also conceptual (publicness requires a sanctified privacy whose function it is to protect). The scene with *The Spectator*—or, to go back to how this scene opened, the scene in the early eighteenth-century coffeehouse—is therefore a social scene in which the male bourgeois subject looks like he is producing himself, all on his own. In reality, it obscures—in its very vividness as a social scene—that entire dimension of the social without which this production would not take place. Just as there was no purely "English" economy without, say, Jamaica, there could be no coffeehouse public discourse without the newly consecrated bourgeois private home and the labor that is done there. Plantation slavery and women's work were essential material and conceptual conditions for the production of the bourgeois spectator.

Though individuals engaging in the practices associated with the public sphere—from reading journals and attending plays to writing both—did, of course, include women, it is clear that, in terms of the construction of gender instantiated by modern patriarchy, the position of the critical bourgeois subject was marked, or rather "unmarked," as neutral. The occupants of this subject position were understood to be male, and cultural production assumed such male subjects as its primary consumers and addressees. This is what allows Mr. Spectator to claim a universal position, characteristic, as we have seen, of "bourgeois philosophy," and to claim it, as it were, on behalf of men and women alike. At the same time, it seems certain that, in the face of a structure that worked to limit or even eliminate their participation in bourgeois cultural production, women would have been more likely than men to disidentify when interpellated in its multiple scenes. The history of feminism is in part the history of these disidentifications. While there is of course ample evidence of male disidentification with class and gender roles—and even with the whole bourgeois business—it is, on the whole, fairly clear that one significant effect of this reorganization of gender in early modern bourgeois culture was the production of spectators as a male subjects who resisted, in the main, the temptation to disidentify (primarily because it would not have been in their interests to do so).

To get a richer sense of what these subjects might be like and what kinds of thing they can do, I'd like to take another step back—this time, into the theatre. Jean-Christophe Agnew's *Worlds Apart: The Market and the Theater in Anglo-American Thought, 1550–1750* has been an important foundation for the ideas I am trying to develop in this book. Its significance for my project lies mainly in its proposition that the English theatre, especially of the first half of the period Agnew discusses, was important—if not exactly as a "moral technology" or "ideological apparatus"—then certainly as a practice or institution that made a distinctive contribution to the production of human subjects at a time of social and economic change. The time in question is, of course, part of the broader transition to capitalism, debates over which I have briefly sketched in Chapter I, "An Essay Regarding the Bourgeoisie." In particular, Agnew argues that the theatre of the period 1550–1650 was a privileged location for negotiating changes in social relations occasioned by the expansion of market activities, in which the increasing abstraction of exchange has raised all sorts of question about who people are, to what extent they can be believed to be who they appear to be, or to have the property or the money they claim to possess or have available. It is not simply that the theatre dramatized or represented the social and economic changes that were taking place, although it certainly did this too, as all kinds of play, from Shakespeare's *King Lear* to the so-called city comedies of Jonson, Middleton, Dekker, and their collaborators, demonstrate. What Agnew insists upon, following Raymond Williams, is that theatre, as an instance of cultural production, was a "true and integral element of the changes themselves; an articulation, by technical discovery, of changes in consciousness which are themselves forms of consciousness of change."[56] Theatre makers—and in this case Agnew primarily has playwrights in mind—are contributing to a process of material cultural change, by means of their production of performances in which changes in social relations are experienced and enacted through the ways actors and audiences witness one another grappling with current questions of social identity. Theatre is not simply an occasion for commenting upon social change, it is a part of that social change.

With Agnew, I would extend the sense of Williams's "technical discovery"—by which he refers to such formal theatrical devices as the aside and the soliloquy—to include the discoveries made by audiences as they respond to and reciprocate the modes of address and new conventions of personation with which playwrights and actors are experimenting. Among the problems that Agnew suggests are being worked over or worked through in this theatre, is the question of credit: questions about what and who might be believed (credited) in both the theatre and the market. In the theatre of this period, he argues, "a new social contract" was worked out in the interactions among actors, the figures they represented, and the spectators for whom they represented them, and who may also have seen themselves represented in stage figures.[57] It did this by reflecting openly upon the conditions of its own performance—in its self-conscious theatricality—which, because it functioned simultaneously as an allegory for what was going on in a "market society" and as an actual instantiation of it, invited consideration of "the questions of authenticity, accountability, and intentionality" that were demanded by the market society taking shape at the time.[58]

My primary concern here is what happened to spectators who signed up to this new social contract generated in the theatre, and what kind of understanding of the self—as constituted through the mediations of theatrical spectatorship—emerged from it and contributed to the production of a bourgeois or protobourgeois subjectivity of the kind I think I am locating in the pages of *The Spectator*, and of which I consider *The Spectator* to be both an effect and a means of further transmission. What happened, I think is that such spectators got used to the idea that the social and personal skills they used in negotiating their relationship with theatrical representation—and with media more generally, especially with the rise of such print media as *The Spectator*, shortly after the period Agnew discusses—are what we have learned to call "transferable skills." They can be adapted into other, nontheatrical, spheres of life, both consciously, as a result of processes of reflection, and (if the term is not too anachronistic) unconsciously, through the kind of taking up and embodying of gestures and attitudes that Carrie Noland has identified as a vital element in such processes of ideological transmission and subject production. They learned, I suggest, that to live with the habitus of a spectator was one way of dealing with the situation in which they found themselves: they learned to observe and evaluate the behavior of others for what it might tell them about what these others might have to offer, in terms of opportunities, financial rewards, benefits, and pleasures in general.

In a world in which it was no longer possible to make assumptions based on stable identities or stable indexes of identity (from familiar faces to familiar ways of dressing), and in which new professional and class identities were in formation, theatre (and theatregoing) offered both the idea that such capacity for spectatorship in everyday life might be possible, as well as opportunities to practice it experimentally. Going to the theatre offered experiences of the self in social relation, both as representations and as actualizations, that could subsequently be deployed as resources for survival and advancement by spectators whose livelihoods would increasingly come to depend upon the new protoprofessional occupations of the colonial state and its commercial wing. Think of all the clerks, inspectors, supervisors, overseers, book-keepers, traders, spies, and administrators, not to mention the professional "observers," "reporters," and "spectators" of the print media, who would spend their working lives looking at people and things and reporting to their employers on what they were up to or what they might be worth. What do these jobs require above all, but a capacity to be in the world while also standing apart from it? Agnew charts, across the first hundred years of his historical period, a shift from a theatre in which participation—such as moving from station to station and immersion within the action—gave way to the separation of the spectator. The theatre gradually produces the spectator, and in the figure of the spectator all the subjects with the capacity to take on these new forms of employment. The spectator in question is simultaneously part of the theatre and at a distance from it; in it and standing outside it. The spectator's relationship to the theatre is like that of *The Spectator*'s relationship to life itself: "rather as a Spectator of Mankind, than as one of the Species," as Addison put it. It is this condition that also makes possible what I have already hinted might be a crucial dimension of the subject produced in this way: its predisposition to irony, facilitated if not yet actively encouraged or even required by being beside oneself, looking in, on everyone else and on oneself. Irony will also characterize the ways many such subjects will learn to perform their professional responsibilities: whether it expresses itself as the dispassionate detachment from one's personal feelings in favor of governmental or business objectives, on the one hand, or the disaffected compliance of the call-center worker and the theatre professor, on the other.

There is a potential criticism of Agnew's historical account, on the grounds that the transition to capitalism as he describes it seems to manifest itself entirely as the expansion of market activity, and does not appear to be the result of changes in production at all. He does not descend, as Marx famously did, from the "noisy sphere" of market circulation, where "everything takes place on the surface and in full view of everyone," into the "hidden abode of production," where one might see "how capital produces."[59] Of course, Agnew has already shown—as Marx, who is, of course, being ironic (he is a bourgeois subject, himself, you see), also knows—that the market is anything but transparent. Nonetheless, does the omission of production from his account weaken it significantly? Does it fail to account for the ways in which the subjects in question may have been produced, not through their acts of consumption and spectatorship, but through their position in the social relations of production? Were they in fact shaped more by work than by leisure? Inasmuch as Agnew is writing about the production of subjects, he is writing about a class of consumers and spectators who are, almost by definition, becoming more and more distant from production, and whose work, as I have suggested, involves the increasing application of the practices and habitus of the spectator. The nature of their participation in both production and consumption appears simultaneously to generate and to demand similar dispositions. If Agnew resembles the subjects of his study, in taking up a position at a distance from production, it might not be too much of a stretch to argue, in both cases, that the distance between these subjects and sites of production is itself an aspect of the composition of their distinctive (spectatorial) subjectivity. The condition of being a spectator, in this respect, is not just that of being a bourgeois consumer, but also that of being a critic, or being an author of a book about theatre.

What began, in Agnew's account, as a kind of social improvisation performed by both theatre makers and audiences, and as a rather anguish-ridden set of responses to collective "distress" in the face of confusing processes of social and economic change, eventually became a fairly familiar and well-scripted routine. As the eighteenth century wore on, he writes, "the theatrical perspective entered into the ideological mainstream as an amusing gloss on the literate ideal of the detached and impartial observer of life, the discriminating consumer of the urban spectacle."[60] The well-scripted routine found perhaps its ideal performance in the writings in *The Spectator*. Spectatorship had, as it were, established itself as an accepted and mainstream mode of social action. But if the experimentation that, in Agnew's account, had characterized the work of the Tudor and Stuart dramatists was no longer, by the time of *The Spectator*, visible in contemporary theatrical production, it had perhaps migrated, he suggests, in keeping with many other accounts of the literature of the period, to what would come to be known as the novel. What critics now tend to identify as some of the novel's inaugurating instances, such as Daniel Defoe's *Robinson Crusoe*, had not yet consolidated in their recognizable hegemonic form either the conventions of fiction or character in any settled way. Neither writers nor readers had yet reached a consensus on the presentation of a seemingly truthful story that could be routinely accepted as if it were true, while simultaneously being known not to refer to any actual historical events or individuals.[61]

Bearing this in mind, I think it is worth reconsidering the extent to which the writings included in *The Spectator* were as well-scripted a routine as critics such as Agnew suppose. It is striking, to this critic, at least, that much *Spectator* criticism tends to attribute views expressed by "characters" written in *The Spectator* (including its fictional "author") to its actual authors while at the same time failing to remark upon what seems to me fairly obvious: that many of the letters published in *The Spectator* and attributed to "real" correspondents, were almost certainly written by Addison and Steele. In other words, *The Spectator*, written as it was by two men both of whom had aspirations and some success as playwrights, continued to experiment with the emergent and unstable categories of fiction and character, just like contemporaries (Defoe, Manley) whose experiments took them closer to writing texts that have subsequently been recognized as fiction, and as novels, while the writings of *The Spectator* have come to be understood as journalism, with the result that what critics would call their "fictionality" has been strangely underemphasized.[62]

So, as Agnew himself recognizes (in spite of his simultaneous assent to the narrative in which energy migrates from theatre to the novel), *The Spectator* does not exactly represent a consolidation and routinization of earlier experimentation associated with the theatre, and might better be regarded as a continuation of the same experimental practice: "But where those dramatists had, to a man, focused on the impostures and impersonations of the actor, eighteenth-century authors declared their epoch the age of the Spectator."[63] The persistence of a theatrical conception of reading as an act of spectatorship in relation to a performance can also be detected, Agnew proposes, in the writings of Shaftesbury, who writes in such a way as to invite his readers to collude with him in the idea that they are not there, creating a "barrier of studied indifference that . . . stood as the textual equivalent of the fourth wall in drama," and that later "became, at the hands of Adam Smith, a startlingly novel, wholly secular, and decidedly functionalist social psychology of market society."[64]

Agnew refers here to, and later discusses at some length, Smith's *The Theory of Moral Sentiments*. In this 1759 work, the philosopher who would later publish a text that would be canonized as the founding theory of capitalism and subjected accordingly to rigorous critique by Karl Marx—*The Wealth of Nations* (1776)—developed a moral philosophy in which the figure of the "impartial spectator," conceived and presented in explicitly theatrical language, plays a central role.[65] I have already suggested that the figure of the spectator, as a figure for a nascent bourgeois subjectivity, is constructed around the need to be simultaneously inside and outside either the theatrical performance or its analogue in the social world. In Smith's philosophy this condition is intensified to the extent that the subject is imagined as irrevocably divided by the ethical and social requirement that they live simultaneously inside and outside, not just the world, but inside and outside their very selves. According to Smith, no one can know what another person is feeling. Everyone has to imagine what it would be like to be another person. At the same time everyone recognizes that other people can grasp how you are feeling only by imagining that they are you, which they can only do in a limited way because they can't know what it is like for you. Aware that other people spectate and evaluate your suffering and your conduct, you organize your behaviors in such a way as you think will elicit sympathy and approval. In an influential essay on Smith's moral philosophy and its relation to theatre, David Marshall insists, as does Agnew, that this condition of spectatorship is now inextricably entwined with those of acting: in life, ethical actors depend for their conduct upon their capacities as spectators.[66] He explains this process of theatrical subject formation for the eighteenth-century spectator-actor as follows: "This condition of constantly imagining ourselves appearing before the eyes of other people inevitably places us in a theatrical relationship to others; but it also creates an internalized sense that determines how we see ourselves, even if we are not in the presence of an actual spectator."[67] In other words, what is proposed in Smith's philosophy represents a full internalization of a practice or habitus that began as credit maximization in business and as theatregoing as a leisure activity. It has turned into a way of being in the world. It is the making of bourgeois subjects, fit for bourgeois life.

The time has come for a quick recapitulation of this attempt to set the scene for the appearance of the Trunk-Maker, which I have delayed long enough. The scene onto which the Trunk-Maker makes his appearance is the scene of the Spectator. It is a scene that is the result of the social and economic processes I have attempted to describe here, and a scene in and for which a new kind of subject has been produced. Such subjects have allowed themselves to be produced as a response to the increasing abstraction and opacity of social and economic life.[68] They have allowed themselves to be produced through their participation in economic prosperity linked to distant (colonial) production. The distinctive characteristics of the subject that interests me here arise from their participation in leisure activities in which spectatorship—or media consumption, more broadly—is the route to self-fulfillment, self-realization, and pleasure, and for which theatre functions as both real and metaphorical point of reference. In allowing themselves to be produced under such conditions, these bourgeois subjects who now make the scene have embraced the condition of living as spectators. In particular, they have learned to place a distance between themselves and the world (of production). They have learned to be both inside and outside at the same time. They have learned to live and act as though they were invisible.

Notes

1. All issues of *The Spectator* are collected in a five-volume scholarly edition. Joseph Addison and Richard Steele, *The Spectator*, ed. Donald F. Bond (Oxford: Clarendon

Press, 1965). A number of complete sets of the original publication exist today. I consulted the set held at the Huntington Library.

2. *The Spectator*, No. 65 (May 15, 1711).

3. Richard Steele and Joseph Addison, *The Spectator*, 5 vols., ed. Donald F. Bond (Oxford: Clarendon Press, 1987).

4. *The Spectator*, No. 235 (November 29, 1711).

5. That he is called Mr. Spectator is not affirmed at this point, and this "name" is not associated with the fictional character supposed to be writing the newspaper until No. 53, when it is the form of address used by one of "his" now "so numerous" correspondents.

6. I am thinking, perhaps a little anachronistically, of twentieth- and twenty-first-century makers and theorists of theatre for whom spectatorship is denigrated as passive. An influential recent critique of this familiar view is to be found in Jacques Rancière, *The Emancipated Spectator*, trans. Gregory Elliott (London and New York: Verso, 2009). Among Rancière's targets are those would-be reformers of the theatre who seek to "emancipate" their spectators, whether bourgeois or proletarian, from the bondage of this passivity: Bertolt Brecht and Antonin Artaud. I shall return to Brecht's ideas about the spectator in relation to bourgeois thought and practice in Chapter IV, "The Scene with the Smoke."

7. Ellen Meiksins Wood and Neal Wood, *Class Ideology and Ancient Political Theory: Socrates, Plato, and Aristotle in Social Context* (Oxford: Blackwell, 1978), 105.

8. Plato, *The Republic*, trans. Desmond Lee, 2nd, rev. ed. (London: Penguin Books, 1987), 94.

9. Wood and Wood, *Class Ideology*, 204, n. 31.

10. Ibid., 153.

11. Aristotle, *Politics*, cited in Wood and Wood, *Class Ideology*, 222.

12. Lawrence E. Klein, "Addisonian Afterlives: Joseph Addison in Eighteenth-Century Culture," *Journal for Eighteenth-Century Studies* 35, no. 1 (2012): 101–18, at 102.

13. Samuel Johnson, *Lives of the Most Eminent English Poets, with Critical Observations on Their Works. A New Edition, Corrected,* 4 vols., London: C. Bathurst et al., 1783, 2: 420.

14. Ibid., 2: 340.

15. Thomas Babington Macaulay, *The Life and Writings of Addison* (London: Longman, Brown, Green and Longmans, 1852), 41.

16. Matthew Arnold, ed., *The Six Chief Lives from Johnson's "Lives of the Poets"* (London: Macmillan and Co., 1886), xii.

17. Key texts for me at the time, and subsequently, included Jean-Christophe Agnew, *Worlds Apart: The Market and the Theater in Anglo-American Thought, 1550–1750* (Cambridge: Cambridge University Press, 1986); Francis Barker, *The Tremulous Private Body: Essays in Subjection* (London: Methuen, 1984); Catherine Belsey, *The Subject of Tragedy: Identity and Difference in Renaissance Drama* (London: Methuen, 1985); Jonathan Dollimore, *Radical Tragedy: Religion, Ideology and Power in the Drama of Shakespeare and His Contemporaries* (Brighton: Harvester, 1984); Jonathan Dollimore and Alan Sinfield, eds., *Political Shakespeare: Essays in Cultural Materialism* (Manchester: Manchester University Press, 1985)—which includes essays by both editors as well as by Graham Holderness and Kathleen McLuskie, along with Margot Heinemann on Brecht and Shakespeare, and an Afterword by Raymond Williams; and Peter Hulme, *Colonial Encounters: Europe*

and the Native Caribbean, 1492–1797 (London: Methuen, 1986). It is perhaps symptomatic, or perhaps even constitutive, of my ongoing blindness to questions of race and British colonialism (which defect I shall discuss in due course), that I came to Hulme's work, which does not in fact focus exclusively on the theatre of Shakespeare and his contemporaries, many years after I encountered the other texts.

18. Belsey wrote, in an outline of her position: "The human subject, the self, is the central figure in the drama which is liberal humanism, the consensual orthodoxy of the west. The subject is to be found at the heart of our political institutions, the economic system and the family, voting, exercising rights, working, consuming, falling in love, marrying and becoming a parent. And yet the subject has conventionally no history, perhaps because liberal humanism depends on the belief that in its essence the subject does not change, that liberal humanism itself expresses a human nature which, despite its diversity, is always at the most basic, the most intimate level, the same. I do not share this belief or the conservatism it implies." Belsey, *Subject of Tragedy*, ix.

19. Terry Eagleton, "The Subject of Literature," *Cultural Critique* 2 (1985–86): 95–104, at 96, 97.

20. Alan Sinfield, "Give an account of Shakespeare and Education, showing why you think they are effective and what you have appreciated about them. Support your comments with precise references," in *Political Shakespeare*, ed. Dollimore and Sinfield, 137–57, at 142.

21. Ibid., 142.

22. Ibid., 147–51; quote at 171.

23. He refers to "a lecture" by Eagleton, from which he takes the term. A year after Roach's article came out in *Theatre Journal*, Terry Eagleton's book *The Ideology of the Aesthetic* (Oxford and Cambridge, MA: Blackwell), in which he explores the concept in depth, appeared.

24. Joseph Roach, "Theatre History and the Ideology of the Aesthetic," *Theatre Journal* 41, no. 2 (1989): 155–68, at 157.

25. Michael Hays, *The Public and Performance: Essays in the History of French and German Theater 1871–1900* (Ann Arbor: UMI Research Press, 1982), 7

26. Judith Butler, *Gender Trouble: Feminism and the Subversion of Identity* (New York and London: Routledge, 1990); Saidiya V. Hartman, *Scenes of Subjection: Terror, Slavery, and Self-Making in Nineteenth-Century America* (New York: Oxford University Press, 1997); Daphne A. Brooks, *Bodies in Dissent: Spectacular Performances of Race and Freedom, 1850–1910* (Durham, NC: Duke University Press, 2006); Robin Bernstein, *Racial Innocence: Performing American Childhood and Race from Slavery to Civil Rights* (New York: NYU Press, 2011); Kyla Wazana Tompkins, *Racial Indigestion: Eating Bodies in the Nineteenth Century* (New York: NYU Press, 2012).

27. Louis Althusser, "Ideology and Ideological State Apparatuses (Notes towards an Investigation)," in *Lenin and Philosophy and Other Essays*, trans. Ben Brewster (New York: Monthly Review Press, 2001), 85–126. See also my earlier discussion in Chapter I, "An Essay Regarding the Bourgeoisie," note 2.

28. Carrie Noland, *Agency and Embodiment: Performing Gestures/Producing Culture* (Cambridge, MA: Harvard University Press, 2010), 30.

29. Ibid., 38, 40. In subsequent chapters she deepens her analysis by working through texts by Maurice Merleau-Ponty, André Leroi-Gourand, Henri Michaux, Judith Butler, and Frantz Fanon.

30. Ibid., 20.

31. I have discussed this tendency, at possibly overemphatic length, in Nicholas Ridout, *Stage Fright, Animals and Other Theatrical Problems* (Cambridge: Cambridge University Press, 2006).

32. J. H. Plumb, *In the Light of History* (London: Allen Lane, 1972), 54–55; for the review's history, see Prologue 1, note 6. Plumb, affectionately described by his colleague and former student, Neil McKendrick, as "the rudest man in Cambridge," was an influential historian whose most important contribution to scholarship was to the social and political history of eighteenth-century Britain. Neil McKendrick, "Sir John Plumb" (obituary), *The Guardian*, October 22, 2001.

33. This monopoly was known as the "asiento" in Spanish, and had been held by France and the Netherlands. My understanding of the historical moment of *The Spectator* is particularly indebted to the work by historians of the period associated with what is now often called "new imperial history." See, for example, Kathleen Wilson, *A New Imperial History: Culture, Identity and Modernity in Britain and the Empire, 1660–1840* (Cambridge: Cambridge University Press, 2004); Stephen Howe, ed., *The New Imperial Histories Reader* (London: Routledge, 2010). For a theoretical account of the entanglements of finance and slavery, see Ian Baucom, *Specters of the Atlantic: Finance Capital, Slavery, and the Philosophy of History* (Durham, NC: Duke University Press, 2005).

34. Influential historical work on the emergence of a "consumer society" in eighteenth-century London includes Neil McKendrick, John Brewer, and J. H. Plumb, *The Birth of a Consumer Society: The Commercialization of Eighteenth-Century England* (London: Hutchinson, 1982); John Brewer and Roy Porter, eds., *Consumption and the World of Goods* (Abingdon, UK: Routledge, 1993); and John Brewer, *The Pleasures of the Imagination: English Culture in the Eighteenth Century* (New York: Farrar, Straus and Giroux, 1997). The work of McKendrick and Brewer has been subjected to a persuasive critique in Jonathan White, "A World of Goods? The 'Consumption Turn' and Eighteenth-Century British History," *Cultural and Social History* 3, no. 1 (2006): 93–104, which argues that by paying no attention to production this work produces a distorted account of its historical moment that reflects, and to some extent endorses, the neoliberal turn in the politics of the 1980s.

35. Zacharias Conrad von Uffenbach, *London in 1710: From the Travels of Zacharias Conrad von Uffenbach,* trans. and ed. W. H. Quarrell and Margaret Mare (London: Faber and Faber, 1934), 88.

36. Peter Smithers, *The Life of Joseph Addison*, 2nd ed. (Oxford: Clarendon, 1968), 000.

37. For Indian Kings, see Eric Hinderaker, "The 'Four Indian Kings' and the Imaginative Construction of the First British Empire," *William and Mary Quarterly* 53, no. 3 (1996): 487–526; for Mohocks, see Daniel Statt, "The Case of the Mohocks: Rake Violence in Augustan London," *Social History* 20, no. 2 (1995): 179–99, and also Chapter III in the present book.

38. Peter Earle, *The Making of the English Middle Class: Business, Society, and Family Life in London, 1660–1730* (Berkeley and Los Angeles: University of California Press, 1989); E. P. Thompson, *The Making of the English Working Class* (London: Victor Gollancz, 1963).

39. Dror Wahrman, *The Making of the Modern Self: Identity and Culture in Eighteenth-Century England* (New Haven: Yale University Press, 2004), 150–51, and *Imagining the*

Middle Class: The Political Representation of Class in Britain, c. 1780–1840 (Cambridge: Cambridge University Press, 1995).

40. Ellen Meiksins Wood, *The Pristine Culture of Capitalism: A Historical Essay on Old Regimes and Modern States* (London and New York: Verso, 1991); Robert Brenner, "Agrarian Class Structure and Economic Development in Pre-industrial Europe," *Past & Present* 70, no. 1 (1976): 30–75; T[revor] H[enry] Aston and C[harles] H. E. Philpin, eds., *The Brenner Debate: Agrarian Class Structure and Economic Development in Pre-industrial Europe* (Cambridge: Cambridge University Press, 1987); Jürgen Kocka, "The Middle Classes in Europe," *Journal of Modern History* 67, no. 4 (1995): 783–806. For debates among largely, but not exclusively, Marxist historians on the class politics of the period, see also Eric Hobsbawm, "The General Crisis of the European Economy in the 17th Century," *Past & Present* 5, no. 1 (1954): 33–53, "The Crisis of the 17th Century II," *Past & Present* 6, no. 1 (1954): 44–65, and "The Seventeenth Century in the Development of Capitalism," *Science & Society* 24, no. 2 (1960): 97–112; Perry Anderson, "Origins of the Present Crisis," *New Left Review* 23, no. 1 (1964): 26–53; E. P. Thompson, "The Peculiarities of the English," *Socialist Register* 2, no. 2 (1965): 311–62; C. H. George, "The Making of the English Bourgeoisie 1500–1750," *Science & Society* 35, no. 4 (1971): 385–414; E. P. Thompson, "Patrician Society, Plebeian Culture," *Journal of Social History* 7, no. 4 (1974): 382–405; Robert Brenner, "The Origins of Capitalist Development: A Critique of Neo-Smithian Marxism," *New Left Review* 104, no. 1 (1977): 25–92; E. P. Thompson, "Eighteenth-Century English Society: Class Struggle without Class?," *Social History* 3, no. 2 (1978): 133–65; Nicholas Rogers, "Money, Land and Lineage: The Big Bourgeoisie of Hanoverian London," *Social History* 4, no. 3 (1979): 437–54; Marvin Rosen, "The Dictatorship of the Bourgeoisie: England, 1688–1721," *Science & Society* 45, no. 1 (1981): 24–51; Lawrence Stone, "The Bourgeois Revolution of Seventeenth-Century England Revisited," *Past & Present* 109, no. 1 (1985): 44–54. There is a recent and helpful survey of these debates in Henry Heller, *The Birth of Capitalism: A 21st-Century Perspective* (London: Pluto Press, 2011).

41. Jürgen Habermas, *The Structural Transformation of the Public Sphere: An Inquiry into a Category of Bourgeois Society*, trans. Thomas Burger (Cambridge, MA: MIT Press, 1991).

42. Significant contributions to the discussion of the public sphere that engage with Habermas include Nancy Fraser, "Rethinking the Public Sphere: A Contribution to the Critique of Actually Existing Democracy," *Social Text* 25–26 (1990): 56–80; Craig Calhoun, ed., *Habermas and the Public Sphere* (Cambridge MA: MIT Press, 1992), which reprints Fraser's *Social Text* essay (109–42) alongside contributions from, *inter alia*, Seyla Benhabib, Moishe Postone, and Michael Warner; Michael Warner, *Publics and Counterpublics* (New York: Zone Books, 2002); and Lauren Berlant, *The Queen of America Goes to Washington City* (Durham, NC: Duke University Press, 1997) and *The Female Complaint: The Unfinished Business of Sentimentality in American Culture* (Durham, NC: Duke University Press, 2008).

43. Habermas, *Structural Transformation*, 15.

44. Fraser, "Rethinking the Public Sphere," 57.

45. Christopher B. Balme, *The Theatrical Public Sphere* (Cambridge: Cambridge University Press, 2014).

46. Terry Eagleton, *The Function of Criticism: From "The Spectator" to Poststructuralism* (London and New York: Verso, 1996).

47. Marcie Frank, *Gender, Theatre and the Origins of Criticism: From Dryden to Manley* (Cambridge: Cambridge University Press, 2002).

48. Brian Cowan, "Mr. Spectator and the Coffeehouse Public Sphere," *Eighteenth-Century Studies* 37, no. 3 (2004): 345–66, at 346.

49. Anthony Pollock, "Neutering Addison and Steele: Aesthetic Failure and the Spectatorial Public Sphere," *ELH* 74, no. 3 (2007): 707–34, at 707.

50. Cowan, "Mr. Spectator," 361.

51. Pollock, "Neutering Addison and Steele," 729.

52. See the discussion in Chapter I of both Silvia Federici, *Caliban and the Witch: Women, the Body and Primitive Accumulation* (New York: Autonomedia, 2004), and Carole Pateman, *The Sexual Contract* (Cambridge: Polity Press, 1988).

53. Elizabeth Maddock Dillon, *The Gender of Freedom: Fictions of Liberalism and the Literary Public Sphere* (Stanford, CA: Stanford University Press, 2004).

54. Ibid., 24.

55. Ibid., 24–25.

56. Agnew, *Worlds Apart*, 11, citing Raymond Williams, *The Sociology of Culture* (New York: Schocken Books, 1982), 142.

57. Agnew, *Worlds Apart*, 11.

58. Ibid.

59. Karl Marx, *Capital: A Critique of Political Economy, Volume 1*, trans. Ben Fowkes (Harmondsworth, UK: Penguin Books, 2004), 279–80.

60. Agnew, *Worlds Apart*, 13.

61. See Catherine Gallagher, "The Rise of Fictionality," in *The Novel I: History, Geography and Culture*, ed. Franco Moretti (Princeton: Princeton University Press, 2006), 336–63.

62. In this context, Lennard J. Davis's contention in *Factual Fictions: The Origins of the English Novel* (Philadelphia: University of Pennsylvania Press, 1997) that the novel as critics know it now was a development of the "undifferentiated matrix of news/novels" (71) is particularly suggestive: writers like Addison, Steele, Defoe, and Delarivier Manley were producing texts in a specific commercial and legal situation in which the need to defend what one had written as neither "true" and thus potentially libelous, nor actually a "lie" and thus vulnerable to simply being dismissed, came to be supported by an appeal to a third category of "fiction." As Davis writes: "The history of that process of defining fact and fiction in a cultural sense, is also the history of the splitting of the undifferentiated matrix of news/novels on the one hand, and journalism and history on the other" (71). Many readers at the time would accordingly not have made clear distinctions of either fact and fiction or their respective genres, regarding writings such as *Spectator* essays and shipwreck narratives as effectively equivalent.

63. Agnew, *Worlds Apart*, 161.

64. Ibid., 169, 13.

65. Ibid., 177–86, quote at 182.

66. Marshall taught an interdisciplinary seminar with Agnew in 1982, in which both critics clearly developed some of their thinking together. See ibid., 247, n. 48.

67. David Marshall, *The Figure of Theater: Shaftesbury, Defoe, Adam Smith and George Eliot* (New York: Columbia University Press, 1986), 174.

68. I have used the active-passive construction "allowed themselves to be produced" in an attempt to articulate my sense that no subject can produce itself, and that no subject

is automatically just produced. In this respect I am of course echoing Marx's frequently cited (including by me) observation that "[m]en make their own history, but they do not make it just as they please; they do not make it under circumstances chosen by themselves, but under circumstances directly encountered, given and transmitted from the past." Karl Marx, *The Eighteenth Brumaire of Louis Bonaparte* (New York: International Publishers, 1963), 15.

III • The Scene with the Trunk-Maker

This is a scene within a scene. In the previous scene, the scene with the spectator (or, The Scene with *The Spectator*), a subject was born—or, as cultural
materialists tend to say, a subject was produced. In any case, this subject, or
rather, these subjects—as there were so many of them, in the end, that they
would come to be considered as a class—lived at least part of their lives at a
distance from the world that had produced them. Both at work and at leisure, they participated in the world through mediation. They read about it in
reports and in journals, and they watched it (and one another) at the theatre.
They were there, and they were not there. They were on the scene, but invisible; they were part of the scene, but apart from it. They were the spectators.
In this scene within a scene, one of these spectators goes to the theatre. He
doesn't go there to see a play, however. In fact no play is even mentioned. Instead he goes to the theatre specifically to see another spectator, a spectator
he has only heard about, presumably from other spectators. Here, at greater
length than the brief citation offered in the previous scene, is what he finds:

> There is nothing which lies more within the Province of a Spectator
> than Publick Shows and Diversions; and as among these there are
> none which can pretend to vie with those elegant Entertainments that
> are exhibited in our Theatres, I think it particularly incumbent on me
> to take Notice of every thing that is remarkable in such numerous and
> refined Assemblies.

> It is observed, that of late Years there has been a certain Person in the
> upper Gallery of the Playhouse, who when he is pleased with any
> thing that is acted upon the Stage, expresses his Approbation by a loud
> Knock upon the Benches, or the Wainscot, which may be heard over

the whole Theatre. This Person is commonly known by the Name of the *Trunk-maker in the upper Gallery*. Whether it be, that the Blow he gives on these Occasions resembles that which is often heard in the Shops of such Artizans, or that he was supposed to have been a real Trunk-maker, who after the finishing of his Day's Work used to unbend his Mind at these publick Diversions with his Hammer in his Hand, I cannot certainly tell. There are some, I know, who have been foolish enough to imagine it is a Spirit which haunts the upper Gallery, and from Time to Time makes those strange Noises; and the rather, because he is observed to be louder than ordinary every Time the Ghost of *Hamlet* appears. Others have reported, that it is a dumb Man, who has chosen this Way of uttering himself when he is transported with any Thing he sees or hears. Others will have it to be the Playhouse Thunderer, that exerts himself after this Manner in the upper Gallery, when he has nothing to do upon the Roof.

But having made it my Business to get the best Information I could in a Matter of this Moment, I find that the Trunk-maker, as he is commonly called, is a large black Man, whom no body knows. He generally leans forward on a huge Oaken Plant with great Attention to every thing that passes upon the Stage. He is never seen to smile; but upon hearing any thing that pleases him, he takes up his Staff with both Hands, and lays it upon the next Piece of Timber that stands in his Way with exceeding Vehemence: After which, he composes himself in his former Posture, till such Time as something new sets him again at Work.

It has been observed, his Blow is so well timed, that the most judicious Critick could never except against it. As soon as any shining Thought is expressed in the Poet, or any uncommon Grace appears in the Actor, he smites the Bench or Wainscot. If the Audience does not concur with him, he smites a second Time, and if the Audience is not yet awaked, looks round him with great Wrath, and repeats the Blow a third Time, which never fails to produce the Clap. He sometimes lets the Audience begin the Clap of themselves, and at the Conclusion of their Applause ratifies it with a single Thwack.

. . .

The Players do not only connive at his obstreperous Approbation, but very cheerfully repair at their own Cost whatever Damages he makes. They had once a Thought of erecting a kind of Wooden Anvil for his Use that should be made of a very sounding Plank, in order to render his Stroaks more deep and mellow; but as this might not have been distinguished from the Musick of a Kettle-Drum, the Project was laid aside.

. . .

As I do not care for terminating my Thoughts in barren Speculations, or in Reports of pure Matter of Fact, without drawing something from them for the Advantage of my Countrymen, I shall take the Liberty to make an humble Proposal, that whenever the Trunk-maker shall depart this Life, or whenever he shall have lost the Spring of his Arm by Sickness, old Age, Infirmity, or the like, some able-bodied Critick should be advanced to this Post, and have a competent Salary setled on him for Life, to be furnished with Bamboos for Operas, Crabtree-Cudgels for Comedies, and Oaken Plants for Tragedy, at the publick Expence. And to the End that this Place should be always disposed of according to Merit, I would have none preferred to it, who has not given convincing Proofs both of a sound Judgment and a strong Arm, and who could not, upon Occasion, either knock down an Ox, or write a Comment upon *Horace*'s Art of Poetry. In short, I would have him a due Composition of *Hercules* and *Apollo*, and so rightly qualified for this important Office, that the Trunk-maker may not be missed by our Posterity.[1]

In this chapter, I want to go behind the scenes of this scene within a scene, to explore what theatrical, cultural, and political realities might lie behind this seemingly rather trivial and lighthearted essay and its recommendation that someone resembling the Trunk-Maker should be appointed as a salaried theatre critic. The salaried theatre critic, is, as I have already suggested from time to time, an ideal figure for the bourgeois spectatorial subject whose production I have been tracking here. What can it possibly mean for Joseph Addison, of all people, to suggest that this ideal bourgeois subject ought to be, or at the very least resemble, "a large black Man, whom no body knows"? To approach this strange proposition, I begin by investigating briefly the historical reality out of which Addison generated this imaginary Trunk-Maker. What made it possible for Addison to imagine such a figure? What historical and cultural circumstances might have enabled his author to imagine him and write him down, and within what horizon of expectations might he have become legible to his readers? First of all, it would be useful to know what sort of a person a trunk-maker would have been, and to think about what Addison might have meant by attributing or assigning to his spectator spectated this particular employment. It will then be essential to establish what Addison might have meant, and what his readers might have understood by the description of the Trunk-Maker as "a large black Man." With a few historical and literary points of reference in hand, I will then attempt a reading of this text that aims to make sense of it as a scene from bourgeois life.

The Trunk-Makers

A trunk-maker made trunks: robust and portable containers for the transport of people's possessions, normally manufactured from wood, and which, by the eighteenth century, were very widely used, even by people of relatively modest means, to keep possessions safe while traveling. As Addison's text makes it clear, this was an artisan occupation and a form of manual labor that required strong arms and the use of hammers. A trunk-maker was not, on the face of it, a bourgeois consumer living a life at a distance from production, although it was apparently possible to make considerable wealth as the owner of such a business (presumably not, however, as someone actually wielding the hammer on a daily basis).[2] Some further indication of the social status of trunk-makers is provided by the fact that, during the War of the Spanish Succession (1701–14), an application was made for John James, a trunk-maker, not to be "imprest" to serve on a ship commanded by Tancred Robinson, on the grounds that he had to care for his widowed mother and his eight younger siblings.[3] Although it appears that most trunk-makers, like most owners of businesses in eighteenth-century London, were men, there was at least one woman trading in 1765: Rachel Bryant, at the sign of the Trunk and Bucket,

St. Paul's Churchyard.[4] A trade card from around 1760 advertises the services of Samuel Forsaith. Engraved by William Clark, this illustrated advertisement identified Forsaith as having been apprenticed formerly to "Mr. Smith, Trunkmaker to his Majesty," and as making and selling "all sorts of Campaign and strong Iron bound trunks for travelling in foreign Roads, Sumpter & Portmanteau Trunks, Budgets & Trunks for Post Chaises, Cover'd Hampers, Canvas and Leather Valeeses for Bedding, Leather Portmanteaus, Saddle Bags, Fire Buckets, Jacks, Powder Flasks, Harvest Bottles, Peruke Boxes, travelling Writing desks, Cases for Plate, China, Glasses, & Musical Instruments. With all other Sorts of Trunkmaker's Goods." The card announced that these goods and services may be obtained at the sign of "Industry and Indolence" in Long Acre, London (which means it would have been located a very short walk from both Drury Lane or the Haymarket). According to Phillippa Hubbard, this illustration also alludes to contemporary discourses on social issues, which had recently been the subject of William Hogarth's *Industry and Idleness* (1747), a series of engravings that depicted the parallel lives of one industrious and one idle apprentice. Cards such as this, Hubbard notes, contributed to the extension during the first half of the eighteenth century of the idea of shopping beyond "the prosaic acquisition of necessities" to include "the pleasures of perusal and decision-making."[5] Trade cards, then, like journals and the theatre, are media with which bourgeois subjects can exercise their capacities for viewing and judging. Forsaith the trunk-maker's card, with its theme of "Industry and Indolence," might even be suggesting to potential customers that such pleasures are (as indeed they must be) the flipside of someone else's industriousness.

By the time of Clark's engraving for Forsaith, the rather more celebrated William Hogarth had left his own mark on the history of the trunk-maker, with an image that reveals a further aspect of the trade and sheds light on what Addison had in mind with his choice of a profession for his imaginary critic. In his 1751 print *Beer Street*—produced as one half of a pair, alongside *Gin Lane*, that together illustrate the social evils of gin in contrast to the healthy enjoyment of beer—Hogarth depicts a pile of books, bundled together with a sign indicating that they are on their way to "Mr. Pastern, the Trunk Maker, St Paul[']s C[hurch]y[ar]d." Books and other printed matter that nobody needs to read any more were used by trunk-makers to stuff the lining of trunks.[6] To be a trunk-maker, then, is to be either a harsh and destructive critic of literary material or an actively antitextual figure, or both.

This trope of the trunk-maker as an ironic figure for the critic (or as a figure through whom to mock the critic) was clearly well established by 1750, as it appears also in Christopher Smart's dedication of his *Horatian Canons of Friendship* to William Warburton—"that admirable critic"—and to "my good friend the Trunk-Maker at the corner of St. Paul's Church-yard" who is, he writes "a man of much more worth and utility." Smart, who published these two dedications under the name of Ebenezer Pentweazle (blatant impersonation or the invention of writing personae for comic effect seems to have remained a standard literary journalistic device), accused Warburton, who was a friend of Alexander Pope and produced an edition of his *Dunciad* as well as an edition of Shakespeare, of "balderdashing the English language," and, in turning from Warburton to the trunk-maker, suggested that the latter's destruction of literature performed a much more valuable public service. He added that nothing in his dedication was "intended to ridicule or reflect upon Mr Nickless, who is an excellent artist in his way, and a very sensible worthy man."[7] Incidentally, the November 1750 edition of *The Universal Magazine of Knowledge and Pleasure* records the death of "Henry Nickless, trunk-maker, the corner of St. Paul's Church yard."[8] One might suppose that Hogarth's Mr. Pastern took over this business, but it appears that this was not in fact the case, as Nickless was succeeded upon his death by his nephew, J. Clements.[9] Mr. Pastern may therefore have been a fiction. Incidentally, both Smart's *Horatian Canons* and the *Universal Magazine* were published at premises on St. Paul's Church Yard. The path from publication to trunk was clearly a short one, and hardly needed to detour by way of Beer Street.

The trunk-maker as fictional conceit seems to have enjoyed a little surge in its cultural visibility at around this time: in 1749, he appears in Henry Fielding's novel *Tom Jones*. He appears here, as in Smart and Hogarth, as a critic, but this time without the emphasis on his role as a paper recycler; rather, in what looks like a clear reference to Addison's text, he is purely a figure for an intuitively excellent critical judgment. Fielding writes that his eponymous hero possessed a principle that incited him strongly to do right and equally strongly restrained him from doing wrong. This is not the same as being able to distinguish between the two: it has instead to do with the strength of the feeling that impels whoever bears such a principle in their heart to act upon it, presumably in an unreflective and even uncritical way. Thus, Tom Jones may be said to resemble "the famous trunk-maker in the playhouse." This principle, Fielding claims, sits "in the mind, like the Lord

High Chancellor of this kingdom in his court . . . with an integrity which nothing can corrupt."[10] In 1752, the same Fielding commends Hogarth for his depiction of literature on its way to the trunk-maker's, in an essay for the *Covent Garden Journal*, now known as "Uses to Which Learning Is Put."[11] Intuitive critical judgment and active destruction of literature seem to coexist for Fielding, suggesting that the figure of the trunk-maker has, by this midcentury moment, come to represent a combination of the two in which sincere and natural good judgment, arising from authentic feeling, inevitably and rightly leads to the destruction of unworthy literature. The books Hogarth consigns to Mr. Pastern's in his 1751 *Beer Street* print appear to be texts which he considered dubious and inauthentic.[12]

That Addison's figure caught on fairly early and endured, at least in literary circles, for quite some time, may be illustrated by three final examples of his appearance in other texts. The first is the earliest, and is in the preface to James Ralph's *The Touch-stone; or, Historical, Critical, Political, Philosophical, and Theological Essays on the Reigning Diversions of the Town*, a book by a Philadelphia-born poet turned journalist (and later, a friend of Fielding's), in which, under this serious-sounding title, he offers a guide to all London's many and various entertainment opportunities. Here Ralph—who begins his prefatory text writing above the name A. Primcock, and proceeds with a personal genealogy of all the other related Stopcocks, Allcocks, Nococks (it is so hilarious), and so on—also confides the following to the reader and his dedicatee:

> I blush not to own, that I was the famous Trunk-Maker, of whom the Tatler so oft made just and honourable mention: as I then gave Laws to the Realms of both Theatres, I am now the only Body that can awe the Footmens Gallery into any tolerable Degree of Order; nor am I less noted for being universally call'd upon, as an infallible Umpire, in all disputes that happen betwixt Men or Brutes, at the Bear Garden.[13]

Here, too, the "famous Trunk-Maker" seems to be presented as a somewhat ambiguous figure for the arbitration of cultural value, with the ambiguity here lying in his capacity to arbitrate in two supposedly very different sites of cultural production and consumption: dramatic theatre and bearbaiting. It is as though the function of this Trunk-Maker is simultaneously to insist both upon a certain infallibility of natural critical judgment and upon the equal meaninglessness (or lack of value) of those productions upon which judgment is being exercised. For Hogarth, he is the destination for worthless literature; for Fielding, he is a destroyer of literature who also has impeccable but passionate judgment; for Smart, he is to be preferred over Warburton but on terms that suggest that the entire enterprise of criticism is risible; and for Ralph, he is a figure for the failure (or refusal) to distinguish between genteel and popular entertainment. Ralph wrongly identifies *The Tatler*, rather than *The Spectator*, as the source for the Trunk-Maker, and also implies that he appears quite often in its pages. He appears nowhere in *The Tatler*, though, and only once in *The Spectator*. One explanation for these errors might be that by 1728 the figure had moved from the pages in which it first appeared, into general conversational circulation among the reading public for such material, yet had retained, in the transmission, at least a trace of its origins, however misleading (that is, in a publication associated with Steele and Addison, even if it was the wrong one).

The final examples to which I briefly refer point more simply to the persistence of the figure of the trunk-maker as the destination for the products of failed literature. Lord Byron, writing in his diary in 1821, and reflecting upon a news item that reported on the appearance, in a butcher's wrapping paper in Tunbridge Wells, of pages of Samuel Richardson's *Pamela*—the significance of which was that they helped reveal the identity of a murderer—commented that "for my part, I have met with most poetry upon trunks; so that I am apt to consider the trunk-maker as the sexton of authorship."[14] Herman Melville, in an 1862 letter to his brother, commenting on his failure to get his poetry published, wrote that "a trunk-maker took the whole stock off my hands at ten cents the pound," and that the next time his brother buys a trunk, he should "peep at the lining & perhaps you may be rewarded by some glorious stanza stareing [*sic*] you in the face and claiming admiration."[15]

So, to conclude this initial foray into the historical conditions of possibility for Addison's Trunk-Maker, the following can be fairly securely affirmed: trunk-makers were manual workers producing goods for widespread use, but perhaps with a particular eye for an emergent class of bourgeois consumer; by the mid-eighteenth century (and probably earlier), trunk-makers were working in premises that made them close neighbors of the expanding business of book and journal publication around St. Paul's cathedral in the City of London; that this probably facilitated the use, by trunk-makers, of unwanted printed matter to stuff the linings of trunks; that this meant that

Addison's figure of the Trunk-Maker could be understood by typical readers, many of whom would have been familiar with this practice and its location, as an anti- or aliterary figure; that this use of the figure of the trunk-maker for these metaphorical purposes persisted in literature in English, with Hogarth's print representation probably doing much to keep it alive; and, finally, that as a figure, the trunk-maker stands—in various ways, all of which have to do with the instability of distinctions between the elite and the popular—for uncertainties about cultural value and aesthetic judgment.

One final clue, which may be of use in the next phase of this investigation, comes in Ralph's explicit identification of Addison's "upper Gallery of the Playhouse" as "the Footman's Gallery." This refers to the tradition that this upper level of the theatre was the territory of liveried footmen, whose behavior was famously disruptive and in some cases violent, as suggested by Ralph's ventriloquial claim for the Trunk-Maker that he was the only person who could keep order there. Some account of questions of class and the threat of violence interfering with (or perhaps contributing to) bourgeois pleasures will need to be taken in what follows.

"a large black Man, whom no body knows"

Here, then, is the question with which this all began. What is to be understood by the word "black" in this description? While teaching a graduate class on spectatorship at Brown University in the winter of 2012, I suggested that we read together a selection of issues of *The Spectator*, which I had selected because they dealt directly with theatre and theatre spectatorship. One text in particular captured our attention, and it did so, I am certain, because it described its central figure as "a large black Man, whom no body knows." What were we to make of this, reading it, as we were, in the United States in the second decade of the twenty-first century, with Barack Obama beginning his second term of office as president, but with all the accumulated damages of slavery and racism making their presence felt in the lives of people and of institutions, including the university itself. Perhaps none of us then anticipated the relegitimation of white supremacy that would follow fewer than four years later with the election of Donald Trump in November 2016. I certainly did not, and as a visitor to the United States from the United Kingdom, I was only beginning to understand the extent to which the experience of slavery had shaped US history and culture, and how much that legacy differed from that inherited in the United Kingdom. This is not to claim that the UK legacy is in any way preferable, but simply to observe differences in both historical experiences and contemporary perspectives.

This difference is visible in many ways, of which two seem of particular significance today. The first is that the consequences of slavery for the formation and development of institutions, identities, and relations of power in the United Kingdom have not received anything like the degree of attention, from historians, politicians, scholars, or citizens in general that they have in the United States. This is now changing, as the impact of important critical work on slavery and its consequences is beginning to be registered in public life.[16] In Bristol, a city whose merchant wealth was largely a product of the slave trade, historians and activists have opened up public debate about how best to acknowledge and respond to this history, resulting in a number of symbolic acts: the attachment of a red ball and chain to a statue of the slave trader Edward Colston; the renaming of Colston Primary School and Colston Hall; and the reopening of the Old Vic Theatre, which had been built in 1766 with funds supplied by Bristol merchants involved in the slave trade, with a season that explicitly acknowledged this relationship.[17] In Glasgow, in response to a report that detailed the financial contribution made by the slave trade to its development, Glasgow University has established a new center for the study of slavery as part of what it has called a program of reparative justice.[18] In London, at Queen Mary University of London, where I work, the university's Pan-African Society organized a campaign to have two plaques commemorating the laying of the foundation of the Octagon (formerly the college's library) by King Leopold II of Belgium, removed and recontextualized. In response the university administration simply had the two plaques quietly removed, without the proposed recontextualization that would acknowledge the relationship between the university and the genocidal slavery for which Leopold had been responsible. The second form of difference is a more discipline-specific and academic one: compared to theatre and performance studies in the United States, there is much less work in the United Kingdom and on UK theatre and performance (especially its history) that engages with these histories, and although attempts are now being made to address the problem, many university theatre and drama curricula tend to reproduce this silence.[19] Moving between academic institutions in these two different countries has made me very conscious of this difference.

At Brown University in Rhode Island—its full name is the State of Rhode Island and Providence Plantations, although this was the subject of a state referendum in 2009 as a result of a campaign to have "and Providence Plantations" removed because of its reference to slavery—it was Addison's use of the term "black" to describe the Trunk-Maker that initially caught our attention.[20] It was impossible then, and would be impossible now, in the UK as well as in the US, to read this without observing and wishing to think about the work of racialization in the text. But what reading of this term would have been possible in the coffeehouse scene with which the preceding chapter opened? What did the word "black" mean, and, assuming it would or could have been read as referring to something readers of today would call "race," what conceptions of race would have been available to readers in 1711, in London, at one of key nodes in the network that was becoming the British Empire?

In 1711, the word "black" applied to a person in this way could have meant a number of different things. It could refer to skin color, or to a broader conception of "complexion" in which it might refer to a constellation of features, including skin and hair color. It could carry a moral implication, arising from Christianity's opposition between light and dark, and, related to this, it could also indicate whether or not the person in question was a Christian. At the beginning of her influential book on this very subject, Roxann Wheeler takes an example from *The Spectator* to illustrate her initial point: that it would only have been possible then (and, indeed, now, for a reader trying to reconstruct reader reception) to determine what precisely was meant by "black" by reference to the context in which it was used. In *The Spectator* No. 262, written by Addison, Wheeler notes the use of the words "a black Man" (one of only two other uses of this phrase in *The Spectator*, other than in relation to the Trunk-Maker). Addison is writing of his desire to avoid ever accidentally giving offence to real people by writing descriptions of invented characters in such a way that readers might think he was referring to someone they could identify by name: "If I write any Thing on a black Man, I run over in my Mind all the eminent Persons in the Nation who are of that Complection: When I place an imaginary Name at the Head of a Character, I examine every Syllable and Letter of it, that it may not bear any Resemblance to one that is real."[21] In this case, Wheeler argues—contradicting both Samuel Johnson and the Donald Bond, editor of the standard scholarly edition—"black" cannot refer to a physical characteristic, despite the use of the term "Complection." Instead "Addison . . .

refers to a wicked man."[22] Although this seems plausible, it may actually be more complex, in that Addison may be using the term "Complection" as a humorous way of suggesting that "wicked" people can be identified by their complexion, or, to be more precise, in this passage he is suggesting that he has to be especially careful lest his characterization lead readers to start thinking that any eminent person with darker skin or hair could be the "wicked" person to whom he is referring. This slippage of meaning in no way invalidates, but actually tends to support, Wheeler's proposition. In this case, even context cannot definitively nail down meaning, not least because there are questions of tone in play as well. In my own reading of *The Spectator*, I have developed a tendency to read for comic effect, and here I think one can detect a trace of comically exaggerated pedantry in Addison's description of the precautions he takes: "I examine every Syllable and Letter of it, that it may not bear any Resemblance to one that is real." The passage reads rather like an ironic use of the familiar modern disclaimer, that "any resemblance to any persons, living or dead, is entirely coincidental," given in circumstances where the resemblances are perfectly apparent.

Wheeler doesn't address another use of the description "black," however, which occurs, as we have already seen, in *The Spectator* No. 1, in which Mr. Spectator introduces himself by promising that he will satisfy his readers' familiar curiosity about whether the author whose text they are reading is "a black or a fair man." Here the context does not seem to support a reading in which "black" carries any moral or religious connotations. The point here is that readers are interpellated as being curious about what Mr. Spectator looks like, and are then frustrated by a self-description that fails to offer such a portrait, presenting instead an account of a man whose identity is known to no one other than his closest associates, even though he is regularly to be seen in all the key locations of London social life. So, although the question of whether he is "black or fair" is left unanswered, it is fairly clear that it is a question about personal appearance, and equally clear, given prevailing assumptions about who is likely to be writing such a text, that it is not a question about race as we would understand it today. Context, in the broadest sense, can guide us reasonably securely in this instance. What of the context in which the Trunk-Maker is described as "a large black Man, whom no body knows"? As in the case of Mr. Spectator's self-introduction, the use of black to carry primarily moral or religious connotations can, I think, be ruled out. There is nothing in the text to suggest that any questions of moral judgment regarding the conduct and character of the Trunk-Maker are at stake. Is he just a man with a darker than average complexion for a resident of London or a theatregoer, or could this description of him as "black" have been understood by its contemporary readers as a reference to race, in anything like the same way it clearly was by its readers at Brown University in 2012?

A first answer to that question might simply be that readers in 1711 did not possess the category of race, at least not with the same set of meanings as it has today. It was not until much later in the eighteenth century, according to Wheeler and others who have considered this question, that the category of race began to take on its recognizable modern form, and only through the nineteenth century that it came to be reified as the organizing principle of "scientific" racism.[23] In other words, Addison's readers would not have seen skin color as the principal term by which human beings could be differentiated from one another. We might venture further, to suggest that the principle of classification, in which people (as well as animals and things) were organized in terms of differences, by which a clear and stable identity could be fixed, had not yet taken hold. The idea that a person was one thing and one thing only, and that this is what constituted who they were and how they would be seen, by everyone, in some imaginary objectivity, had not yet come to dominate bourgeois thought as it did later—and, to a very large degree, still does. So rather than trying to answer a question that may have no definitive answer, about a category that may have had no currency for Addison's readers, we could take up a different kind of task, which is to read the text in relation to the use of the term "black," in order to reach a more holistic than identarian sense of who the readers of this text could have imagined the Trunk-Maker to be.

This would involve bearing this conceptual gap in mind and—without conceding too much to anachronism, but rejecting the idea that either race or blackness is an inappropriate analytical category—giving proper attention to the ways in which subjects who will have been racialized (as black) in subsequent discourses might have been perceived and understood by readers of *The Spectator*. The remainder of this chapter is conceived, therefore, as an extended contextual reading of the word "black" in the description of the Trunk-Maker, and as an exploration of what critical potential is released by deciding to accept it as referring to what we have since come to understand as race. The preceding section of this chapter considered the choice of Trunk-Maker as the job for Addison's imaginary theatre critic and the range of connotations that choice may have had for readers. This section, accordingly, looks for historical, visual, and textual evidence that might indicate what experiences of and ideas about "black" men it would be reasonable to assume might be shared by some or all of the readers of *The Spectator* in 1711.

Lingering a moment longer with the text itself, however, a few further aspects of Addison's imaginary theatre critic are worth bearing in mind as we sift the historical evidence that follows. First, he is not only a "large black Man" but also someone "whom no body knows." This phrase could be read in at least two ways. Either he is a man who is completely unknown to any-one, or he is someone whom nobody *who matters* knows (nobody who could be imagined reading *The Spectator*, perhaps). It is also worth noting that this description points toward some affinity or correspondence with Mr. Specta-tor himself, whose identity, as we have seen, is unknown among the society in which he moves and observes. Like Mr. Spectator, but probably for rather different reasons (even if to similar critical effect), the Trunk-Maker (who is not known as Mr. Trunk-Maker, incidentally) stands outside society. Of course, if we accept a modern sociological meaning for society, then he can-not stand outside it. The Trunk-Maker *can* stand outside "society," however, if we understand by society what used to be called "polite society": those classes of people who participate in the dominant institutions of public life, or what Habermas called the "public sphere." Unlike Mr. Spectator, who is recognized there despite "no body" being able to put a name to his familiar face, the Trunk-Maker is recognized nowhere—except in the "upper Gallery of the Playhouse," of course, where he is a familiar, if still anonymous figure. Among the many thousands or millions of people living in or passing through London in 1711 whose lives and faces "society" would not have recognized—people who would have been numbered among those "whom no body knows" and not counted as participants in the public sphere—would have been the footmen who habitually occupied this part of the theatre, who could have been identified by "society" only by the liveries they wore to iden-tify whose household they served.

Second, not only is the Trunk-Maker unknown to society, but he is also represented as being without speech. Perhaps, Addison speculates, he is "a dumb man," who expresses himself at the theatre in this unusual manner be-cause he cannot speak. One other possibility worth bearing in mind, as we pursue the possible (fictional) explanations for his being (imagined) this way, is that although he does not speak in the theatre, he speaks elsewhere—

not, of course, to anyone whom anyone might know—but among people who speak his own language. In other words, he may not be a speaker of English. Were he to speak, he would not be understood. Indeed, he might not even be recognized as speaking a language at all, and assumed to be merely making a noise: the kind of noise that the Greeks of antiquity identified with "barbarians." This possibility is intriguingly consistent with the choice of Trunk-Maker as his job: a figure who is being made to stand for the destruction of the printed word is also presented as someone with no participation in speaking the language that is printed. He is not outside language, then, but outside the production of the English language—the medium in which, of course, he appears. He thus contradicts the means of his own production: he is the antitext within the text, the non-English within English. His "language"—his theatre criticism, in other words—is experienced by the literate spectator, quite literally, in this case, as "Noises," indistinguishable, by some spectators, from the exertions of the "Playhouse Thunderer" on the roof of the theatre.

There may even be a literary and theatrical reference within this text to a play much performed during this period. In Shakespeare's *The Tempest,* the magician Prospero has enslaved Caliban, an indigenous native of the island over which he has, in his exile from Milan, asserted his control. The word "slave" appears in Prospero and his daughter Miranda's speeches to Caliban four times during his first brief appearance in the play. He is made to perform manual labor to sustain Prospero's microsociety. Miranda claims to have taught him how to speak properly, when before he could only "gabble, like a thing most brutish" (act 1, scene 2). Despite the conditions in which he lives, Caliban is later capable of expressing in poetic terms his aesthetic appreciation of the musical sounds and voices of the island:

> the Isle is full of noyses,
> Sounds, and sweet aires, that giue delight and hurt not:
> Sometimes a thousand twangling Instruments
> Will hum about mine eares; and sometime voices,
> That if I then had wak'd after long sleepe,
> Will make me sleepe againe, and then in dreaming,
> The clouds methought would open, and shew riches
> Ready to drop vpon me, that when I wak'd
> I cri'de to dreame againe.[24]

Might readers of Addison's text, attentive not only to its playhouse setting but also to its reference to *Hamlet*, another Shakespeare play with supernatural elements, also observe some correspondence between Caliban—the island native, who once spoke no English, who hews wood, draws water, and displays a remarkable capacity for aesthetic appreciation—and the Trunk-Maker, who seems to share so many of these attributes?

In looking beyond the text itself, at last, and to the historical conditions in which it was read, I begin with two simple questions: were there any "black" men in London, and would the readers of *The Spectator* have known that they were there? The answer on both counts will turn out to be Yes, as the burgeoning literature on this historical presence and pervasive representations of people of color in eighteenth-century (and earlier) London has clearly demonstrated.[25] I can't do justice here to the wealth of scholarly research on the topic of this historical presence and its various media representations, so a short summary of some key points will have to suffice, by way of a more substantive answer to the first of these simple questions. After that I will attempt to develop a further understanding of the representation of such figures, focusing primarily, although not exclusively, on material drawn from *The Spectator* and related print publications.

To begin, then, with the simple question about the presence of black people in London, and in England more generally, at the time of the Trunk-Maker text, it has for a long time been very clear—notwithstanding a strong residual public understanding that the black presence in Britain began in 1948 with the West Indian immigrants aboard the *Empire Windrush*—that there have been black people (or rather, people who would be described as black according to present-day understandings of race) in Britain, albeit mostly in fairly small numbers, at least since African soldiers were among the Roman armies that subjugated Britain.[26] There are references to Africans at the courts of James IV of Scotland, Henry VII of England, and James VI of Scotland, on each occasion appearing as musicians or performers. These fleeting appearances in the historical record have been supplemented through archival research by Imtiaz Habib, who identifies eighty-nine citations of black residents of England in Elizabethan records, involving at least ninety-five individuals—a numbers that, he proposes, suggests there would have been around ten times that many.[27] With the development of English colonial projects from the mid-seventeenth century, as we shall see, these numbers increased considerably, both as enslaved people started to feature more

frequently in wealthy households, and as free seamen and other largely unknown entertainers and laborers arrived. A few educated figures, such as
Olaudah Equiano and Ignatius Sancho, who left their own written accounts
of their lives, also began to appear in port cities such as London.[28] One interesting indication of their presence and its impact upon the economy of London is that the Lord Mayor of London issued an order in 1731 that banned
the employment of "Negroes or other Blacks" as apprentices. This would
have prevented any "black Man" from becoming a Trunk-Maker, of course,
but it also suggests that until this ban came into effect there were indeed
black apprentices in London.

Among the most widely discussed materials showing the presence of
black people in England in the early modern period are a series of three open
warrants issued in the name of Queen Elizabeth I, two of which are dated
July 1596, and a third found, in draft form only, in the papers of Robert Cecil,
the Queen's Secretary of State, which is assumed to have been written in
1601. The first notes that "there are of late divers blackamoores brought into
this realm, of which kinde of people there are allready here to manie," and
specifies that ten of those recently brought to England by Sir Thomas Basker-
ville should be removed. The second also notes that the presence of the
"blackamoores" deprives her own subjects of gainful employment, and or-
ders that the very precise number of eighty-nine should be transported to
Spain by Caspar van Senden, a merchant from Lübeck. The third also refers
to van Senden, noting, as did the second, that his role in the proposed removal of "blackamoores" is a reward for previous services (in obtaining the
release of English prisoners in Spain). These texts have been frequently, and
quite rightly, read as evidence, not only of a significant presence of "blackamoores" in England in the late sixteenth century, but also of sentiment that
there are too many such people and that they are threatening the livelihoods
and well-being of the supposedly indigenous English population.[29]

They have also usually been read as edicts of expulsion. Emily Weissbourd, however, argues persuasively that they were not, and that far from
demonstrating the existence of a government policy that sought to remove
such people from the realm, they are actually evidence of English participation in the growing Iberian slave trade.[30] The documents in question were
not public proclamations and did not enjoy wide circulation: they were used
for the very specific and limited purposes that they clearly stated—in the case
of the first two (which are the only ones that we know were actually com-

pleted), the removal of ten and eighty-nine "blackamoores," respectively. By identifying these warrants as evidence of an exchange between the English state and the merchant (slave trader) Caspar van Senden, in which van Senden gains access to enslaved people as commodities in exchange for his services rendered to the state, Weissbourd argues that in the late sixteenth century the association of slavery with race and the idea of the enslaved person as a commodity were already established in England, thus complicating and challenging those accounts that suggest that the racialization of the enslaved was a later development. The warrants, Weissbourd concludes, "represent blacks as a uniquely commodifiable subset of the population."[31] So, far from there being no category of race, linked to blackness and to slavery, available to readers of *The Spectator*, it appears that over a hundred years earlier, just such a constellation of concepts was already in use. Weissbourd's essay suggests that it is precisely the identification of enslaved Africans as "things" that allows the consolidation of the term "black" in a recognizably modern way.

Beyond the contribution that she makes to our understanding of these Elizabethan warrants, Weissbourd's work also therefore contributes to a wider discussion about the development of the category of race in early modern English culture. Some theorizations of race have suggested that the category of race, as such, cannot be applied to periods that preceded, variously, the Enlightenment, modernity, the birth of capitalism, or the beginning of European colonialism.[32] Others—and Weissbourd's work would appear to support such arguments—contend that, although the category of race may not have had the same meanings as it has in post-Enlightenment, postcolonial capitalist (post)modernity, it is clear that there was a concept of race, marked strongly by differentiations on the basis of belonging and not-belonging as well as superiority and inferiority. Cedric Robinson, for example, has argued that there was a "racialist" dimension to European society and culture that predated New World slavery. It emerged, he argues, out of the organization of feudal society, in which substantial work was carried out by a variety of "other" people, whose presence and social position means that a framework of "otherness" associated with "Slavs" and "barbarians" already existed and was available for Europeans to draw upon as they sought to define their relations with the "others" of Africa and the New World.[33] The connection between slavery and race was already present, in other words, in European culture, before the period of capitalist growth and colonial expansion. What these later developments gradually added, as Weissbourd's analysis seems to corroborate, was the concept of commodification. It is in this sense that the modern concept of race can be understood as typically modern, capitalist, colonial, and even "enlightened." An earlier concept of race existed in medieval Europe, with some but not all of the social and political meanings with which it is now associated.[34] In other words—those of Bryan Wagner, in fact—"Blackness does not come from Africa. Rather, Africa and its diaspora become black at a particular stage in their history. It sounds a little strange to put it this way, but the truth of this description is widely acknowledged. *Blackness is an adjunct to racial slavery*."[35] Race, yes, but blackness, not yet.

It was during the period between Elizabeth's warrants and Addison's Trunk-Maker that the more familiar "modern" social and political meanings of the word "black" as a racializing term seem to have established themselves. For, if the Elizabethan warrants and research such as Habib's offer evidence of the black presence in sixteenth- and early seventeenth-century London, developments in the century that followed would generate further and substantial evidence of increased presence and visibility as a direct result of both state and commercial investment in colonial projects. It was this increased presence, and the new colonial circumstances under which larger numbers of people of African heritage came to England, that would bring these new meanings into focus.

Returning to the London of 1711, then, there is sufficient evidence and analysis to support the idea that literate Londoners of the kind who were readers of *The Spectator* would have known about the longstanding presence of black people in London, and would have been likely to associate them strongly with manual labor, the colonial project, slavery, and the traffic in humans as commodities. They would also have been familiar with the use of the word "black" to describe such people, even if the precise referent for this term may not have always been clear, even if other terms were also used, and even if the word "black" did not have quite the same connotations as it does for readers in the twenty-first century. How might they have read this word in relation to the social reality they inhabited? What might "a large black Man" mean to them?

Many readers of *The Spectator* are very likely to have also been readers of the *Daily Courant* (1702–35), and to have been well-informed, as a result, about London's economy and politics, and the sources and means of circulation of the multiple products and people whose presence and whose labor was making the economy possible. Generally regarded as the first daily news-paper, it was, like *The Spectator*, a single sheet, and, like *The Spectator*, it car-ried advertisements after the (mainly foreign and diplomatic) news items that were its main texts. This means that on a single sheet, published on Janu-ary 14, 1707, a reader might have been able to read about the passage of the Act of Union through the Edinburgh Parliament (thus creating the United Kingdom), the sale of some books, a cure for wind, details of the evening's offering at the Theatre Royal, and a notice offering a reward for the recapture of an escaped 'Negro'. On other days they might have encountered reports on deliberations in France as to the legal status (are they "Movable" or "Immov-able")[36] of "Negroes" in "Saint Domingo" (i.e., Saint-Domingue: present-day Haiti, then a French colony with a growing enslaved African popula-tion), notice of the arrival at Falmouth of a "Pacqet-Boat" out of Jamaica, and a few days later, the arrival at the same Devon port of the "Susan Privateer with a Prize called the Frances Robert of and from Nantz laden with Wine and Brandy: As also the Mariana of and from Rochelle another Prize taken by the Neptune Privateer, with Provisions, bound for the West Indies," an advertisement for "A New and Accurate Description of the Coast of Guinea, divided into the Gold, the Slave, and the Ivory Coasts, and Natural History of all the Kingdoms and Countries therein," and another for "Bohee-Tea, Coffee Roasted, Chocolate all Nut or with Sugar, Ipococaan-Roots, Jesuites-Bark, Sold by Robert Fary Druggist on London-Bridge, with great Encour-agement to the Buyer," requests for the return of lost items (etuis, dogs, ser-vants, snuffboxes, and apprentices).[37] Enslaved peope, pirates, mass luxury consumer goods (coffee, tea, chocolate, snuff), exotic herbal products, maps of Africa, islands in the West Indies: these were not only the stuff of colonial Britain, but the daily reading of its literate bourgeoisie in the early eighteenth century. Even if these readers never saw anyone from Africa or the West Indies—which in many cases would be unlikely, as recent historical research suggests—they will have known that they existed, that they in some sense at least shared a social space with them, and they will have known something of the colonial relations into which the "long-distance trade" (see Chapter II) was organizing them. In other words, such figures appeared primarily either as the objects of representation, or as bodies whose distance and proximity were matters for regulation: are they "Movable" or "Immoveable Goods"; can they be returned to "the Africa-house in Leaden-hall Street," please; and might the maps perhaps show where they come from and where they are bound (the Slave Coast, Jamaica, "Saint Domingo")? These are some of the distances that might enable such readers, such a bourgeoisie, to behave, to read, and to write as though a "black man" is always someone "whom no body knows."

As well as representations encountered through this reading, they—and fellow Londoners less inclined toward or with less time for this particular leisure activity—will also have encountered other images of black figures. London, as David Dabydeen writes, "if not actually 'swamped' (to borrow the infamous term from the present Prime Minister) by flesh-and-blood alien blacks, was 'swamped' by *images* of blacks. London in the eighteenth century was *visually* black in this respect."[38] Dabydeen is referring here to the popularity of signboards bearing images of black men, which identified businesses (primarily grocers and tobacconists selling goods associated with the colonial trade) at the signs of "The Blackamoore's Head," "The Black Boy," "The Black Boy and Sugar Loaf," and "The Black Boy and Tobacco Roll."[39] This feature of the urban landscape is offered as background, as it were, for Dabydeen's more extensive analysis of the appearance of black subjects in "hundreds of seventeenth and eighteenth century English paintings and prints," including those of William Hogarth.[40] He observes that black subjects are represented in such images as occupying multiple social positions: "footmen, coachmen, page-boys, soldiers, sailors, musicians, actresses, prostitutes, beggars, prisoners, pimps, highway robbers, streetsellers,"[41] but not, typically, as theatre critics, journalists, owners of land or property, or occupants of any other bourgeois positions that might have made them participants in a public sphere, nor any people of whom it could *not* be said that "no body knows" them. For the owner or viewer of such prints and paintings, these subjects would therefore, for the most part, appear as "other" than themselves (pretty much all such owners and nearly all viewers would have been white property owners, either bourgeois or aristocrat), rather than as figures with whom they could imagine themselves identifying. Although the black subjects in such pictures were, as Dabydeen observes, represented as "very much a part of white society," they were, on the whole, a clearly defined part of that society, a society that, as Dabydeen's own phrasing acknowledges, *was* a "white society."[42] Particularly in representations of black subjects as members (or servants of) aristocratic households, Dabydeen notes, they are frequently depicted as somehow detached from the rest of the image, rather than as fully participating in the life of the household. Such images tend to emphasize "the solitude of blacks in the alien environment of the aristocratic household." Often, as in Hogarth's *The Wollaston Family* (1730) or Francis Wheatley's *A Family Group in a Landscape* (1775), the black subject is a background presence or little more than a silhouette, included, Dabydeen suggests "only as a token of their [the family's] affluence and colonial business interests . . . to whom he does not really belong, except in the economic sense."[43] In a more recent study of the relationship between the actual lives of black subjects in Britain and their representation in the artifacts of what he calls eighteenth-century Britain's "culture of taste," Simon Gikandi observes that the presence of black figures in such representations of aristocratic and bourgeois lives were "deployed in a subliminal, subordinate, or suppressed relation" to that culture.[44] In other words such figures were included in order to emphasize the value attached to the mode of life from which, in reality, they were excluded. Furthermore, they appeared in such images, even when they were in fact enslaved, without becoming visible as such. Unlike the much larger enslaved populations of the Caribbean, whose work was far more vital to the economic prosperity of British society, they wore no chains and performed no plantation labor. Enslaved people as such, then, were "difficult to conceptualize or represent . . . as a visual or palpable ingredient of British society"; slavery was thus, Gikandi writes, "part of the political unconscious of Britishness."[45] It was literally beyond the horizons of most of the viewers and owners of such images and the readers of *The Spectator*.

The political unconscious of *The Spectator*

What was it that Britishness knew but did not know? What was (or what is, now) the political unconscious of Addison's account of the Trunk-Maker? During the period in which English settlers were consolidating their political hold over West Indian plantation islands such as Barbados and Jamaica, with their growing populations of enslaved Africans—from the middle of the seventeenth century—there were significant acts of resistance to the imposition of the new order. In both Barbados and Jamaica, organized resistance to the development of the English plantocracy took the form of both isolated acts of arson and sabotage and more substantial organized attacks on white planter power.[46] Some of the most significant of these were reported in London and circulated in texts such as Richard Ligon's *A True and Exact History of Barbadoes* (1657), Nicholas Foster's *A Briefe Relation of the Late Horrid Rebellion Acted in the Island Barbadas, in the West-Indies* (1650), and the anonymous *Great Newes from the Barbadoes; or, A True and Faithful Account of the Grand Conspiracy of the Negroes against the English, and the Happy Discovery of the Same* (1676). Texts such as these, with their sensationalized accounts of the actions of the insurrectionists and of the violent punishments (including executions and castrations) carried out against those accused of participating (and even those who protested against the cruelty of some of the punishments), will have contributed to shaping the way contemporary and later reading publics viewed the people they were coming to think of as "black." The events they described also contributed to the development of legal codes that would determine the limits to be placed upon "black" subjectivity—limits upon their ability to associate with one another or to produce their own culture. A rebellion on Barbados in 1675 (the "Grand Conspiracy" reported in *Great Newes*) led the Barbados Assembly (the colony's legislature) to update its 1661 "Act for the Better Ordering and Governing of Negroes" with a "Supplemental Act" that prohibited weekend movements of enslaved people, restricted the extent to which they could be hired out from one plantation to another, banned public gatherings of enslaved people, and forbade them "to beat drums, blow shells, or use any other loud instrument."[47] The planters' legislators saw a clear connection between the performance of African music and the potential for slave insurrection, even if they did not quite understand what the nature of the threat posed by such activities might be, or how the connection might work in practice: "From the beginning of the Atlantic slave trade, Europeans knew that drums were powerful tools of state among many West African peoples, but could not quite comprehend *how* this was so. English planters in the West Indies early associated African drum and horn music with mass uprisings of enslaved Africans seeking their freedom."[48] In the centuries of slavery and oppression that followed, both the enslaved and those who escaped their chains to form maroon communities of resistance and freedom would challenge and circumvent the provisions of such laws and their prohibitions on expression through the development and practice of their own performance cultures, involving music, dance, and impersonation.[49]

Such laws, which would include subsequent legal codes enacted on the model of the Barbados legislation in the plantation colonies of what would become the southern United States (Virginia, Maryland, South Carolina), were an explicit codification of the consequences of what Orlando Patterson called the "social death" of the enslaved. They named and made visible the simultaneous namelessness and hypervisibility of the black (non)subject.[50] Stripped of identity and culture by the violence of their enslavement and reduced to the status of property (or commodity) the enslaved person was also the object of systems of visual surveillance and legal classification that were established in conjunction with one another at this time.[51] In the eyes of the white settler class, the enslaved is visible primarily as a threat of violence, though invisible and anonymous as a human subject.[52] This combination of visibility and anonymity seems to me crucial, and needs to be considered in relation to highly differentiated relations to textual production and self-reproduction. Although it will still be several decades before colonial laws introduced bans on teaching black people to read, the fact that literacy was so closely tied at this time to whiteness is already significant. As this very text demonstrates, much of what the Londoners of the early eighteenth-century could have understood of the lives of black people would have reached them, not just in textual forms, but in textual forms that constructed the black person in the negative: by means of bans, restrictions, and makings-absent. This is why the later eighteenth-century textual self-representations by Sancho and Equiano will be so important.

But now, in 1711, the figure of the unknown and unnamed black man, whose actions might be construed as simultaneously violent (destroying property) and musical (resembling drumming), and who is sufficiently visible to warrant the attentions of Mr. Spectator but not sufficiently social to encourage Mr. Spectator (who, after all, wants to find out who he is) even to speak to him, is more than a little suggestive of the conditions that produced the social death of the black subject, even if the superficially benign form in which he is presented might obscure his relation to those conditions. The figure might also be imagined to combine, in a somewhat improbable fashion, a dim Addisonian imagining of the performance cultures of Caribbean slave societies with an appreciation of the finest offerings of the white bourgeois culture of the colonial metropolis. In this act of imagination, on the part of writer and reader alike, the figure of the "large black Man, whom no body knows" is placed at a distance but also utterly present in the everyday life of London. He is over the horizon, unintelligible, and potentially violent. He is in London, in the theatre, a recognizable yet unknown part of a familiar social world. In that familiar social world he is also a potential source of violence, of a reasonably familiar and on the whole nonthreatening kind: he stands amid the footmen in the Upper Gallery, at least some of whom, even in London, could very well have been black, and whose behavior in the theatre was notorious for its unruliness (at least in the accounts of that familiar world offered to history by its largely elite and protobourgeois citizens). The Trunk-Maker, presented here, at least on the face of it, as the ideal theatre critic, capable of shaping an audience's responses to theatrical production, is also the very opposite of such a spectator, a potential troublemaker and a disturbingly close-to-home realization of fears and fantasies of "black" insurrection. In the political unconscious of this text, then, these antithetical things appear to be condensed into one and the same: bourgeois criticism and black rebellion; white spectatorship and proletarian action.

The knowledge produced in this unconscious might be simply this: that black rebellion is what makes bourgeois criticism possible. This is not the same as the argument that black slave labor makes it possible, in the sense that the wealth it generates creates the economic conditions for the leisurely exercise of aesthetic and consumer judgement. It is to suggest that the critical disposition—a crucial dimension of the bourgeois subject in formation—is produced precisely in order to deal with the fact of black rebellion. It installs within the subject in question—as a kind of safety mechanism—a psychic replica of the necessary distance between insurrection in the West Indies and comfortable spectatorship in the metropolis. It does so in the face of the impending collapse of this very distance. It is the production of the bourgeois subject's whiteness, as a consequence and corollary of the (imaginary) blackness of the enslaved. But Addison's text is also working to distance itself from this troubling connection that it reveals but cannot know. Its preferred technique is irony, a characteristic attitude of the critical disposition itself. For just as it makes the humorous proposition that when a successor is needed for the Trunk-Maker, someone of comparable attributes (of both intellectual and manual labor, of Apollo and of Hercules) should be appointed, and paid for the position, it is simultaneously suggesting—as part and parcel of this praise for the Trunk-Maker—that the position in question may not be worth having. Theatre criticism, or even criticism more generally, is just not a worthwhile occupation. All it amounts to is the wordless banging of a "dumb" black laborer. This is no basis for the construction of any kind of public sphere. The irony is clearly directed partly at Addison himself, and at the entire *Spectatorial* project. Inasmuch as the Trunk-Maker is the black double of the white Mr. Spectator—both anonymous observers of the theatre of London—he reveals the essential triviality of Mr. Spectator's own undertaking, and by extension, Addison and Steele's. So once again, the two figures, which irony might have been expected to pull apart from one another, appear to converge, as it becomes impossible, with the double-edged sword of the ironic intervention, to cut into the figure of the Trunk-Maker without lacerating yourself. This irony, whatever damage it might inflict upon its executor, functions, nonetheless, to domesticate slightly the figure of the Trunk-Maker, by subordinating him to a quasi-allegorical role in a self-mocking story. But the irony never quite settles the matter. One subordination cannot entirely mask the other. If an enslaved illiterate could be a bourgeois critic, well, whatever next?

"Indian Kings" and "Mohocks"

A few supplementary scenes may reveal more. Sir Roger de Coverley is thinking of going to the theatre. He's not been for twenty years, and he's a little worried about being out in town late at night, in case he might fall foul of the Mohocks. The previous night he had been followed on his way home along Fleet Street by "three lusty black Men," and despite having used his fox-hunting skills to dodge them on this occasion, he requests that he be accompanied to and from the theatre by Captain Sentry. Sir Roger is one of the fictional members of Mr. Spectator's club—a Tory landowner who has retired to his country estate but makes occasional trips up to town—and this report of his theatregoing, interlaced with his anxieties about Mohocks, appears in *The Spectator* No. 335, of March 25, 1712. The Mohocks—of whom the "three lusty black Men" may or may not have been members—were a rather different kind of "Club," and were discussed in several issues of *The Spectator* at around this time (Nos. 324, 332, and 347). They, too, may have been partly or entirely fictional: there is no very strong evidence to support their existence, besides the substantial media attention that their supposed exploits attracted—not just from *The Spectator*, but from numerous other writers, including Daniel Defoe, Jonathan Swift, and John Gay (who wrote a short play about them). Whether real or imagined, they were, it seems, a group of young, presumably aristocratic men (of the kind who might have aspired to the generic character type of the "rake") who amused themselves by terrorizing and assaulting people on the streets of London, mainly at night, and mainly after having got themselves sufficiently drunk. They took—or were given—their name from the indigenous American people known in English as the Mohawks, who offered, presumably, an appropriate analogy (or imagined model) for their own acts of "savage" violence.

The resonance of this choice of name for London readers and audiences is generally assumed to have been made possible by the much talked-about visit to London, about two years previously, of "four Indian Kings," who met Queen Anne, made numerous public appearances, including at the theatre, and who were the subjects of extensive media coverage, including paintings, poems, broadsides, and woodcuts, as well as, of course, an essay by Joseph Addison, published as *The Spectator* No. 50, on April 27, 1711. It is this essay that will provide the material for this subsidiary scene, although we will also return in due course to the street scene with Mohocks that Sir Roger nervously anticipates. For now, what matters, in the light of the previous (main) scene's concern with the question of "a large black Man," is that, in the imagination of the imaginary Sir Roger, at least, it makes sense that the Mohocks are "black men," too. In other words, this text is a minor piece of evidence to support the arguments of historians of race and culture that Londoners in the early eighteenth century did not routinely distinguish between Africans and Native Americans, and that the term "black" could apply equally well to both. Sir Roger's fears for his safety may be a joke for urban sophisticates about the nervousness of country folk who only occasionally dare come up to the big city, but it functions as just such a joke precisely because it draws upon racializing stereotypes about the sort of people most likely to be committing violent crimes in the modern metropolis. It may also be evidence, accordingly, of the cultural fears about blackness that are producing the very category of the white bourgeois spectator who remains the subject of this book: a subject that produces itself, in part, by making jokes about being scared of black men. Such black men are always in some sense imaginary. But real black men keep getting killed, all the same.

Even imaginary black men can still show up for real. That is what happened in April 1710, when "four Indian Kings" arrived in London on a diplomatic mission, supposedly on behalf of the Haudenosaunee, known in English as the Iroquois Confederacy (of which the Mohawks were one participating people, along with the Oneidas, the Onondagas, the Cayugas, and the Senecas), to secure Queen Anne's renewed support for a joint

Iroquois–British military campaign to take Canada from the French. These "black men" were imaginary in the sense that they were by no means the "Kings" they were represented to be (no category of "king" existed among the Iroquois), but instead four relatively young Native Americans, only three of whom were actually from people that were then part of the Iroquois Confederacy, and who represented only one (pro-British) strand of Iroquois political opinion on the military campaign in question. Three of them were Mohawks—Sagayenkwaraton, Onioheriago, and Tejonihokarawa—and the fourth, Etowaucum, was a Mahican, whose people had allied themselves with the Haudenosaunee in 1675. The British organizers of their visit gave them fictitious titles and announced them with Anglicized versions of their names (Sa Ga Yeah Qua Rah, Oh Nee Yeath Tow No Riow, Tow Tee Yee Neen Ho Ga Row, and E Tow Oh Kaom). They were fitted out with clothing apparently acquired from the playhouse, and gained an audience with Queen Anne, in which one of the British organizers pronounced a speech in English on their behalf. They met with influential political figures, particularly Tories whose approach to foreign and military policy was thought to be potentially favorable to the project of taking Canada from the French, and whose political fortunes were, at that time, taking a turn for the better: Queen Anne was about to replace her Whig government with a cabinet led by Tories. They were also the lead performers in a spectacular public performance apparently designed to enhance their political credentials by demonstrating their status as "Kings" through participation in activities consistent with the role of a visiting monarch. This included making an appearance, on April 24, 1710, as spectators, at a performance of Shakespeare's *Macbeth* at the Queen's Theatre, which was advertised in advance as being expressly "for the Entertainment of the FOUR INDIAN KINGS, lately arriv'd." A report of this evening at the Queen's Theatre, published some forty years later, claimed that spectators in the Upper Gallery had disrupted the performance to demand that, since they had paid to see the "Kings," the "Kings" should be given seats onstage. Robert Wilks, the theatre manager, who was playing the part of Macbeth, complied with this request, and the performance apparently continued. This anecdote—whether or not it is an accurate account of the events of the evening in question—reveals something crucial, I think, about how the visit of the "Kings" was understood by the reading public. The program of entertainments in which the Native American visitors were taken to see the society they were visiting was a program of double spectatorship. In showing their guests the sights, the hosts simultaneously created occasions for the guests to be the sights. But it was not just a matter of exposing exotic visitors to the curious gaze of multiple London publics. The London publics also witnessed the visitors in acts of spectatorship, watched them as they watched the entertainments laid on for them, presumably interested not just in seeing the visitors themselves but in seeing what they made of the culture they were visiting.

This visit, with its various scenes of performance, has been the subject of a number of rich and interesting analyses, and my account does not aim to add much to these.[53] My aim instead is to linger a little longer with *The Spectator*, in order to extend the previous scene's suggestion that the culture of early eighteenth-century London, in the process of producing the bourgeois subjects I am interested in, did so at least in part by producing "black" doubles of its ideal self. It did so, in the case of the "Indian Kings," by imagining the doubles, not so much as objects of spectatorship, but as spectators.

The Spectator No. 50—written, like No. 235 on the Trunk-Maker, by Joseph Addison—is another fiction in which Mr. Spectator's curiosity leads him into a scene of fantasy about another spectator. In this case, acknowledging his earlier fascination with the visit of the "Kings," whose progress around town he had "followed . . . a whole Day together," he reports that he has secured the services of a "Friend" to contact the "Upholsterer" in whose house the "Kings" had stayed, to find out what he can about "their Manners and Conversation." He does this not simply to form "a right Notion of such Strangers" but also to learn from any "Remarks" they may have made "what Ideas they have conceived of us." In response to the inquiries of this "Friend," the "Upholsterer" handed over "a little Bundle of Papers, which he assured him were written by King *Sa Ga Yean Qua Rash Tow*, and, as he supposes, left behind by some Mistake." Mr. Spectator claims that the papers in question have now been translated and a "Specimen" offered in "this Paper," with the suggestion that more may follow in subsequent editions (a sequel that does not in fact materialize). Unlike in the case of the Trunk-Maker, for which Mr. Spectator did the legwork and went to the theatre to see his subject for himself, even if he apparently made no effort to ask him anything, Mr. Spectator here relies upon a "Friend" (who may, of course, simply be the sort of "friend" on whose behalf one asks questions) to contact the Upholsterer, then upon the Upholsterer to provide the bundle of papers, and finally upon the labor of a translator to render into English the words he attributes to

Sagayenkwaraton. The act of ventriloquizing this Native American "Spectator" comprises a series of mediations, as though Mr. Spectator (and, at a further remove, Joseph Addison) was keen to put as much distance between himself and Sagayenkwaraton as possible, in order to set out for his readers the conventions of the genre in which the following text is to be read, so that they can be in no doubt that this performance of ethnographic spectatorship is a fiction.

The text attributed to Sagayenkwaraton comments on four aspects of London life. Critical commentary has tended to focus on just three of these. It is the fourth that interests me most. The three familiar passages are those that deal with St. Paul's Cathedral, which is presented as a building carved and scooped out of rock into a huge interior space that the "Natives of this Country" are imagined to have used, in some distant past, for "some sort of Worship"; with the mythical beasts called "*Whigs*" and "*Tor[ies]*," who supposedly inhabit this land, but of whose existence the fictional author is clearly skeptical; and with the extravagant fashions for both male and female hair and wigs. In each case there is a clear critique of contemporary mores: of the decline of religious observance, of political factionalism, and of fashionable excesses. Each critique is a familiar bourgeois trope of moderate common sense, in which the preferred subject position for reader and writer alike is one that finds complacent amusement at the obvious follies of less sensible fellow citizens. People who go to church are just going through the motions; politicians—they're all the same; aren't modern fashions ridiculous? The fourth topic (which actually appears as the third and briefest in the text itself) is the theatre:

> We were invited to one of their publick Diversions, where we hoped to have seen the great Men of their Country running down a Stag or pitching a Bar, that we might have discovered who were the Persons of the greatest Abilities among them; but instead of that, they conveyed us into a huge Room lighted up with abundance of candles, where this lazy People sat still above three hours to see several Feats of ingenuity performed by others, who it seems were paid for it.

The "Indian Kings" are represented as though they came from a culture in which hunting and athletic prowess were both the main "publick Diversions" and the basis for allocating social status. This is of course a casual and fairly familiar fantasy about "native" life, offered as a counterpoint to London's supposedly overcivilized and decadent entertainments. But the main target of this brief passage is of course the theatre itself, and in particular, the idea that one group of people might pay to sit for hours to see others be paid to perform for them. In other words, it is the practice of spectatorship—and the economic arrangement that it involves—that is in question, contrasted as it is here with the imaginary practices of another culture, which involve action and participation. These other practices are presented, albeit ironically, as superior. They help constitute the persistent tropes of both the "Indian" and the "noble savage" in white European culture, and one of their uses for that culture has been to permit its bourgeois participants to espouse imaginary "authentic" and "manly" values in opposition to the perceived decadence of their own "inauthentic," "effeminate," or theatrical leisure pursuits. In this case the figure of the "Indian" as commonsense bourgeois subject serves as a position from which a bourgeois practice—theatre spectatorship—can be ridiculed.

The text's emphasis upon its own mediations serves, particularly, perhaps, for twenty-first century readers, as a reminder of what this text stands in for—or, rather, supplants. In presenting it so clearly as *not* being the words of Sagayenkwaraton himself, it draws attention to its own role in an ongoing silencing of voices such as Sagayenkwaraton, and their comparative absence from a history written on the basis of archives compiled in the languages of the colonizers. In rendering Sagayenkwaraton as a moderate bourgeois Englishman, the text simultaneously erases the real Sagayenkwaraton and makes visible the substitution by which his perspective is eliminated. The bourgeois subject position attributed to Sagayenkwaraton is possible only by imagining that there might be some other subject position, some other place (of spectatorship, of participation) from which to view the culture of eighteenth-century London. The joke, such as it is, works only because the revelation of an utterly familiar bourgeois sensibility relies upon the prior assumption by the reader that a Native American would, in reality, see things very differently. It is only possible, in other words, to invent a bourgeois by imagining the not-bourgeois. (To be bourgeois is to be in relation to others.) The Native American "black man" stands for that not-bourgeois subject in the very moment of the substitution by which he is made to appear as the typical bourgeois.[54] It is the role of spectator that makes this substitution so easy.

Would this sort of substitution produce different meanings if it were achieved by way of action rather than in a text that imagines an "Indian" as a spectator? In turning from the "Kings" to the "Mohocks," I want to see if it is possible to deepen my presentation of the figure of the "Indian" as it features in the pages of *The Spectator*. Others have written about what the Mohock phenomenon might reveal about both the sexual and party politics of early eighteenth-century London, and I draw on their work here for my sense of its contemporary social meanings.[55] My aim here is at once narrower and wider: to examine the role played by writing about the Mohock phenomenon in the production of bourgeois spectatorial subjects, and to do so with a view to the broader question of the hybrid figure of the "black" and the "Indian" and its function in the production of bourgeois subjectivity. What was going on in London in 1712 that might make it plausible for Sir Roger de Coverley to be afraid to venture out at night, and for no fewer than four issues of *The Spectator* to contain letters on the topic of the Mohocks?

Media reports of violent attacks committed on the streets of London by a gang of men referred to as Mohocks started appearing in February 1712, and a wave of sensational accounts of Mohock assaults followed, many of which made political use of the alleged attacks. Tory journalists were eager to associate the Mohock violence with Whig opposition to the relatively newly established Tory government, while some of their political opponents made the counterclaim that the reports of Mohock attacks were a Tory fabrication, designed to distract public attention from the negative consequences of government policies. Some subsequent scholars, viewing the phenomenon as a media sensation, have suggested that it was in fact largely or entirely fabricated, either for political purposes or to generate sales.[56] But, as Daniel Statt shows, to my mind fairly convincingly, there is sufficient evidence of attacks and of responses from city authorities, including a commission of investigation and the arrest of a number of young male aristocrats, to establish that a wave of violent attacks did indeed take place, with victims including both men and women, with the assailants typically described as "like gentlemen." It is clear from most accounts that there was a strong misogynist dimension in many of the attacks: Statt notes that the attacks on women were both more frequent than those on men (at least some of whom were law enforcement officers) and that they were "strikingly brutal."[57]

What is less clear is where the title of "Mohocks" came from. Was there an organized group of that name, or was the name taken by a number of different groups and individuals? Was "Mohocks" perhaps a name created by the media to describe, or even, in effect, to create the group in question? Who, in other words, was responsible for the racial mimicry involved? Four young men—a baronet, his servant, a captain, and a "gentleman"—were eventually convicted of offences of assault and riot, and sentenced to very small fines, after unsuccessfully offering the defense that they had been on the streets in order to track down and apprehend Mohocks. This at least suggests that the defendants were fully aware that they were being tried as Mohocks, even if they had not initially claimed the name. According to Statt, this unsuccessful defense might suggest that they were familiar with John Gay's play, in which a gang of Mohocks capture and swap clothes with law enforcement agents and bring them up before judges to accuse them of being Mohocks.[58] In this respect, at least, they may have been playing along with an already established narrative role. However, neither Statt nor Erin Mackie, who draws on Statt's work for her analysis, address either the question of who decided on the name, or the issue that the name itself raises—the racialization of urban violence. This is the issue I want to tackle briefly here, in a consideration of the four appearances of the Mohocks in the pages of *The Spectator*. What use, conscious or unconscious, were its authors making of the phenomenon and the cultural figures it evoked?

The Spectator's contributions to public discourse on the Mohocks began on March 12, 1712, less than two weeks before the story of Sir Roger de Coverley's fearful theatregoing appeared. In that day's issue, *The Spectator* No. 324, a letter is published that purports to make a contribution to the paper's earlier project of compiling a history of clubs, by adding information about the Mohocks. The letter looks like a fairly typical example of the pretend letters regularly published in *The Spectator*. Statt includes it in his survey of Mohock-related accounts, which, he notes were of "varying degrees of probability," without commenting on its authorship.[59] Certainly there is no good reason to assume that the "Informations" it provides is genuine: neither the claim that the group is led by the self-styled *"Emperor of the Mohocks,"* nor that he bears a tattoo of the Turkish crescent on his forehead, nor yet the names offered to describe the various forms of Mohock assault should be treated as anything other than imaginative. What these details reveal instead, I suggest, is the kind of imaginative processes at work: the tattoo would have come from some familiarity with the use of tattoos by Native Americans (perhaps acquired through the visit of the "Indian Kings" and the circulation of their images); the term "Emperor" is suggestive of real American powers, such as those dramatized by Dryden in *The Indian Emperour* (1665); and the association with the Islamic crescent points to the prevailing cultural habit of condensing both the language used to describe and the images used to evoke the non-European cultures that were at that time coming to be seen as those of "black" people.

Nine days later, on March 21, 1712, *The Spectator* No. 332 is also in the form of a letter, again probably from a fictional or pretend correspondent, who offers some further inside information on the Mohocks' preferred techniques of violence, as well as an account of his own encounter with them while out on the street seeking sex. This letter might be understood as a setup for the final appearance of the Mohocks in the pages of *The Spectator*, on April 8, 1712 (No. 347), in which are printed two texts, which may not, readers are warned, be "Genuine and Authentic." These are a letter from the "Emperor of the Mohocks," who gives his name—in a clear echo of the names by which the "Indian Kings" were known in London—as Taw Waw Eben Zan Kaladar, followed by the group or club's "Manifesto." The "Manifesto" expresses, in typically ironic vein, the commitment of the Mohocks to law and order in the cities of London and Westminster. The Mohocks will not countenance violent assaults on law-abiding citizens going about their business, but will act only against those—like the pretend author of the letter published in No. 332—who are out late and seeking to engage in immoral activities. The Mohocks, in other words, are the police, or, as they are called at the time—for example, in John Gay's play—the Watch. The "Manifesto" aligns the Mohocks with the social and moral reform agenda associated with *The Spectator*, and it does so precisely by laying claim to the socially beneficial character of keeping a watchful eye on what society is up to. The defendants in the subsequent trial of alleged Mohocks in June could as well have been drawing on this text as on Gay's play for their claim that, far from being Mohocks, and constituting a threat to the social order, they were actually vigilante upholders of both law and order.

What does this reversal mean? It seems to bear some resemblance at least to the reversal offered in the case of the Trunk-Maker, the "large black Man" who is proposed, ironically, as we have seen, as a figure for the bourgeois critic. What can an early eighteenth-century publication, associated with the ascendancy of a protobourgeois class, be doing by proposing, however tongue-in-cheek, that responsibility for the regulation of both law and order and aesthetic judgment might be handed over to those subject to the new

United Kingdom of Great Britain's intensifying colonial domination? Even jokes—or jokes, especially, if Freud is to be taken at his word—have something to say, both about those who make them and those who their authors imagine might find them funny. What might these authors and readers have had collectively in mind, even without knowing it, when they were thinking about what we would now call race, culture, and the police?

Eric Hinderaker and Robbie Richardson both suggest that the political and cultural significance of the "Indian Kings" lay, at least in part, in their status as aliens like us. Earlier English experiences and conceptions of people from alien cultures—who would have been, in this context, non-Christians—involved understanding them as being outsiders. They would have been Muslims, for example, located beyond the borders of Christendom. Indeed, to some extent, the difference between Christians and Muslims, and existence of borders (often violently contested, of course) between the lands in which they lived, had come to be constitutive of European Christian ideas of difference. What changed with the advent of settler colonialism was that the indigenous people of the Americas (of the Caribbean and North America, in the case of British settlement) were non-Christians contained within, if not the borders, at least the imaginary cultural space of the colonizing nation, and could not be conceptualized in this straightforward way.[60] The case of the "Indian Kings"—all of whom, furthermore, had converted to Christianity—offered a particularly powerful example of a new kind of Other, and gave the Londoners who paid attention to their visit a basis for imagining and entering into a new kind of relation with cultural others. Dressed for the occasion in playhouse costumes chosen to help produce familiar images of royalty, the "Kings" could stand for a version of the Other with whom colonizing subjects could imagine themselves existing in a relation of both amity and equality, to whose dignity and nobility they might even aspire. In that respect, in their playhouse costumes, in the portraits painted of them by Jan Verelst, in the woodcut variants of these portraits, as well as in Addison's ventriloquism of Sagayenkwaraton, the "Kings" can be taken as a representation of an ideal colonial subjectivity, into which the colonizers can imaginatively project themselves and, thereby, at least in Addison's case, represent their own values as those of a dignified nobility. This is, of course, a variant of the well-known European trope of the "noble savage."

If Londoners' experience of the "Kings" subtended their reception of the "Mohocks," we might expect some trace of this identification here too, and that is clearly present, in the ventriloquism through which the "Emperor of the Mohocks" expresses his program for the maintenance of urban peace. In the case of the Mohocks, however, the identification of the "Emperor" and his "Manifesto" with a bourgeois moral order and its policing contains a further twist on the figure of the alien Other. I have already suggested that one important dimension of the figure of the "large black Man" for readers of *The Spectator* in 1711 would have been background knowledge about the violence involved in slave rebellions and their suppression in the American colonies. I think this is a factor in the construction and reception of the Mohocks narrative, too, and that, quite possibly, this knowledge would have been combined, with varying degrees of accuracy and discrimination, with an awareness that, like plantation slavery, the broader settler colonial project was encountering resistance from indigenous people. What I want to suggest, in keeping with the logic of reversal that is so clearly at work in both *The Spectator* texts—and in Gay's play about the Mohocks (as well as in the legal defense offered in the June 1712 trial)—is that it is not just that the Mohocks could be associated with the violent aspects of indigenous American resistance to settler colonialism. Instead, in their ironic depiction as agents of law and order on the streets of London, they indicated an unconscious recognition of the incipiently genocidal violence that settler colonialism was visiting upon the indigenous people of the Americas. The violence of slave rebellions and "Indian" wars was imported to the streets of London in fantasies of "Mohock" violence, but then, in this strangely persistent reversal of roles, the perpetrators of the violence in question were revealed to be secret sharers in the settler colonial project, disclosing, in the process of the reversal, the true origins of the violence that London is worrying about so enthusiastically in the early months of 1712: the violence that has been and will continue to be necessary to secure and continue bourgeois rule.

But even in this disclosure on the part of the bourgeois spectator's political unconscious, there may be a further displacement. After all, slave rebellions and "Indian" wars were by no means the only threat to the orderly progress of early modern English capitalism. The civil war in the middle of the previous century had made it fairly clear that there was a struggle much closer to "home," in which protoproletarian subjects had succeeded in organizing themselves not just in opposition to Stuart rule, but on the basis of developing critiques of the economic order that the landowner–bourgeois alliance was seeking to establish. The enslaved and native Americans were only two heads of Linebaugh and Rediker's "Many-Headed Hydra":

From the beginning of English colonial expansion in the early seventeenth century through the metropolitan industrialization of the early nineteenth, rulers referred to the Hercules–hydra myth to describe the difficulty of imposing order on increasingly global systems of labor. They variously designated dispossessed commoners, transported felons, indentured servants, religious radicals, pirates, urban laborers, soldiers, sailors, and African slaves as the numerous, ever-changing heads of the monster.[61]

While attributing urban violence to "Mohocks" involves the making conscious of one reality—that the peace and prosperity of London depends on the effectiveness of bourgeois and state violence in the distant colonies—it may also involve a distantiation that reverses the importing of American violence to the streets of the metropolis. In the idea that the violence is "Mohock" it effectively exports the problem straight back out: there is not really any problem here in London, the real threat is (safely) over there. What this twist suggests is that the political unconscious of the bourgeois spectator is inclined to constant reversal; it is, in the strongest sense of the term, ironizing. Anything that appears in this unconscious can always become its opposite, in a logic that is much more both–and than it is either–or. The Trunk-Maker is both a sophisticated critic and an enslaved illiterate. The exotic Indian King is also a familiar bourgeois moralist. The Mohocks are both anticolonial violence on the streets of London and the forces of metropolitan law and order. Figures of colonial alterity are also masks for the threat of rebellion close at hand. Small wonder, then that bourgeois spectator in possession of (or possessed by) such an unconscious should also possess the capacity for disidentification. A fair man can always be a black man.

The Brazilian

The Trunk-Maker had a predecessor, a grandfather, perhaps, who appeared to the philosopher Baruch Spinoza in a dream. In a letter written on July 20, 1664, to his friend Pieter Balling, Spinoza was trying to explain the difference between images produced in the mind as a result of "corporeal causes" and those that are the product of the imagination. It is only the latter, claims Spinoza, that can be omens of the future. To illustrate this distinction he recounts a dream he remembers from a year earlier, images from which remained with him, in his waking condition, "as vividly as if they had been real." The image he remembers having retained most vividly in this way, as he awoke, was of "a black, scabby Brazilian [*cujusdam nigri & scabioisi Brasiliani*], whom I had never seen before." He found he could make this image disappear by concentrating on "a book or some other object," but, as soon as his attention wandered again, "the same image of the same Ethiopian kept appearing with the same vividness again and again."[62] Let's briefly note some points of comparison between this figure and Addison's Trunk-Maker: both are "black"; one is a man "whom no body knows," the other is someone whom the philosopher had "never seen before"; neither of them speak; both seem to exist in some kind of oppositional relationship to the conscious intellectual practice of reading—the Trunk-Maker because of his profession that makes books disappear into trunk lining, the "Brazilian" because reading will make him disappear, at least temporarily. I propose the Brazilian as a predecessor for the Trunk-Maker, however, not merely because of these similarities between them, but because, considered together, they suggest that both Spinoza and Addison were capable of imagining the collapse of the colonial relation's appropriate distance, a collapse that, in the case of Spinoza's Brazilian, at least, is the fearful content of the future—his dream image being, as he sees it, the omen of what is to come (unlike the auditory hallucinations that had troubled his friend, Balling).

Warren Montag, in his book on Spinoza entitled *Bodies, Masses, Power*, offers a historical contextualization of the Brazilian that is similar in some respects to that I have attempted for the Trunk-Maker. This contextualization, which I shall briefly summarize momentarily, enables him to identify the Brazilian as a figure for what Spinoza termed the "multitude," just as I have sought to identify the Trunk-Maker as a figure for a potentially rebellious colonial subject.[63] In associating Spinoza's dream image with the potential of the "multitude," Montag is clearly taking his cue from Antonio Negri's brief engagement with the same figure in *Savage Anomaly*, where he identifies the Brazilian with Caliban—an identification that echoes Silvia Federici's nomination of Caliban as the theatrical and philosophical figure for all the unruly proletarian bodies to whom Negri (with Michael Hardt) would extend the term "multitude."[64] In *Savage Anomaly*, Negri reads the Brazilian as an example of "the Caliban problem"—that colonial capitalism must contend with the force of its subaltern subjects' imaginative force—and observes that here, in Spinoza's dream and the philosophical use to which he puts it in his letter to Balling, the "Caliban problem" is "located within the highest abstraction of philosophical meditation."[65] As in the case of the Trunk-Maker, part of the force of the imaginary figure derives from its anomalous appearance in a realm of rational discourse—philosophy, theatre criticism—from which its real-world referents—actual "black" people—are typically excluded. It is for this reason that such figures appear, for Negri, as instantiations of Caliban as "contemporary hero."[66]

Montag notes that Spinoza's correspondent, Pieter Balling, was "a merchant engaged in trade with Spain and the Spanish holdings in the Americas," and that Isaac Aboab, one of the elders who had excommunicated Spinoza from the Jewish community (in 1656) had previously served as the chief rabbi in the Dutch colony of Pernambuco in Brazil, until its conquest by the Portuguese in 1654.[67] Residents of Amsterdam, like Spinoza, would have been well aware of their colonial relations with Brazil (and other American locations, to which Africans had been enslaved): like the Londoners of the early eighteenth century, the Dutch of the latter half of the seventeenth would have known all about slave revolts and the threat posed by maroon communities to the colonial project. All of these will have been present for both parties to the Spinoza–Balling correspondence, as familiar materials from everyday life. In Montag's reading of the image of the Brazilian it is not, however, just a case of the potentially threatening presence of "a black, scabby Brazilian" as a figure for slave rebellion, but a rather more complicated scenario in which Spinoza makes an unconscious identification between himself and this "battle-scarred rebel slave" on the grounds that they both faced the hostility of Rabbi Aboab, who stands in the wings of this scene as both colonial ruler and religious leader, exercising punitive authority on Spinoza and his Brazilian alter ego.[68] Spinoza identifies with the Brazilian, then, albeit unconsciously, just as Addison, somewhat more consciously, would identify the Trunk-Maker with Mr. Spectator, and, by extension, himself. Montag's reading of the image is supported by his analysis of Spinoza's *Ethics*, where, as he shows, Spinoza wrote far more explicitly than other philosophers of the time, such as Hobbes and Locke, of the potential significance of these subaltern subjects who would one day (for Negri and others) constitute the multitude. In this, writes Montag, Spinoza is not entirely anomalous; it is simply that "he addresses directly what haunts the others as the absent centre of their political projects."[69] In other words, he suggests, Spinoza's thought, and this image of the Brazilian that seems to rise up within it, asks a question very similar to the one I have been teasing out of the Trunk-Maker: "to what extent was early liberal philosophy [or 'bourgeois life'] shaped by its fear of the masses"?[70] If Spinoza's image is indeed an omen, as he claims it must be, it presumably presages a revolution to come that is already under way, a distant threat to metropolitan and philosophical order that is also already within the gates. But that is, of course, to get way ahead of ourselves.

Notes

1. *The Spectator*, No. 235 (November 29, 1711). See also Joseph Addison and Richard Steele, *The Spectator*, ed. Donald F. Bond (Oxford: Clarendon Press, 1965), 2: 413–16.

2. Henry Nickless, whom we will encounter again shortly, apparently died with a fortune of £20,000 in 1750. See Ambrose Heal, *The Signboards of Old London Shops:* A Review of the Shop Signs Employed by the London Tradesmen during the XVIIth and XVIIIth Centuries (London: B. T. Batsford, 1947), 172.

3. G. Hinchliffe, "Impressment of Seamen during the War of the Spanish Succession," *Mariner's Mirror* 53, no. 2 (1967): 137–42.

4. See Heal, *Signboards*, 171.

5. Phillippa Hubbard, "Trade Cards in 18th-Century Consumer Culture: Circulation, and Exchange in Commercial and Collecting Spaces," *Material Culture Review* 74–75 (2012): 30–46, at 35.

6. See Denise Gigante, "Sometimes a Stick Is Just a Stick: The Essay as (Organic) Form," *European Romantic Review* 21, no. 5 (2010): 553–65.

7. Christopher Smart, *The Horatian Canons of Friendship* (London: J. Newbery, 1750), i, v, iv, iii, viii.

8. "Births, Marriages, Deaths, Preferments, Promotions, and Bankrupts," *Universal Magazine of Knowledge and Pleasure* 7 (November 1750) [monthly; London: John Hinton]: 238–39, at 238.

9. See Heal, *Signboards*, 172.

10. Henry Fielding, *The History of Tom Jones, a Foundling* (London: Vintage Books, 2007), 122.

11. Henry Fielding, ["Uses to Which Learning Is Put"], *Covent Garden Journal*, 1, no. 6 (January 21, 1752); reprinted in Alexander Drawcansir [Henry Fielding], *The Covent Garden Journal*, vol. 1, ed. Gerard Edward Jensen (New Haven: Yale University Press, 1915), 167–72, at 169, and in Denise Gigante, ed., *The Great Age of the English Essay: An Anthology* (New Haven: Yale University Press, 2008), 169–74, at 171–2.

12. For an account of these prints see Ronald Paulson, *Hogarth's Graphic Works*, 3rd, rev. ed. (London: The Print Room, 1989), 145–48, and for reproductions of the prints see plates 185–86. Paulson suggests that Hogarth may have taken the idea of the books being sent to the trunk-maker from Smart's *Horatian Canons*.

13. James Ralph, *The Touch-stone; or, Historical, Critical, Political, Philosophical, and Theological Essays on the Reigning Diversions of the Town* (London, 1728), xvi.

14. George Gordon Byron, *The Life, Letters and Journals of Lord Byron*, ed. Thomas Moore (London: John Murray, [1830] 1932), 471.

15. Herman Melville, *Correspondence*, ed. Lynn Horth (Evanston and Chicago: Northwestern University Press, and Chicago: Newberry Library, 1993), 377.

16. See, for example, the "Legacies of British Slave-ownership" project at University College London.

17. Vanessa Thorpe, "New Life for Historic Theatre as It Faces Up to 'Slave Trade' Past," *The Observer*, September 9, 2018; online at https://www.theguardian.com/stage/2018/sep/09/bristol-old-vic-slave-trade-theatre-reopens-25m-facelift (accessed September 28, 2018).

18. Martin Belam, "Glasgow University to Make Amends over Slavery Profits of Past," *The Guardian*, September 17, 2018; online at https://www.theguardian.com/education/2018/sep/17/glasgow-university-to-make-amends-over-slavery-profits-of-past (accessed September 28, 2018).

The report itself is Stephen Mullen and Simon Newman, *Slavery, Abolition and the University of Glasgow* (Glasgow: University of Glasgow, History of Slavery Steering Committee, 2018), and is available at https://www.gla.ac.uk/media/media_607547_en.pdf (accessed September 28, 2018).

19. Some of the most significant scholarly contributions on this dimension of British theatre have been by writers and researchers working in North America. See for example, Felicity Nussbaum, "The Theatre of Empire: Racial Counterfeit, Racial Realism," in *A New Imperial History: Culture, Identity and Modernity in Britain and the Empire, 1660–1840*, ed. Kathleen Wilson (Cambridge: Cambridge University Press, 2004), 71–90, and *The Limits of the Human: Fictions of Anomaly, Race, and Gender in the Long Eighteenth Century* (Cambridge: Cambridge University Press, 2003). See also Daniel O'Quinn, *Staging Governance: Theatrical Imperialism in London, 1770–1800* (Baltimore: Johns Hopkins University Press, 2005). One area in which there has for a long time been significant British scholarly work on race and colonialism in the theatre has been in the study of Shakespeare, where significant interventions have made since the 1980s. Much of the early work of this kind was clearly part of the cultural materialist turn in literary scholarship, much of it focused on Shakespeare and the early modern period, which I discussed in Chapter II, "The Scene with the Spectator." See, for example, Paul Brown, "'This Thing of Darkness I Acknowledge Mine': *The Tempest* and the Discourse of Colonialism," in *Political Shakespeare: New Essays in Cultural Materialism*, ed. Jonathan Dollimore and Alan Sinfield, 48–71 (Manchester: Manchester University Press, 1985); Peter Hulme, *Colonial Encounters: Europe and the Native Caribbean, 1492–1797* (London: Methuen, 1986); Ania Loomba, *Gender, Race, Renaissance Drama* (Manchester: Manchester University Press, 1989), and many other books and essays since.

20. For an indication of student and institutional engagement with the history of colonial slavery in Rhode Island and the role of Brown University in promoting that engagement and reflecting upon its own involvement, see the following articles by Anne Wootton in the university newspaper, the *Brown Daily Herald* (all accessed online September 28, 2018):

"In Colonial Rhode Island, Slavery Played Pivotal Role," October 17, 2006; http://www.browndailyherald.com/2006/10/17/in-colonial-rhode-island-slavery-played-pivotal-role/

"Campbell Introduces First-Years to Slavery and Justice Committee," *Brown Daily*

Herald, October 23, 2006; http://www.browndailyherald.com/2006/10/23/
campbell-introduces-firstyears-to-slavery-and-justice-committee/
"Slavery & Justice Report to Be Released Today," October 23, 2006; http://www.
browndailyherald.com/2006/10/23/slavery-justice-report-to-be-released-today/

21. *The Spectator*, No. 262, December 31, 2011.

22. Roxann Wheeler, *The Complexion of Race: Categories of Difference in Eighteenth-Century British Culture* (Philadelphia: University of Pennsylvania Press, 2000), 3.

23. See Introduction. Other work that complicates this account will be discussed below.

24. William Shakespeare, *The Tempest*, act 3, scene 2; online at https://en.wikisource.org/wiki/Page:Shakespeare_-_First_Folio_Faithfully_Reproduced,_Methuen,_1910.djvu/38 (accessed August 26, 2019). *The Tempest*, especially in a 1667 adaptation by John Dryden and William D'Avenant entitled *The Enchanted Island*, was a staple in the repertoire of the London theatre through the first two decades of the eighteenth century.

25. Peter Fryer, *Staying Power: Black People in Britain since 1504* (Atlantic Highlands, NJ: Humanities Press, 1984); David Dabydeen, *Hogarth's Blacks: Images of Blacks in Eighteenth Century English Art* (Manchester: Manchester University Press, 1987); Gretchen Gerzina, *Black London: Life before Emancipation* (New Brunswick, NJ: Rutgers University Press, 1995); Kathleen Chater, *Untold Histories: Black People in England and Wales during the Period of the British Slave Trade, c. 1660–1807* (Manchester: Manchester University Press, 2009); and others.

26. Fryer, *Staying Power*, 1–2.

27. Imtiaz Habib, *Black Lives in the English Archives, 1500–1677: Imprints of the Invisible* (London and New York: Routledge, 2016), 115.

28. See, for example, Gerzina, *Black London*, esp. 57–67 (Sancho), 152–57 (Equiano). Gerzina cites the estimate made by the antislavery campaigner Granville Sharp of a black servant population in London in 1768 of about 20,000, which, she notes, would have been augmented by sailors, students, musicians, and others (5–6). She regards Sharp's number as on the high side (on what basis is not clear). But it is nonetheless worth bearing in mind that if this number is anywhere near correct, and taking into account the sailors and so on, this would have represented about three percent of the population of the city. For Equiano, see Olaudah Equiano, *The Interesting Narrative of the Life of Olaudah Equiano, or Gustavus Vassa, the African*, 9th ed. (London, 1794). For Sancho, see Ignatius Sancho, *Letters of the late Ignatius Sancho, an African. To Which Are Prefixed, Memoirs of His Life* (London: J. Nichols, for C. Dilly, 1784).

29. See, for example, Fryer, *Staying Power*, 10–12; Kim F. Hall, "Reading What Isn't There: 'Black' Studies in Early Modern England," *Stanford Humanities Review* 3, no. 1 (1993): 23–33; Ania Loomba, *Gender, Race, Renaissance Drama* (New York, 1989); and Emily C. Bartels, "Too Many Blackamoors: Deportation, Discrimination, and Elizabeth I," *Studies in English Literature, 1500–1900* 46, no. 2 (2006): 305–22, whose work sought to connect what had been assumed to be only an expression of a racist expulsion policy to other political and economic factors involved.

30. Emily Weissbourd, "'Those in Their Possession': Race, Slavery, and Queen Elizabeth's 'Edicts of Expulsion,'" *Huntington Library Quarterly* 78, no. 1 (2015): 1–19. See also Miranda Kaufmann, "Caspar van Senden, Sir Thomas Sherley and the 'Blackamoor' Project," *Historical Research* 81, no. 212 (2008): 366–71, for an earlier engagement with

the same archival evidence that also challenges the view that these texts are evidence of an expulsion policy.

31. Weissbourd, "Those in Their Possession," 17.

32. There is a useful survey of much relevant literature supporting this kind of argument in Charles Hirschman, "The Origins and Decline of the Concept of Race," *Population and Development Review* 30, no. 3 (2004): 385–415.

33. Cedric J. Robinson, *Black Marxism: The Making of the Black Radical Tradition* (Chapel Hill: University of North Carolina Press, 2000).

34. See Lisa Lampert, "Race, Periodicity and the (Neo-) Middle Ages," *Modern Languages Quarterly* 65, no. 3 (2004): 391–421; Geraldine Heng, "The Invention of Race in the European Middle Ages I: Race Studies, Modernity, and the Middle Ages," *Literature Compass* 8, no. 5 (2011): 258–74, and "The Invention of Race in the European Middle Ages II: Locations of Medieval Race," *Literature Compass* 8, no. 5 (2011): 275–93; and Peter Erickson and Kim F. Hall, "'A New Scholarly Song': Rereading Early Modern Race," *Shakespeare Quarterly* 67, no. 1 (2016): 1–13.

35. Bryan Wagner, *Disturbing the Peace: Black Culture and the Police Power after Slavery* (Cambridge, MA: Harvard University Press, 2009), 1–2; emphasis mine.

36. "Movable" means that they are deemed to be chattel slaves. In other words they are not attached to the land or property where they work ("Immovable") but, as the personal possessions of their owner, may be used as collateral for borrowing purposes. Their status was in fact established in *Le Code noir* of 1685, issued by Louis XIV and supposedly drafted by Colbert, which governed the treatment of slaves in all French colonies: "Déclarons les esclaves être meubles." In French the terms "meubles" and "immeubles" refer, with the same basic sense, to "furniture" and "buildings." This decision in France would have aligned the position in Saint-Domingue with the legal position established by the British slave colony of Barbados in 1661, and followed in subsequent slave codes in colonies that would later become part of the United States, such as South Carolina, Virginia, and Maryland. The settlement of this "remarkable Question" in such codes represent significant legal moments in the process by which the personhood of the "black" subject was obliterated and their character as commodity established. Presumably the decision referred to in the *Daily Courant* is a legal confirmation of this status.

37. *Daily Courant*, 1707. Jesuit's bark is a Peruvian bark used as a malaria cure. Ipococaan root was found in Costa Rica, Nicaragua, Panama, Colombia, and Brazil and was used an emetic.

38. Dabydeen, *Hogarth's Blacks*, 17. As the 1987 publication date of Dabydeen's book indicates, the prime minister in question was Margaret Thatcher. Dabydeen refers to a 1978 interview, when the then leader of the opposition said: "If we went on as we are, then, by the end of the century, there would be four million people of the new Commonwealth or Pakistan here. Now, that is an awful lot and I think it means that people are really rather afraid that this country might be rather swamped by people with a different culture." Margaret Thatcher, TV interview for Granada *World in Action*, broadcast January 30, 1978, transcript online at https://www.margaretthatcher.org/document/103485 (accessed February 12, 2019).

39. A directory of such signs may be found in Heal, *Signboards*. Subsequent work has identified trade cards, like that printed for "Samuel Forsaith, Trunkmaker," as another source for such representations that, like signboards, would have been part of the everyday life of even fairly modest bourgeois consumers who might not have had the chance

to admire the paintings Dabydeen analyses. See Catherine Molineux, *Faces of Perfect Ebony: Encountering Atlantic Slavery in Imperial Britain* (Cambridge, MA: Harvard University Press, 2012), particularly Chapter 5, "Pleasurable Encounters," which examines trade cards for tobacco products.

40. Dabydeen, *Hogarth's Blacks*, 18.

41. Ibid., 20.

42. Ibid., 18.

43. Ibid., 21.

44. Simon Gikandi, *Slavery and the Culture of Taste* (Princeton and Oxford: Princeton University Press, 2011), 26.

45. Ibid., 28. Gikandi's use of the term "political unconscious" encourages a consideration of his analysis in relation to Fredric Jameson's work, which does indeed appear in Gikandi's bibliography even though it is not referred to explicitly. In my own attempt to deploy the kind of interpretative strategy outlined by Jameson in *The Political Unconscious*, it is not slavery as such that is rendered visible, but rather the relationship between slavery and the production of bourgeois subjects. My suggestion is not that British culture was unconscious of slavery, but rather that its white bourgeois participants were unable consciously to articulate the terms of the relationship between themselves and the system of slavery that made their way of life possible. See Fredric Jameson, *The Political Unconscious: Narrative as a Socially Symbolic Act* (Ithaca, NY: Cornell University Press, 1981).

46. Slave rebellions, portrayed with varying degrees of sensitivity, sensationalism, and sympathy, provided dramatic material for theatrical productions from William Shakespeare's *The Tempest* (1611) to Thomas Southerne's *Oroonoko* (1695), adapted from Aphra Behn's prose fiction of 1688, which was rewarded with favorable comment from Addison in *The Spectator*, No. 40 (April 16, 1711).

47. "A Supplemental Act to a Former Act for the Better Ordering and Governing of Negroes," April 21, 1676, CO (Colonial Office papers) 30/2, 114–25, PRO (Public Record Office, London); cited in Jerome Handler, "Slave Revolts and Rebellions in Seventeenth-Century Barbados," *Nieuwe West-Indische Gids / New West Indian Guide* 56, no. 1–2 (1982): 5–42, at 17. Bans on musical instruments, and particularly drums, were in force in Jamaica by 1688, according to Hans Sloane, and were enforced in St. Kitts in 1711 and again in 1722, and were included in a new slave act in Jamaica in 1717. See Dena J. Epstein, *Sinful Tunes and Spirituals: Black Folk Music to the Civil War* (Urbana and Chicago: University of Illinois Press, 1977), 58–59.

48. Richard Cullen Rath, *How Early America Sounded* (Ithaca, NY and London: Cornell University Press, 2003), 79.

49. Kathleen Wilson, "The Performance of Freedom: Maroons and the Colonial Order in Eighteenth-Century Jamaica and the Atlantic Sound," *William and Mary Quarterly* 66, no. 1 (2009): 45–86. Paul Gilroy explores with exemplary care and historical attention the possibility that such practices might constitute an alternative black aesthetics, recognizing that to do so involves risking drinking from a "poisoned chalice," but nonetheless affirming "that the history and practice of black popular music point to other possibilities and generate other plausible models . . . that bourgeois democracy in the genteel metropolitan guise in which it appeared at the dawn of the public sphere should not serve as an ideal type for all modern political processes." He adds that we "need to make sense of musical performances in which identity is fleetingly experienced

in the most intensive ways and sometimes socially reproduced by means of neglected modes of signifying practice like mimesis, gesture, kinesis and costume. Antiphony (call and response) is the principal formal feature of these musical traditions. It has come to be seen as a bridge from music into other modes of cultural expression, supplying, along with improvisation, montage, and dramaturgy, the hermeneutic keys to the full medley of black artistic practices." Paul Gilroy, *The Black Atlantic: Modernity and Double Consciousness* (Cambridge, MA: Harvard University Press, 1993), 77–78.

50. Although slave traders clearly recognized that the Africans they had taken prisoner and transported across the Atlantic came from what eighteenth-century discourses understood as separate African "nations," their enslavement and transport sought—not always successfully—to erase such distinctions. Such erasure was thus a contributory factor to the development of "race" during the eighteenth century as the term by which to distinguish them from people of European birth or origin—who, of course, retained their national identities, and failed to recognize their own whiteness as "race." See Nicholas Hudson, "'From Nation to Race': The Origin of Racial Classification in Eighteenth-Century Thought," *Eighteenth-Century Studies* 29, no. 3 (1997): 247–64.

51. For an argument about the development of "visuality" enabled by systems of plantation surveillance, see Nicholas Mirzoeff, *The Right to Look: A Counterhistory of Visuality* (Durham, NC: Duke University Press, 2011).

52. This argument is indebted to numerous theorizations of blackness and the historical legacy of slavery, particularly as it has been experienced in the United States, but from which geographical distance provides the United Kingdom, then as now, with no alibi. The following texts have been of particular significance for the present argument: Orlando Patterson, *Slavery and Social Death* (Cambridge, MA: Harvard University Press, 1982); Saidiya V. Hartman, *Scenes of Subjection: Terror, Slavery, and Self-Making in Nineteenth-Century America* (Oxford and New York: Oxford University Press, 1997); Fred Moten, *In the Break: The Aesthetics of the Black Radical Tradition* (Minneapolis: University of Minnesota Press, 2003); Hortense J. Spillers, *Black, White and in Color: Essays on American Literature and Culture* (Chicago: University of Chicago Press, 2003); Frank Wilderson III, "Gramsci's Black Marx: Whither the Slave in Civil Society?," *Social Identities* 9, no. 2 (2003): 225–40; Wagner, *Disturbing the Peace*; Jared Sexton, "The Social Life of Social Death: On Afro-Pessimism and Black Optimism," *InTensions Journal* 5 (2011): 1–47, online at http://www.yorku.ca/intent/issue5/articles/jaredsexton.php (accessed August 18, 2019).

53. Richmond P. Bond, *Queen Anne's American Kings* (Oxford: Oxford University Press, 1952); Eric Hinderaker, "The 'Four Indian Kings' and the Imaginative Construction of the First British Empire," *William and Mary Quarterly* 53, no. 3 (1996): 487–526; Coll Thrush, *Indigenous London: Native Travelers at the Heart of Empire* (New Haven: Yale University Press, 2016), 73–82; Robbie Richardson, *The Savage and Modern Self: North American Indians in Eighteenth-Century British Literature and Culture* (Toronto: University of Toronto Press, 2018), 25–33. See also, for an analysis highly attentive to theatre and performance, Joseph Roach, *Cities of the Dead: Circum-Atlantic Performance* (New York: Columbia University Press, 1996), 119–78.

54. For earlier and much fuller articulations of this broader political and cultural phenomenon, as well as the history and present-day issues of recognition and refusal that it has entailed for Native Americans specifically, see Philip J. Deloria, *Playing Indian* (New Haven: Yale University Press, 1998); Glen Sean Coulthard, *Red Skin, White Masks: Re-*

jecting the Colonial Politics of Recognition (Minneapolis: University of Minnesota Press, 2014); Audra Simpson, *Mohawk Interruptus: Political Life across the Borders of Settler States* (Durham, NC: Duke University Press, 2014); Jace Weaver, *Red Atlantic: American Indigenes and the Making of the Modern World* (Chapel Hill: University of North Carolina Press, 2014). The work of Coll Thrush, particularly in *Indigenous London*, represents an attempt to move beyond the limits imposed by white European historiographical practice to recover at least something of the experiences whose reality is simultaneously alluded to and denied in texts such as *The Spectator* No. 50.

55. Daniel Statt, "The Case of the Mohocks: Rake Violence in Augustan London," *Social History* 20, no. 2 (1995): 179–99; Neil Guthrie, "'No Truth or Very Little in the Whole Story'?: A Reassessment of the Mohock Scare of 1712," *Eighteenth-Century Life* 20, no. 2 (1996): 33–56; Erin Mackie, *Rakes, Highwaymen and Pirates: The Making of the Modern Gentleman in the Eighteenth Century* (Baltimore: Johns Hopkins University Press, 2009).

56. See, for example, Ian A. Bell, *Literature and Crime in Augustan England* (London and New York: Routledge, 1991).

57. Statt, "Case of the Mohocks," 194.

58. Ibid., 183–90. John Gay's play, *The Mohocks*, was published in April 1712. The trial was in June 1712. Statt's supposition that the defendants may have read the play is very plausible: it seems highly likely that young men involved in a media sensation of this kind would have been avid readers of material about themselves.

59. Statt, "Case of the Mohocks," 191.

60. Hinderaker, "'Four Indian Kings,'" 505; Richardson, *Savage and Modern Self*, 13–38.

61. Peter Linebaugh and Marcus Rediker, *The Many-Headed Hydra: Sailors, Slaves, Commoners, and the Hidden History of the Revolutionary Atlantic* (London and New York: Verso, 2003), 3–4.

62. Baruch Spinoza, "Letter 17," in Spinoza, *The Letters*, trans. Samuel Shirley (Indianapolis and Cambridge: Hackett, 1995), 125–26. "Ethiopian" does not, unlike "Brazilian," indicate a geographical identity, but is instead a term used to describe people of African origin, whatever their actual place of origin.

63. Warren Montag, *Bodies, Masses, Power: Spinoza and His Contemporaries* (London and New York: Verso, 1999), 123.

64. Silvia Federici, *Caliban and the Witch: Women, the Body and Primitive Accumulation* (New York: Autonomedia, 2004); Michael Hardt and Antonio Negri, *Multitude: War and Democracy in the Age of Empire* (New York: Penguin, 2004). See also Roberto Fernandez Retamar, Lynn Garafola, David Arthur McMurray, and Robert Márquez, "Caliban: Notes towards a Discussion of Our Culture in America," *Massachusetts Review* 15, no. 1–2 (1974): 7–72.

65. Antonio Negri, *Savage Anomaly: The Power of Spinoza's Metaphysics and Politics*, trans. Michael Hardt (Minneapolis and Oxford: University of Minnesota Press, 1991), 86. Negri's Italian text was first published as *L'anomalia selvaggia: Saggio sul potere e potenza in Baruch Spinoza* (Milan: Feltrinelli, 1981).

66. Negri, *Savage Anomaly*, 98. The figure of Caliban had already been deployed, well before Negri and Federici, in the work of Caribbean thinkers and writers, most notably Retamar et al., "Caliban"; and Edward Kamau Brathwaite, "Caliban, Ariel, and Unprospero in the Conflict of Creolization: A Study of the Slave Revolt in Jamaica in 1831–32," *Annals of the New York Academy of Sciences* 292, no. 1 (1977): 41–62.

67. Montag, *Bodies, Masses, Power*, 87.

68. Ibid., 88–89, 123.

69. Ibid., 89.

70. Ibid. Willi Goetschel makes a related point, and one that complements both Montag's reading of the Brazilian and mine of the Trunk-Maker and the Mohocks, observing that "Spinoza's dream thus serves as a reminder that the modern subject is a product of the material conditions that colonialism produces—and not just in the colonies but also in equal measure and intensity 'at home.' The dream represents the threshold where the domestic serves as the scene for the construction of the postcolonial." Willi Goetschel, "Spinoza's Dream," *The Cambridge Journal of Postcolonial Literary Inquiry* 3, no. 1 (2016): 39–54, at 54. The point in all these lines of argument is that the distant revolutionary threat is imagined at the very heart of the bourgeoisified colonial metropolis: in the philosopher's Amsterdam bedroom, in the "upper Gallery of the Playhouse," and on the streets of London.

IV • The Scene with the Smoke

This final scene opens, perhaps rather predictably, with a spectator sitting in the stalls. In defiance of the conventions of the bourgeois theatre, he is smoking a cigar. His cigar possesses magical properties: while smoking it, the spectator is able to see right through the illusions presented on the stage. Or, more strangely and more magically still, because he is smoking, the illusions presented onstage have acquired the capacity to see through themselves. In place of the ideological deceptions of capitalism's preferred theatrical mode—realism—which is supposed to have produced him over and over again as the compliant bourgeois subject, the stage now offers the smoking spectator an astonishing vision of how capitalism really works. That is the theory. But it is complicated, of course, not least because the spectator in question is almost certainly bourgeois.

The early eighteenth century is long gone (but it can always be revived). At a writing table in his apartment at Hardenbergstraße 1A in Charlottenburg, a distinctly bourgeois district of Berlin, a playwright enjoying recent commercial success is making some notes in which he will explain what he thought was up to when writing and producing his collaborative update of John Gay's theatrical hit, *The Beggar's Opera* (1728). These notes will include his famous suggestion that the ideal spectator for the new kind of theatre that this playwright will develop should be "a man" (yes, once again, a man) who is smoking. In the years between the successful production of Bertolt Brecht and Kurt Weill's *Threepenny Opera* (1928) at the Theater am Schiffbauerdamm in Berlin, the playwright, for it is he, has been reading a lot of Marx. This might go some way toward explaining a certain ambivalence he clearly feels about his current lifestyle, although he had already adopted a recognizably antibourgeois stance long before his encounter with Marx:

In my bedroom, which is small, I have two tables, one big and one small, an old wooden bed, which is not longer than me but a bit wider even though it's not wider than most beds, two low Norman chairs with straw seats, two Chinese bedside rugs and a large wooden trunk with canvas straps for manuscripts. On it I've got a film projector, a projection lamp and an electric bowl fire as well as *a plaster cast of my face*. My clothes, linen and shoes are in two built-in wardrobes. My linen includes shirts, bedding to make the bed, seven suits, eight pairs of shoes. There's a lamp hanging from the ceiling and a second one on the table by the bed. I like the room and most of these things, but I am embarrassed about the whole thing because it is too much.[1]

This kind of embarrassment is a persistent background affect for a certain kind of bourgeois subjectivity, particularly in the twentieth century. For those subjects whom I have earlier described as "left-wing or in other ways dissident children of bourgeois parents" (see Chapter 1, "An Essay Regarding the Bourgeoisie," § "Bourgeois"), such embarrassment arises from knowing that they are in some way complicit in the structural injustices created by and sustaining the society they inhabit. By insisting on his preference for an ascetic way of life—by presenting as "too much" the distinctly modest furnishings of his new apartment—Brecht is expressing his embarrassment at his class position, an embarrassment exacerbated, presumably, by his recent success in the commercial theatre, which would seem to confirm him in the class to which he was born, and from which he had been distancing himself through repeated acts of disidentification for many years. In other words, he is embarrassed to be living in Charlottenburg, and tries to mask that fact by making out that he is embarrassed to have any furniture or clothes at all, even though, as he makes a point of revealing, his bed is too small. There will be more to be said, in due course, about this background affect and its relation both to Marxism and to bourgeois life.

Why, though, having taking our leave of the eighteenth century so abruptly, have we found ourselves in Berlin in the early 1930s? In the intervening years, which the present volume omits, at least in its selection of scenes, two crucial and intimately related developments have unfolded. The first was the progression, beyond the "transition," into what we might call a fully realized capitalism. The second was the emergence of a critical tradition that identified capitalism as such and made it the object of its critique. These two nineteenth-century formations—industrial capitalism and Marxism—are what this book has just overleaped, but not without picking up along the way the conceptual wherewithal for its own critical operations. Without Marxism's critique of industrial capitalism there would have been no way for Dobb, Brenner, Wood, Federici, and others to have identified the "transition to capitalism" and to have contested its nature and its reality, nor, by the same token, any way for me to have imagined such a figure as the bourgeois subject, or to have identified it with acts of spectatorship. The leap into 1930s Berlin, then, allows me to land in a historical moment at which the kind of critique I am trying to develop here had become possible, a moment at which the bourgeoisie had developed for itself the means to make its own subjectivity the object of its inquiry, its discourse, and, quite frequently, its disdain. It allows me to make a very particular spectator the new subject of my own inquiry, replacing, as it were, Joseph Addison and Mr. Spectator with their twentieth-century successors: Bertolt Brecht and a cigar-smoking man in the audience, who may well turn out to be one and the same. I am going to suggest that this figure represents the bourgeois against the bourgeoisie—as well, perhaps, as the theatre against the theatre. The former might be also a way of describing an influential tradition in twentieth-century thought to which the name of "Western Marxism" is often attached, and to which I turn now as a way of preparing the stage for the appearance on the scene—which scene is, of course, the auditorium—of this chapter's central figure, complete with his cigar.

Western Marxism; or, The Bourgeois Critique of the Bourgeoisie

The term "Western Marxism" was initially used in condemnatory fashion by Soviet Marxists of the "East" and subsequently adopted by Maurice Merleau-Ponty as the title for a chapter of his *Adventures of the Dialectic*, in which he identified it as a coherent philosophical project.[2] It was historicized, in a largely critical manner, by Perry Anderson in *Considerations on Western Marxism*; György Lukács's *History and Class Consciousness* is widely seen as one of the inaugural moments of this philosophical project.[3] Lukács's contemporaries, to whom the term is also applied, included a group of thinkers associated with the Frankfurt School—with whom Sohn-Rethel's thought shared many connections, although he had no formal relation with its institutional structure—Max Horkheimer, Theodor Adorno, Walter Benjamin, Herbert Marcuse. Their contemporary and frequent interlocutor Ernst Bloch is also seen as part of this German-language constellation of thinkers. Bertolt Brecht was a friend of Benjamin's, of course, and participated in, as well as being the subject of, debates among many of these writers on questions of politics and aesthetics.[4] Among non-German figures generally regarded as part of this tradition (and included in Anderson's survey) are the Italians Antonio Gramsci (the single member of this conceptual group whom Anderson exempts from his main lines of criticism, as we shall see), Lucio Colletti, and Galvano Della Volpe and the French philosophers Henri Lefebvre, Jean-Paul Sartre, and Louis Althusser.[5]

Leaving aside for the moment the wide range of topics and perspectives covered in the work of these writers, one historical reality cannot be avoided: they were all white European men. That they are dead is, in my view, far less of a problem, although surely regrettable. This reality is absent from Anderson's historicization, and far more than simply a question of representation and canon formation, although it is all that, too. Merleau-Ponty's essay is also a historicization of the work in question. Merleau-Ponty asks whether Western Marxism, and, in particular, Lukács—who so successfully demonstrated the failure of bourgeois thought (including that of his earlier mentors Max Weber and Georg Simmel) to accept its own historicity—might also be capable of generating a properly historical account of itself. Here I want to take my cue from Merleau-Ponty's question to suggest that the entire tradition of Western Marxism—which has been an enormous influence upon my own habits of thought—still possesses a blind spot as regards its own historical conditions of possibility and conceptual limitations. It is a blind spot that Anderson, notwithstanding his demonstration of other limitations he ascribes to this body of work, appears to share, and from which I am also most unlikely to be immune. The real problem associated with this tradition, and the variations upon the bourgeois subjectivity that is the topic of the present book, is that it shares with bourgeois thought in general a failure to attend properly to the colonial relation and to the alternative political potential in thought generated by those subjects systematically excluded from positions of power and authority by European capitalism. In other words, this is a tradition that largely reflects the subjectivity of its authors (and those who view it as a tradition, of course) in paying no attention to the contributions—to historical developments or their critique—of women and people of color.

After briefly outlining the contours of Western Marxism in order to explain its relation to bourgeois life—which is still the subject at hand, after all—I will make an attempt to direct a small mirror toward the blind spot.

Anderson is not alone in identifying as bourgeois the social origins of the thinkers whose work he considers under the rubric of Western Marxism. Stuart Jefferies, in his recent group biography of the Frankfurt School, does so too, and Michael Löwy, addressing the question in a more theoretical register in his study of Lukács's work, raises the issue by asking what are the historical circumstances under which intellectuals (whom he sees as characteristic members of the "petty bourgeoisie") "join the struggle of the proletariat."[6] Löwy explains this phenomenon, at least for German-speaking intellectuals of the early twentieth century, such as Lukács, as the consequence of a gulf that opened up very rapidly between, on the one hand, the "ethico-cultural and socio-political values" held by this fraction of the bourgeoisie—which, he suggests, occupied varying positions on a broad spectrum of "romantic anti-capitalism"—and, on the other, the "ruthless spurt of industrial monopoly capitalism in Germany."[7] Confronted with this gulf, such intellectuals initially adopted a tragic or despairing attitude to the possibility of the culture being able to resist this process; some, at least, including Lukács, were able to translate this despair at their own culture and class into an affective and intellectual affiliation with Marxism and the proletariat. Of the various thinkers to whom Anderson applies the term "Western Marxism," this movement toward affiliation with the proletariat is probably strongest in Gramsci and Lukács, and weakest in the apparently more despairing and politically withdrawn figure of Theodor Adorno. The proposition, nonetheless, is that each of them to some extent (with the possible exception of Gramsci) shared a bourgeois background, and, in many cases, especially those of the Frankfurt School, considerable affluence and cultural capital. This is not a way of calling into question the sincerity or authenticity of their various political or intellectual commitments (as though only authentic proletarians can really identify with and participate in revolutionary politics or Marxist thought), but nor can it simply be put to one side as a merely accidental contingency, especially in light of Merleau-Ponty's question about Western Marxism's capacity to do what bourgeois philosophy is supposedly (according to Lukács) unable to do: understand its own historicity (that is, relativize its relativization of bourgeois philosophy).

Anderson's essay presents Western Marxism as a response to political defeat on three fronts: the defeat of a genuinely revolutionary communism by Stalin, the rise to power of the Nazis, and, finally, the postwar economic success of US and Western European capitalism. In the Soviet Union and the communist parties of Western Europe that took their lead from Moscow, the kind of thinking that Lukács inaugurated—which had begun to question and move beyond the newly established orthodoxies of Marxist thought associated with the earlier generation of theorist-politicians such as Lenin—faced actual suppression or strong discouragement. Nazism was of course a devastating setback for progressive thinkers of all kinds, including Marxists, as well as posing a direct threat to their institutional positions, livelihoods, and in many cases, including, of course, that of Walter Benjamin, their very lives. After the defeat of Nazism, Western Marxists secured institutional positions in the capitalist-democratic regimes of West Germany, France, and Italy, and either had no connection to a mass socialist movement (especially in Germany, where membership of the Communist Party was subject to a "Berufsverbot," or professional ban), or, if they remained formally as members of the Communist Party—as did Lefebvre and Althusser in France—felt obliged to abstain from direct political or economic work that might dissent from party policy. The overall result, argues Anderson, was that Western Marxism became a largely theoretical project, almost exclusively pursued in universities (he notes that all of its major postwar exponents were professors of philosophy), and came increasingly to focus on social and cultural questions—perhaps, above all, questions of art (that part of the superstructure typically considered as the most remote from the determining conditions of the economic base). I would put this observation of Anderson's slightly differently: Western Marxism took shape, above all, as a Marxist theorization of bourgeois life—its social structures and practices, its cultural production and consumption, and its aesthetics.

Those bourgeois subjects (some of whom may even be Western Marxists, or theatre professors, or even both) who start to experience something of the split between who they feel they are expected to be and who they really want to be—the "disidentification" I have already briefly discussed in Chapter I, "An Essay Regarding the Bourgeoisie," and that has reappeared here regarding Brecht's Charlottenburg discomfort—learn to conceptualize this split (or organize their critical distance) in terms, to put it at its most simplistic, of a choice between the life of an accountant or commercial traveler and the life of a poet or rock guitarist. To think of this in a more nuanced and perhaps everyday register, bourgeois aesthetic production and appreciation (of music, painting, novels, theatre) emerges as a means by which subjects who are becoming uncomfortable with their bourgeois selves can establish a little critical distance from their philistine coworkers or co-owners, but without needing to join a revolutionary political organization. This kind of distance is far from fatal: indeed it may be vital to the reproduction of bourgeois life. In other words, the ideal subject products of bourgeois education may in fact be those who both feel and understand the inadequacies and injustices of the bourgeois capitalist world but who continue to live within it, enjoying string quartets, voting for whomever seems to offer something that resembles social democracy, and sometimes even writing books in which they ironize their own subjectivity and political affiliations. Understood as an ensemble of attitudes and positions, then, distance is simultaneously both the condition that produces and maintains the bourgeois capacity to ignore the violent foundations of their well-being and hegemony, and the condition that enables the production of a critique, not merely of bourgeois well-being and hegemony, but even of the capacity for willful ignorance upon which those conditions depend. Going to the theatre, I am suggesting, helps cultivate a subjectivity disposed to entertain such an ensemble of distances. It is, of course, a subjectivity inclined to the production and contemplation of scenes.

Those bourgeois subjects of this type who became Western Marxists managed to maintain—despite their searching critiques of every dimension of bourgeois life, and their personal and intellectual commitments to various forms of political struggle—one very particular distance in the scenes they produced for contemplation, exhibiting in this regard what seems today to be a very specific willful ignorance on one crucial dimension of the capitalism that is the object of their critical analysis. Among all the writers that Perry Anderson identified with this tradition, none—with the crucial exception of Sartre, for whom the Algerian War of Independence was an event of considerable political significance, and who engaged intensely with the work of Frantz Fanon (writing a preface for *The Wretched of the Earth*)—paid any significant attention in their work either to the colonial dimension of capitalism, or to questions of race. The tradition has been the subject of extensive critiques on these grounds (and, as we have already seen in Chapter I, for its parallel failure to account for the gendered dimensions of capitalism's "originary" or "primitive accumulation"), and there is a rich literature in which such critiques can be considered and their implications weighed.[8] My aim here is not to add to this literature but to address two more limited questions: What might have caused this strange error of omission, and what might Western Marxism's race blindness have to do with both the production of the spectatorial bourgeois subject in eighteenth-century London and the question of Brecht's cigar in early twentieth-century Berlin?

Some preliminary answers to these question might be developed by paying attention, once again, to the Trunk-Maker: the "large black Man, whom no body knows." He is socially invisible. No one who knows anyone, or whom anyone else knows, knows him. He is not a participant in the world of the colonial metropolis but appears there almost as the emblem of what that social world cannot see, despite it being right there, in plain sight. Addison was not, of course, a Western Marxist. But his consigning of the black man to this social invisibility is a gesture repeated in one of Marxism's central categories: the gesture that makes wage labor central to an understanding of how a capitalist economy functions. In centering wage labor in this way, Marx and subsequent Marxists have performed a structural exclusion of a whole category of unwaged labor, which, as we have argued already, is in fact an integral part of that economy: the enslaved. Thus the arguments offered—by historians such as Eric Williams, for the role of slavery in early capitalism's accelerated growth; by those, like Silvia Federici, who see other proletarian subjects (and their subjection) as an essential component of a patriarchal capitalism; and by those who, like Nicholas Mirzoeff, see the plantation system as the organizational model for later industrial capitalist factory system—may now be complemented by an argument made at the more abstract philosophical level at which a Marxist understanding of subject formation is in operation.

That argument is made with particularly clarity by black scholars such as Saidiya Hartman and Frank Wilderson III. It is a phrase of Hartman's that gives the title to a conversation between them, "The Position of the Unthought," in which they discuss the enslaved's occupation of this position in ways that clearly invite a consideration of the figure of The Trunk-Maker, or, indeed, of Caliban, in precisely such terms: as figures who stand entirely outside the discursive frameworks and social categories that (mis)hail them.[9] If you are a Western Marxist looking for subjects to fulfill the demanding role of the agent of revolutionary change, you will simply not think of the enslaved, because, as Wilderson explains, the enslaved operates outside the system of wage labor: the enslaved is not "approached by variable capital—a wage," but with "direct relations of force."[10] Thus, while white wage laborers can sustain claims for the "universal applicability" of their relation to capital, the laboring black body is denied any subject position at all, by virtue of not having entered into the definitive wage relation.[11] For Wilderson, then, it is white supremacy and its direct violence that plays a more fundamental role than wage labor in the position (of the unthought) occupied by black (non) subjects. Slavery, he writes, "is closer to capital's primal desire than is waged oppression." In perhaps his most direct formulation of the position of the black subject in capitalism, and one that has particular resonance for the present project's consideration of theatregoing as a bourgeois leisure activity, Wilderson writes that "[b]lack death is the modern bourgeois-state's recreational pastime."[12]

One striking aspect of this "black death" is that it takes place in plain view. Although it could be said, in Marx's terms, that, like wage labor itself, slavery takes place in the "hidden abode of production,"[13] even those who, like Marx, insist that we turn our gaze in that direction (to conjure scenes from proletarian life, perhaps, to complement Adam Smith's sunny scenes of the self-regulating bourgeois market), seem not only to have been unable to catch sight of this black presence, but appear, at least in their construction of a philosophy of (universal) history, to have been responsible not just for not seeing the black presence on the scene, but for effecting its erasure. This is the substance of Susan Buck-Morss's historicizing consideration of Hegel's master–slave dialectic, which, she argues, has consistently been read as a largely abstract and allegorical account of the production of self-conscious human subjects in a universal historical process. What Buck-Morss shows is that, in writing this famous passage in the *Phenomenology of Spirit*, Hegel could not have conceived the struggle between master and slave in such abstract and ahistorical terms. Instead, his awareness of the revolutionary struggles of the actually enslaved in the French colony of Saint-Domingue (the very colony in which the question of the chattel status of the enslaved was discussed in the *Daily Courant* in early 1707; see Chapter III, "The Scene with the Trunk-Maker") demands that his text be read in this specific historical context. One of the principal reasons, she writes, for the failure of Hegel scholarship to attend to this material reality was that the single most influential materialist development of Hegel's thought—in Marx's dialectical historical materialism—subsumed the specific figure of the enslaved under the more abstract figure of the proletarian, whose presumptive whiteness (along with his unmarked masculinity) made him the privileged subject of Marxist conceptions of political struggle and historical change. This is why it was that "[e]ven when theoretical claims of freedom were transformed into revolutionary action on the political stage, it was possible for the slave-driven colonial economy that functioned behind the scenes to be kept in darkness."[14] The same darkness, perhaps, in which "a large black Man, whom no body knows" would have lived his life, had he not been momentarily propelled into theatrical visibility in the imagination of a colonial administrator-*cum*-essayist. I would like to be able to claim a further parallel here, proposing that the critical literature on the Trunk-Maker has stripped him of this racialization (a crucial part of his historical specificity as a subject), just as the literature on Hegel has rendered his "slave" as both abstract and white. But sadly the critical literature on the Trunk-Maker hardly approaches the scale and scope of the work that has been written about Hegel's "slave." In fact, this is pretty much all there is. The "black death" of the Trunk-Maker, as an "unthought" figure, is thus more complete than that of Hegel's "slave", while simultaneously yet to have been enacted.

Brecht's America

Brecht was, of course, an inheritor and a participant in this Western Marxist tradition, and his critique of capitalism, of bourgeois society and of the bourgeois theatre, too, was strongly shaped by his reading of Marx, as well as by his extensive discussions with other Marxist thinkers and writers of his own time. His work might be said to suffer from some of the same blind spots over colonialism and race that I have attributed in general terms to the Western Marxist tradition. His work does not—despite its use of imaginary non-European locations such as India (*Man Equals Man*) or China (*The Good Person of Szechuan*)—address the material realities and histories of slavery, colonialism, and racism. Although the "Chinese" aspects of his critical thought can produce a recognition that the agent of revolutionary struggle might not simply be the white industrial proletarian, but could emerge from rural laborers or "peasants," no more than any of his illustrious contemporaries did he extend the implications of this thought into considerations of the subject position of the unwaged and invisible black subjects of colonial capitalism. Brecht, however, developed his own critique of bourgeois culture, and, to some extent, of capitalism as such, before any sustained intellectual engagement with Marxism. Through much of the first half of the 1920s this critique developed alongside his fascination with America, and it is in the imaginary America that Brecht produced for himself at this time—itself a kind of placeholder, as we shall see, for capitalism as such—that traces of an alternative perception of capitalist history and reality may be found in his work. At the heart of this chapter is the suggestion that one particular trace of America can serve as a key to this alternative perception. I will suggest that it is an American commodity—the tobacco out of which the ideal spectator's cigar has been fashioned—that permits a revised account of Brecht's conception of spectatorship and, with it, of the relationship among colonialism, consumption, and the bourgeois theatre that has been the topic of this book. I want to let tobacco usher America and its (racial and colonial) histories into a consideration of Brecht's calls for a new critical spectatorship, just as I have asked the Trunk-Maker to adjust our understanding of the emergent bourgeois public sphere of the early eighteenth century. Before we think about tobacco, though, a brief sketch of Brecht's America is in order.

Brecht would not visit the real America until 1935, and would eventually live there from July 1941 (when he arrived in Hollywood) until October 1947, when he returned to Europe immediately after his appearance before the House Un-American Activities Committee. But this was not the America I have in mind. Before he ever set foot in the real America—or, more precisely, the United States of America—Brecht had invented an America of his own, one that functioned as a cartoonish capitalist-leisure complex associated with a strange intuition about what is now often called "settler colonialism." That Brecht understood his own America to be something entirely different from the "real" America he would one day visit is clear from a poem that appears to have been his response to his brother Walter's enthusiastic reports from New York, which urged him to join him in this brave new world:

I can hear you saying
He talks of America
He understands nothing about it
He has never been there.
But believe you me
You understand me perfectly well when I talk about America

And the best thing about America is:
That we understand it.[15]

In other words, there exists another America, which has a higher purpose than the America over which Walter Brecht is enthusing. The function of this America will be, eventually, to offer the critic of capitalism a heuristic device by means of which to generate a clear vision of what capitalism really is, freed from the illusions about it suffered by those who are living in it on a day-to-day basis. For the device to work, it is vital that you don't get too close. Better to keep your distance if you want to understand what is going on.

What is this imaginary America in the distance? Brecht's comes in two versions, and there are both gains and losses in the transition from one to the other. The first is really just Brecht's own variant of a pervasive fascination in the German (and other European) culture of the time with America as a distinctly modern society, compared to which Europe appears variously dull, decadent, weak, fading, or degenerate. It is an America of skyscrapers and motorcars. It is virile and frank. Its poetry is to be found in its popular culture, including jazz, spirituals, and other "black" cultural production. Other admirable characteristics include pleasures and entertainments in keeping with America's modernity—fighting, drinking (whiskey), and smoking (cigars)—which feature prominently in Brecht's imaginary social landscapes of the 1920s, and which would become explicit subject matter in one of his most fully realized "American" works, *The Rise and Fall of the City of Mahagonny* (a further collaboration with Kurt Weill, first produced, in Leipzig, in 1930). Brecht's frequent expression, in his early writings on theatre, of his preference for "fun" and "sport" as models for alternative modes of cultural consumption to those offered by the established bourgeois theatre of his day, his interest in boxing, in particular, and, of course, his special interest in the pleasures and virtues of smoking were all aspects of this phase of his "Americanism." This first version of America is by no means entirely positive, in that those aspects of "America" that appear so much more exciting and attractive than their tired old European counterparts are precisely those that will represent the underlying cruelty of American society. Brecht will simultaneously recommend an "Americanization" of Berlin culture and his own theatrical practice—replace a bourgeois reverence for the classics with a proletarian embrace of entertainment—and offer, in *Mahagonny* and elsewhere, a critique of an entertainment culture that is both "culinary" and fatal.[16]

Mahagonny presents the story of the foundation and destruction of a city dedicated entirely to the pleasures of consumption. Leokadja Begbick, Trinity Moses, and Fatty the Bookkeeper, all on the run from the law in an imaginary America, stop right where they are in the middle of nowhere (it could be California and it could be Florida) and start up an entertainment industry. Their enterprise begins with a small sex-work industry before expanding to encompass food, drink, tobacco, cabaret, and boxing. The city attracts eager customers, including a quartet of Alaska lumberjacks, seeking recreation after the almost unendurable pain of "seven years of felling timber / seven years of cold and squalor / seven years of bitter toil." At the height of its economic boom the city narrowly and miraculously avoids destruction by a hurricane and thereafter enshrines as its governing principle the radical free-market motto that "everything is permitted." When Jimmy Mahoney, one of the four Alaskans, fails to pay his bar bill, however, he is arrested, put on trial, convicted, and condemned to death, "for the penniless man / is the worst kind of criminal / beyond both pity and pardon." Everything is permitted, as long as you can pay for it. This America, then, offers a vision of capitalism in its most "natural" and unadulterated form—with no compromising accretions of precapitalist historical formations or cultural practices (no religion, no cathedrals, no renaissance painting, poetry, theatre, or any of that stuff). Just the logging and then the drinking (and the smoking), the producing and the consuming.

This first version of Brecht's America, which culminates in *Mahagonny*, also contains an intuition that this America has something to do with colonialism. In a notebook entry from September 1921, in a line of thought that would lead to the composition of *In the Jungle of Cities*, Brecht wrote:

> As I considered what Kipling did for the nation that "civilizes" the world, I came to the epochal discovery that actually nobody had yet described the big city as a jungle. Where are its heroes, its colonizers, its victims?[17]

Here Brecht performs a reversal not unlike Joseph Conrad's in *Heart of Darkness*, by suggesting that the real "jungle"—the location of the savagery that colonialism claims to eradicate—is to be found not in the "darkness" of India, but in the "cities" of "white" civilization.[18] The reversal is not, of course, identical to Conrad's, because of America's double valence in the colonial equation: on the one hand, it is the cutting edge of a formerly European society and "civilization"; on the other, it is, of course, just like India, or Conrad's Congo, the site of colonial expropriation. In other words, it is America as a settler colonial society that creates the material conditions of possibility for Brecht's imaginative work with it. It contains within it, in ways that are perhaps not as apparent in other colonial scenarios (such as in India and Congo), both the beneficiary agents and the victims of the colonial process.

This means that his imaginary America is not without racialization. Schlink in *In the Jungle of Cities* is identified as "Malay," suggesting that his relation to the otherwise predominantly white migrant world of Chicago might have its origins in the British Empire in Asia. As a theatrical figure Schlink also seems to come out of a more general modernist-primitivist fantasy, in which such orientalized characters function as ciphers for unknowability: Schlink's existential challenge to John Garga materializes inexplicably, out of the blue, and without any discernible motivation. One key feature of American racialization, however—slavery—is largely absent from the social and economic structure of this imaginary world, notwithstanding its author's interest in African American musical production, shared with many of his Berlin contemporaries.[19] Even here, although slavery as such does not feature, one of its historical legacies—lynching—is the focus of perhaps the single most racially charged scene of *In the Jungle of Cities*, in which Garga first tells Schlink that there have been lynchings earlier in the day, and then uses a familiar American racist trope in an attempt to get the men in the bar to take his side against Schlink, remarking that yellow-skinned men are sleeping with their daughters.

Although he does not make it the subject of any of his numerous American works, Brecht was also fully aware that the America he imagined was made possible by the genocide of Native Americans.[20] In a poem that was initially composed in 1924 for inclusion in an unfinished opera, fragments of which appear in the archive (first as *Man from Manhattan* and then as *Sodom and Gomorrah*), Brecht has a character, Ane Smith, speak explicitly about what happened.

One day a man with white skin arrived
He made a noise and spat chunks of iron
When he was hungry and he was
Always hungry

...
And soon
In red men chunks of iron were found and in bears and buffalo
For thrice one hundred years between
The Atlantic Ocean and the quiet Pacific
The red men died

...
Buffalo and red men
Were dead but
There was oil and iron and gold more than water
And with music and screaming the white people sat
In the everlasting prairies of stone[21]

Brecht's own first encounter with an idea of America seems to have been—as with many other Germans of his generation—with the "Wild West" fictions of Karl May, whose mythologized encounters between white men and "Indians" formed part of a pervasive discourse that translated the realities of genocide and dispossession into narratives of heroic struggle. This poem indicates very clearly that this childhood image had stayed with him and acquired a new and much more sinister aspect.[22]

The significance of these aspects of Brecht's America of the 1920s is that, however fantastical and secondhand it may have been, it served as an imaginary space for an emerging intuition that capitalism, in its most modern, most dynamic, and cruelest form, had something to do with colonialism, race, and genocide, even if the nature of the relationship among them was not fully articulated. In the account constructed from the Brecht archive by Patty Lee Parmalee, this intuition was interrupted and superseded in the process of Brecht's encounter with Marxism, which was itself motivated, she argues, by questions Brecht formulated in the course of his research into the America he was trying to use as material for further theatrical work. In particular, she suggests, it was a direct result of his attempts, in collaboration with Elisabeth Hauptmann, to understand properly the economics of Chicago's market in commodity futures specifically for *Joe Fleischhacker*, a play about a Chicago wheat speculator, as well as research for *The Book of Daniel Drew*, about a Vanderbilt-style millionaire, on which he was working in the mid-1920s. Of his problems with *Joe Fleischhacker*, Parmalee writes:

He pieced together a plot, worked out the very mathematics of the trading, but could not understand the logic of the system. The more he read, the less possible it was for him to write the play, nor could he finish any other projects he had been working on—which were all on similar themes—as long as he could not make clear the rationale behind the market.[23]

Parmalee concludes that Brecht reached an impasse in his writing about (and imagination of) America around 1926, and that it was this that prevented him from proceeding with these projects. Elements of them appear in later work, including, of course *Mahagonny*, but not because the problem of representing the economic system of American capitalism had been solved. (*Mahagonny* certainly offers no such analytical payoff, and the Chicago of *Arturo Ui* is little more than an appealing and movie-related setting for his allegory of the rise of Hitler.) Instead of pursuing these projects, Brecht devoted more and more of his time to reading Marx and Marxist literature.

Brecht's engagement with Western Marxism was motivated, at least in part, then, by his attempt to move from his initial conception of an imaginary America toward a deeper understanding of its real underlying economic realities. This involves some analytical gains, inasmuch as it provides Brecht with a historical and theoretical framework and conceptual tools to understand America as an instance of capitalism. This understanding of capitalism will be adapted to multiple further terrains, and, indeed, will involve a gradual withdrawal from the use of his imaginary America as a kind of Ur-capitalism. It also entails some countervailing losses, in that in leaving the imaginary America behind for a more universal and less idiosyncratic vision of capitalism as a global system, his work no longer engages with those particularities of the American experience that, while local and particular in some senses, are also part of capitalism's systemic global operations. As his new understanding of capitalism takes shape, Brecht's work attends increasingly to social, political, and cultural questions arising from a specifically European historical experience, and one that tends not to take into account the interconnectedness of, say, European industrialization and American plantation slavery. Brecht's early intimations, in his construction of an imaginary America, that lynching, genocide, originary accumulation, and the enjoyment of pleasures such as those of tobacco have something to do with one another, fade away in favor of an understanding of capitalism's histories that is distinctly European in perspective, and in which lynching and genocide are part of some other story, on the far distant shore of the Atlantic Ocean. What I want to show in what follows is that what has been forgotten is in fact still there, in the hands and mouths of the ideal spectators of the "new" theatre Brecht sets out to make as a result of his engagement with Marx. The cigar, in other words, will restore this "American" dimension to the critique of capitalism it is supposed to facilitate.

Complex Seeing

In the text I imagine Brecht having composed at his writing desk in Harden-bergstraße, he sets out the relationship between the new kind of theatre he proposes to make—and claims to have been making, in the case of *The Three-penny Opera*. The key moment for present purposes is as follows, presented here first in German and then in the most recent English translation:

> Das komplexe Sehen muß geübt werden. Allerdings ist dann beinahe wichtiger als das Imflußdenken das Überdenflußdenken. Außerdem erzwingen und ermöglichen die Tafeln vom Schauspieler einen neuen Stil. Dieser Stil ist der epische Stil. Beim Ablesen der Tafelprojek-tionen nimmt der Zuschauer die Haltung des Rauchend-Beobachtens ein. Durch eine solche Haltung erzwingt er ohne weiteres ein besseres und anständigeres Spiel, denn es ist aussichtslos, einen rauchenden Mann, der also hinlänglich mit sich selbst beschäftigt ist, "in den Bann ziehen" zu wollen.[24]

> Complex seeing must be practised. Then, however, thinking across the flow is almost more important than thinking in the flow. Moreover, the use of screens facilitates and imposes a new style of acting. This is the *epic style*. The spectators, as they read the projections on the screens, adopt a watching-while-smoking attitude. Such an attitude immediately extorts a better and more respectable performance from the actors, since it is hopeless to try to "cast a spell" on a man who is smoking and whose attention is thus already occupied.[25]

Some attention needs to be paid here, first of all, to questions of translation. It strikes me that there is something significant about the German term "Rauchend-Beobachten" that is not quite captured in the English translation. I do prefer this English translation to an earlier version, in which it is rendered as "smoking and watching," because it communicates better, for me at least, the simultaneity of the two activities: the idea that there is some smoking going on, and that the watching is a parallel activity to that smoking. "While" does this much more effectively than "and." But what doesn't work so well, I think, even in this more recent and revised translation, is the term "watching." I am not convinced that there is an alternative that would flow particularly elegantly in English, but I do want to note that there is something quite particular going on when a "Zuschauer"—a spectator—is imagined as a "Beobachter"—an observer. "Beobachten" seems to suggest a higher level of attentiveness than "zuschauen," in that it suggests that you are not just looking ("schauen"), or even just looking at something in particular. Instead you are attending, noting, even remarking upon what is going on. One observes in order to be able to report. The act of observation has a purpose beyond the moment and act of observation itself. Mere spectating consumes itself in its accomplishment.

This means that what Brecht calls the observer's "Haltung," which is translated into English as "attitude," is quite distinct from that of a mere spectator. And it is the smoking, apparently, that plays some part in producing that "Haltung." There's a small but important translation issue here, too, especially when thinking about theatrical performance (and the performance, or practice, of the theatrical spectator). "Haltung" is best thought of as an attitude that involves both a point of view or intellectual disposition and a habitual bodily posture. This is what Brecht is interested in. It is the particular articulation of bodily attitude and quality of attention that he suggests is produced by the act of smoking that matters. And the key thing, it seems, is that it is impossible to "'cast a spell'" on a spectator who is "already occupied." For two reasons: I have already hinted at the first, and the term "already" makes this point a little clearer, I think. The German "hinlänglich" does so to, in that it suggests that there is an adequate or satisfactory level of occupation in place at the time that the watching (or observing) begins. The smoker is smoking before starting to watch (or observe). The play is something to which the smoker turns his attention after he has lit his cigar and started to

enjoy it. The play comes as an interruption, then. "Oh, look," says the smoking spectator, "a play is happening over there. Let me pay it some attention."
The second reason—which is not quite captured by this English translation—is that this spectator is occupied with himself: "mit sich selbst be-
schäftigt." What does this mean? The spectator is already attending to his
own pleasure. Organizing hands, eyes, mouth, throat, smoke, and lungs in a
circuit that involves a satisfying and more than adequate articulation of sensation, attention, and manipulation. It is an activity that can be complete in
itself, but also, because it soon leaves the mind relatively free to do other
things, at the same time, it is an occupation that can readily be combined
with something else—like paying attention to a play, for example. It is for
this reason, I think, that it also functions very well as a way of making another activity feel good: I am thinking about communicational activities
here, such as talking to a stranger at a party, running a theatre rehearsal,
speaking in an academic seminar. In such situations, I think, the act of smoking rounds out the activity at hand, filling that space between you and the
people you have to engage with in such a way as to mitigate the social and
intellectual vulnerability you might otherwise experience. The act of smoking, the "Haltung" it encourages, the gestures to which it leads, rolls up a
range of human faculties in such a way as to make you feel somehow at home
in the situation. To feel at home in the situation, in this way, is to place other
things at a distance, to create, if you like, a little bubble of self-occupation
and security from within which you can manage the social interaction at
hand. John Berger explains the spatial dimension of the social relationship
shaped by the activity of smoking in theatrical terms, in an interview with
Sean O'Hagan in *The Guardian*: "Here is Berger on smoking, which he does
with the fierce enjoyment of a true addict. 'A cigarette,' he says, inhaling
deeply, 'is a breathing space. It makes a parenthesis. The time of a cigarette is
a parenthesis, and if it is shared you are both in that parenthesis. It's like a
proscenium arch for a dialogue.'"[26] His use of the theatrical structure of the
proscenium here suggests, interestingly for the present argument, that the act
of smoking achieves a separation and distance that helps the participants in
the act of conversation to know, and to feel that they know, that they are in a
conversation. Of course, as I have noted already in my observations about the
casual use of theatrical metaphors for communicative situations, the theatre
is not in fact a space of conversation. The proscenium is usually a frame that
allows two groups of people with different functions in an interaction (speak-

ing and being seen, for one group; listening, watching, and being unseen for the other) to recognize the terms of the interaction. In a conversation the proscenium of the smoking does something similar, however, except that in this case it is a frame that both parties recognize as marking the time and space of an activity for people whose functions in the interaction are effectively identical: both speak and both listen. The idea that this proscenium is also a parenthesis is helpful too, as though, as in the theatre, part of the function of the frame is to set the time of the interaction aside from the flow of "normal" time: time that has not been dedicated to the performance and enjoyment of theatre, or to the pleasures or pains of conversation. Smoking introduces "theatrical" distance into everyday conversation. At least, it does so in the mainly bourgeois smoking scenarios familiar to people like theatre professors.

For the theatre spectator, then, this kind of self-occupation, assisted by smoking, is what protects you from being overwhelmed by theatrical illusion. (Although, pursuing Berger's logic, one might think that the proscenium would do this. The conventional account of the effect of the proscenium is, of course, that it does the very opposite.) With this distance in place, the observer is able to view with clear and untroubled vision the representation of social life presented on the stage, and to see beyond the mystifications that might make these relations appear natural and unchanging, to a true understanding of their historical contingency. So here is the problem. Brecht's suggestions for how his ideal spectator might view his work, and thus for the kind of work his "new theatre" should make for this spectator, bear a striking resemblance to the descriptions of bourgeois philosophy and the scientific or experimental attitude or "Haltung" identified by Marxist philosophers György Lukács and Alfred Sohn-Rethel (see Chapter I), and which they both suggest should be overcome through the very same proletarian class-consciousness and socialist thought with which Brecht is increasingly coming to associate his new theatre project.

It is this position as the "pure observer" and the attitude of the "experimenter" that encourages both commonsense bourgeois subjects and their specialist representatives—scientists, detectives, philosophers, theatre professors, and so on—to treat the social world as if it were a natural world, and to see it as a closed system which they somehow stand, or sit, outside of. In short, to see it as something that has always been the way it is, and that no intervention is going to change. Of course, it is precisely this kind of com-

mon sense that Brecht, too, wants to unsettle and challenge. But it is characteristic, I suggest, of his essentially bourgeois conception of science, that he
should fall back on precisely this attitude that Lukács and Sohn-Rethel critique, in order to make his challenge. Brecht's proposals for a new theatre—
and the production, with it, of a new kind of spectator, the smoker-observer,
if you like—attempt to achieve antibourgeois aims, inasmuch as they seek to
render visible the historicity of the social relations represented onstage, but
do so in a manner that still appears confined within the philosophical epistemology Sohn-Rethel, like Lukács, wishes to move beyond. However, there is
something in Brecht's figure of the smoker-observer that, perhaps inadvertently, might point us toward that beyond. That something is, of course, tobacco.

The Four Alkaloids of Capitalist Modernity

In particular, I am interested in what historical residues—performance
remains—tobacco may have brought with it when it was first introduced
into Europe, and smoking was adopted as a leisure practice to be enjoyed by
such consumers as, eventually, Bertolt Brecht. What might we gain from
paying attention to the tobacco itself, and its histories, rather than just the
"Haltung" it induces? To start to answer that question requires that we pay
some attention to what tobacco did, and what tobacco meant, before it was
brought to Europe. Much of the evidence for this comes from two kinds of
source—conquistadors and other colonial actors, and anthropologists. This
poses a number of problems, many of which we might consider as questions
of translation. These issues of translation carry greater political significance
than my earlier concerns about the translation of German into English. The
various uses made of tobacco by indigenous peoples of the Americas reach
me in translation: of speech to writing, of one language into another, of performance into ethnographic observation. The understandings of human relations, power, nature, spirit, healing, death, and so on that have shaped the
uses of tobacco (and the ways they are spoken about by their participants) in
each of these contexts differ from those that underpin their translation into,
say, Spanish or English, or from the practices themselves into their representation in ethnographic accounts. So nothing I say here should be understood
as a statement about the actual meanings or functions of tobacco in any in-

digenous American community. What I am concerned with is what the translation has produced, in terms of a European imagination (reconstruction, transcription, explanation, adaptation) of indigenous tobacco practices, because it is this imagination that has shaped (if not actually controlled) the transculturation/refunctioning of tobacco in its transatlantic movement. I limit myself, that is, to what I think Europeans have been able to imagine tobacco might do for them.

The word "tobacco"—along with "canoe," "hurricane" (which appears, of course, in *Mahagonny*, but not in Shakespeare's *The Tempest*), "hammock," and other useful things—comes from the Taino language, that is, the language spoken by the first people to encounter the Spanish colonialists in 1492. These are people who, or so we had been taught, vanished entirely only fifty years after this encounter, yet who turn out still to be there—there, in this case, referring not only to those areas of the Caribbean, such as contemporary Cuba, Haiti, the Dominican Republic, and Puerto Rico, but also to a range of diasporic locations—and whose cultural practices and perspectives persist, often in complex relations with practices acquired and assimilated over five hundred years of transculturation. The Taino, like many other people of the Americas, North, South, and Central, used tobacco in a range of social, sacred, and political situations, often alongside other "drugs." It was sniffed, chewed, eaten, drunk, and, of course, smoked, in pipes and cigars and tubes. As I have already suggested, the range of uses and the cosmologies and social practices with which they were associated is a subject too vast for this chapter. What interests me is fairly straightforward: tobacco's social uses in the Americas broadly share the idea that the use of tobacco, and perhaps most particularly its consumption through smoking, is a way of communicating with spirits, and it therefore relies upon a conception of the world in which the spirits are available for communication, and in which an altered state of consciousness—sometimes understood as a kind of trance—is all that is needed to effect the communication. An alternate reality is ever present, and tobacco is one of the ways of entering into it. This, at least, is how a European like the theatre professor might best understand it.

I have twice used the word "transculturation," which is a term I am adopting—and perhaps even slightly adapting—from a remarkable book by the Cuban writer Fernando Ortiz. First published in 1940, Ortiz's *Cuban Counterpoint* is an essay on the history of Cuba told through the opposition and interaction between two of its most notable commodities, sugar and tobacco. For Ortiz, transculturation described the process in which, in Cuba, successive generations of its inhabitants have shed some cultural practices and ideas and adopted others, creating a new ensemble of practices and ideas that might be recognizable as a culture. He sees transculturation as fundamental to Cuba's past five hundred years of history, and also identifies the way tobacco, in its passage East across the Atlantic, participates in a transculturation experienced by Europeans. I'd like to let you hear Ortiz in person, as it were, because, even in English translation, there is something about the literary character of his text that I think it's important to experience and retain, as part of our understanding of his ideas. So here is Fernando Ortiz on tobacco:

> The extension of tobacco from the Indies to Europe was a phenomenon of transculturation of the most radical sort. Tobacco was as nothing to the whites; it had to be transplanted to their consciences before it could be adapted to their soil and their habits. If tobacco was accepted by the whites in a somewhat clandestine fashion, they soon attempted to rationalize its use, not for the true reasons, which smacked of diabolism and witchcraft in that feverish epoch of religious conflicts and intolerance which was the sixteenth century, but for reasons that could find justification in the morality and trends of the Renaissance....

> Tobacco reached the Christian world along with the revolutions of the Renaissance and the Reformation, when the Middle Ages were crumbling and the modern epoch, with its rationalism, was beginning. One might say that reason, starved and benumbed by theology, to revive and free itself, needed the help of some harmless stimulant that should not intoxicate it with enthusiasm and then stupefy it with illusions and bestiality, as happens with the old alcoholic drinks that lead to drunkenness. For this, to help sick reason, tobacco came from America. And with it chocolate. And from Abyssinia and Arabia, about the same time, came coffee. And tea made its appearance from the far east.

> The coincidental appearance of these four exotic products in the Old World, all of them stimulants of the senses as well as of the spirit, is

not without interest. It is as though they had been sent to Europe from the four corners of the earth by the devil to revive Europe when "the time came," when that continent was ready to save the spirituality of reason from burning itself out and give the senses their due once more. . . . Other spices and nectars were needed that should act as spurs of the senses and the mind. And the devil provided them, sending in for the mental jousts that initiated the modern age in Europe the tobacco of the Antilles, the chocolate of Mexico, the coffee of Africa, and the tea of China. Nicotine, theobromine, caffeine, and theine—these four alkaloids were put at the service of humanity to make reason more alert. . . .

These four alkaloids, solace for the senses and subtle nervous stimulants, all arrived at the same time to prolong the Renaissance. They were supernatural reinforcements for those of revolutionary ideas.[27]

In other words, tobacco underwent a process of transculturation, not in spite but because of its associations with religious (magical, supernatural, shamanistic) practices. This is why there must have been something "clandestine," in Ortiz's view, about the way it was adopted for use by Europeans. More recent historical support for this suggestion comes from Marcy Norton, who sets out explicitly and persuasively to contradict the widely accepted idea that tobacco had been adapted for use in Europe because of its supposedly medicinal, and thus (according to the conventional wisdom) secular and scientific properties.[28] In what reads to me as a clear echo of Ortiz, and also rests on close reading of both textual and other visual material, Norton sees the presumptive scientific legitimacy of tobacco as medical commodity as an alibi or cover under which it entered Europe. Once it had infiltrated this new cultural space, it became free to perform something rather more closely resembling the functions for which it had previously been used in the Americas than Europeans or Euro-Americans have generally been inclined to acknowledge. In other words, in the process of transculturation it retained something of what Europeans imagined, at least, to have been its spiritual powers.

Ortiz's proposition is not as simple as this, however. Tobacco comes to Europe, bearing with it spiritual powers that had made it an integral part of numerous American religious practices. Yet in the European context it now enters, it serves not to strengthen the existing institutions of religion, but instead to give fresh impetus to a new, ostensibly antireligious spirit. It is a supernatural reinforcement for what we have come to see, historically, as a progressive triumph of the rational over the supernatural. It plays a contradictory role, then, and it is this contradiction that I want to explore further here, not least because it might help us trouble the simple distinction between a secular, rational epistemology and what we might variously call a spiritual or poetic one (or maybe, even, a theatrical epistemology). Or, to state it in terms closer to those that might be used by Brecht, between science and illusion.

Ortiz says that these four alkaloidal stimulants—which I am calling the Four Alkaloids of Capitalist Modernity—give sustenance to the ongoing development of modern secular European reason and its triumph over the religious obscurantism and social tyranny he identifies with the preceding medieval period and its domination by Church and nobility. It is in this sense, I think, that we might appropriately say that the alkaloids ride, ultimately, to the aid of the bourgeois revolutionary cause. As Sohn-Rethel has indicated, the ongoing development of the reason Ortiz is talking about here is contingent upon certain real, historical, and material developments. It is not just that the economic base—as a vulgar Marxist analysis might have it—is forcing a transformation of the so-called superstructure. It is, rather, that a whole new relationship between base and superstructure is taking shape. The mediation between material reality and consciousness, the secret of which Sohn-Rethel suggests from the outset might be the aim of his project, is transformed because the social pervasiveness of the exchange abstraction and its realization in the paradigmatic commodity of commodities—money—make possible, and increasingly widely spread, the conscious apprehension of the underlying abstraction at work in exchange. (In other words, the mediation between base and superstructure becomes apprehensible as such, or, we might even say, this conceptual understanding of a social totality becomes possible for the first time.) This conscious apprehension of the underlying abstraction, you will recall, is, for Sohn-Rethel, what makes possible the rapid intellectual advances and eventual hegemony of modern scientific rationalism. It is no less than the basis for the philosophical epistemology that is the object of his critique.[29]

It should be therefore be no surprise to find, as we translate between Ortiz's idealist and Sohn-Rethel's materialist languages, that tobacco is not simply a valuable ally for the spiritual or intellectual dimension of the process they both describe, but that its presence in Europe is a direct result of one of the historical processes that is substantially responsible for the unprecedented pervasiveness of the exchange abstraction: namely, the colonial expropriation of the Americas that acted as such a powerful driver for early European capitalist expansion. Tobacco is indeed summoned, in a way Ortiz perhaps intuits but does not state, by the very forces to which it comes as a supernatural reinforcement. To translate this proposition back into Ortiz's language, this process is the "devil" that "provided" Europe with what it didn't quite yet know that it needed. The devil delivers tobacco to Europe in the midst of, and indeed as a part of, a process in which the consolidation of capitalist labor relations is strengthening the distinction between intellectual and manual labor. This is a process in which it is the bourgeoisie, who are gaining ownership of the means of production, who are becoming the intellectual laborers, and those from whom the means of production have been appropriated, manual laborers. As a result, tobacco establishes itself as an element in the leisure–entertainment complex in two ways. It becomes the accompaniment and eventual ideological or brand guarantee of the contemplative intellectual in search of truth, emblematized in the closely related bourgeois occupations of the philosopher and the detective. In other, often less bourgeois contexts, however, it becomes the instrument or pretext for the interruption of manual labor. Although manual laborers cannot smoke while working (because they don't have enough hands), and they often have more reason than bourgeois smokers to seek an interruption or slowdown of their labor, the bourgeois whose labor is intellectual may smoke while working. This means that working and smoking is typically done while seated. For the bourgeois spectator, very little adjustment in "Haltung" is required for the move between work and the leisure.[30] Since this is a project on bourgeois life (even if bourgeois life is, of course, always unavoidably related to proletarian and other subaltern lives), my attention here is to these bourgeois intellectual uses of tobacco in modernity.

Brecht's figure of the "Rauchend-Beobachter," then, is fully legible within the framework offered by the category of the bourgeois who makes a living from intellectual rather than manual labor, and who has learned, since at least the early eighteenth century, to find his or her entertainment in the contemplation and observation of productions and performances made by others. To smoke at the theatre, in the manner suggested by Brecht, is to consume two things at the same time (tobacco and performance), and it is to reproduce and consolidate the progressive interrelation of consumption, spectatorship, and an orientation toward truth. The observant-contemplative subjects imagined by Brecht are at once the bourgeoisie at leisure and the bourgeoisie going about their philosophical business. But at the same time, Brecht hopes, such subjects might become the "experts" whose mode of attention, whose "Haltung," if you like, will transcend the reification of bourgeois philosophy by means of a still more critical recognition of the contingent social relations that produce both the entertainment they are enjoying, and their own subjectivity. In order to do this, however, they will need, I suggest, to take some account of the history of tobacco that has made this contemplation possible.

Smoke gets in your eyes. That is to say, that there is something else in the scene, in the scene of spectatorship, that is working insidiously against both bourgeois and revolutionary clarity. That something else, drifting across the scene, is not just the secret of the expropriation that made tobacco a commodity in the leisure and entertainment economy of modern Europe, but the possibly equally scandalous secret that it never really lost its old magic in the process. That its spiritual reinforcement is still in force; that in this modern bourgeois theatre, smoke in the auditorium is doing some supplementary work, and that in the mind and body of the "Rauchend-Beobachter," some kind of spiritual and bodily transformation is taking place. Or even that the clear-sightedness that Brecht seeks here is not so far removed as he might imagine from the capacity to communicate with the spirits that tobacco encouraged in the cultures from which it had been transculturated. Is it perhaps because they hold in their hands and between their lips this secret trace, this residue of the past, reignited in the present, that Brecht's spectators offer the prospect of an alternative epistemology? Because Brecht's figure is doing more than just taking an attitude of critical contemplation; he participates, even if unwittingly, in the kind of seeing that bourgeois modernity has assigned to its own dark, distant prehistory—a kind that threatens always to slide into a state of consciousness routinely condemned as superstition and naive enchantment. This is not so very far, indeed, from the state of consciousness that Brecht himself condemns in his diagnosis of the failings of the operatic "Gesamtkunstwerk," in fact, in the very theatre and opera to which Brecht opposes his own practice:

The smelting process takes hold of the spectator, who is also melted down and represents a passive (suffering) part of the *Gesamtkunst-werk*. This sort of magic must of course be contested. Everything that aims to induce hypnosis, or is bound to produce undignified intoxication, or makes people befuddled, must be given up.[31]

The question, then, is what sort of critical spectatorship might be possible if we were to reject Brecht's strict opposition between magic, hypnosis, intoxication, or befuddlement, on the one hand, and clear critical thinking in the interests of political transformation, on the other? The invitation to ask this question comes from within Brecht's very own figure for the ideal spectator: the figure of the smoker who, it now seems, achieves critical detachment by means of a magical stimulant. For this alternative epistemology to emerge from within the contradiction inadvertently introduced by Brecht into this figure, a further twist in the process of transculturation must be applied. Those who long for a revolutionary spectatorial practice don't need to settle, after all, for the somewhat melancholy proposition with which this discussion began, that Brecht's "Rauchend-Beobachter" is simply the bourgeois philosopher in a new and only superficially revolutionary guise. If Brecht's observant expert critic were really only the old bourgeois philosophy claiming not to have been taken in by the illusions of bourgeois theatre and bourgeois post-Wagnerian opera, then there would be no place for tobacco in this story. But with tobacco center stage, as it were, blowing its smoke in the face of bourgeois claims to have successfully disenchanted the world, things look a little different.

They might look something like this. Seeing clearly in the present is not the only route to a critique of modernity. Complex seeing may involve seeing in more than one way at the same time: attending to the show, to the cigar, to the smoke; to the present and the past. It means recognizing not just that the world presented onstage may involve reifications and mystifications of actual contingent social relations, but also that the (now gender-neutral) spectator cannot simply remove themself from that process of reification and mystification through a self-willed act of critical detachment. The transculturation in which tobacco participates in the modern theatre, then, might involve the spectator recognizing that they, too, have a history, and that they are putting a part of that history in their mouth. That the smoke takes them to another time and place. That the act of smoking repeats something that may have been forgotten, but that has not really been eliminated, after all. That complex seeing involves seeing something of this history of your seeing. And that history, especially in the theatre, will turn out always to have involved moments of clarity and moments of hypnosis. A transculturation of Brecht's ideal spectator, by way of the smoking of tobacco, then, might encourage us to think that clarity cannot claim a monopoly on truth—that truth is not simply the reality uncovered beneath the illusion. And that *could* be an alternative to bourgeois philosophical epistemology, even if it is not quite the one that either Sohn-Rethel or Lukács, or even Brecht, might have imagined.

Toward a Theatrical Epistemology

I have no idea what that alternative might be. Only certain thoughts are available to consciousness at any given historical moment. All I can propose here, therefore, is a "Haltung" that might permit the workings of a political unconscious to be dimly apprehended. It is not exactly an approach—that might be too purposive—so much as a receptive disposition. Bourgeois philosophy's demand for clarity would keep these dim apprehensions in the dark. An alternative might take its cue from Spinoza's lucid dream of the "scabby Brazilian," in which a figure from the unconscious—encountered, that is, in a dream—was prolonged or repeatedly revived whenever the philosopher turned away from his "book or some other object."[32] Unwittingly I may have adopted this disposition throughout my work on this book. The Brazilian took his place in the text quite belatedly. He had been forgotten and then recovered in the course of my rereading notes made over a year and a half earlier.[33] His relevance is perhaps questionable. But I have included him, all the same, and now, as I reach the end of the book, he seems to offer himself not just as a figure for the "Other" against which the bourgeoisie organized themselves politically and philosophically, but also as a figure for the kind of things that appear in shadows, away from the light of center stage, and to which it seems to be my predilection to pay too much attention. He joins the Trunk-Maker and the tobacco smoke, so that all three become images (maybe even rebuses) that inhabit a political unconscious (maybe even mine, now). The work of analysis, as regards such images, is to pay too much attention to them in order to make of them some sense that differs from the common sense that would normally pay them no attention at all. The hope is that, whatever the scenes in which they first appear (the philosopher's room, the theatrical auditorium), they might open up wholly other scenes (in the Caribbean, for example), and suggest to whomever is paying this excessive attention some relations that might otherwise not occur to them. This procedure might involve a sort of free association or intellectual suggestibility that, once activated, transforms itself into a hyperactive scrutiny, worrying away at the images and the scenes they conjure until they can be made to give up something that can be claimed as a secret or a discovery about a culture—in this case, the bourgeois culture of theatrical spectatorship—and the subjectivity it produced, and which, in turn, produced it. Perhaps the best that might be said about such a procedure is that it involves the strategic misapplication of the contemplative techniques of bourgeois philosophy. For it certainly cannot make much of a claim to have overthrown them, or anything else.

Why call this practice a theatrical epistemology? The theatre, as I have already suggested, in discussions of its habit of malfunctioning as a ideological apparatus, is a very strange way of knowing what you know. This is clearly the case, even if from time or time (or even most of the time) state or corporate interests either deliberately or by sheer force of the normalization of their conceptions of the world may end up using it to try to make sure that people know the things they are required or supposed to know. So this epistemology is theatrical inasmuch as it tends to work with, rather than against, the confusion of reality with illusion, and against, rather than with, whatever clarity the bourgeois theatre (in both its moral-liberal and its political-agitational forms) might imagine itself to offer. It is a theatrical epistemology because it attends to those aspects of spectatorship that, while by no means exclusively theatrical, appear frequently in the theatre. There is always the possibility—in the theatre and in its remediations, too—that spectators may not always be paying attention to what they are supposed to be paying attention to. They are capable, therefore, of losing sight of the subject they are supposed to have become (the coherent figures onstage, for example). They are capable, too, of catching a glimpse of the processes by which they are being produced. This might happen, for example, when they are attending to the tobacco instead, and get caught in a dissociative loop of some kind that takes them to Cuba. It might happen when a theatre professor starts attending to spectatorship rather than to what is happening in theatre (onstage, in other words). In such moments of distraction or misplaced focus, they are attending, in both cases, I suggest, to the conditions of their own production. This makes them strong candidates for recruitment to that multitude of the one in ten who sometimes fail to respond appropriately to their interpellation as subjects in bourgeois life in that little scene that Althusser imagines.

Think about this in relation to the discussion of Stanley Cavell's essay with which I partly introduced this book (see "Prologue," §2). For Cavell, Shakespeare's *King Lear* (exceptionally) offers spectators a glimpse of how their predicament as spectators—for whom the characters are present, but who can never make themselves present to the characters—might have tragic real-world consequences. By thematizing the "avoidance of love," Cavell argues, this play (exceptionally) alerts its spectators to the danger that their continued spectatorship (in the world) might promote further avoidance of love, or what I might choose to call instead a renunciation of solidarity, performed by bourgeois subjects who know they are responsible for the plight of others but will do nothing to take responsibility for that responsibility. This is what I have called until now the "production of distance" (see Chapter I). What I have argued in the course of this book is that this spectatorial predicament is far from "exceptional." It is, as Cavell claims, "exemplary,"[34] but only inasmuch as a far wider range of theatrical experiences actually produces the same effects: to allow what I called in the second Prologue a "recognition that this experience of spectatorship . . . is not inevitable but historically contingent." This recognition involves the capacity of a particular kind of theatre—the bourgeois theatre whose spectators are the subject of this book—to direct spectators "attention to the historicity of the conditions of their own spectatorship" (see Prologue §2). This was, of course, part of the bourgeois project of *The Spectator*, in which the bourgeoisie, from the beginning, are interested at looking at themselves looking.

The subject possessed of this theatrical epistemology may, perhaps, be a theatre professor and have acquired this epistemology without much thinking about it, as an occupational hazard; or, if not a theatre professor, would almost certainly reject the proposition that this way of paying the wrong kind of attention amounts to an epistemology. Either way, as I have repeatedly insisted—usually by adverting to Marx's observations about the historical contingency of the histories (and other things) that subjects make—it is not possible to think entirely beyond or outside the frameworks for thought available in one's own historical moment. It would be foolish, therefore, to claim that this theatrical epistemology is anything other than bourgeois through and through, or that its subjects can claim any privileged position in the revolutionary struggle on this basis. A preference for irony and paradox will always make this impossible. The point is that, although such subjects are unable to project an alternative in any realizable form, they are at least susceptible to invitations to resist the demands for clarity that bourgeois philosophy and its cousin, common sense, so often make upon them—in the theatre, in the classroom, and at work.[35] They live perilously close to the subjects they wish to critique, and are as fully implicated as any other bourgeois subjects in the same historical conditions, growing up, as some of them may have done, *in a family home in an English provincial town at some point in the late twentieth century.*

Notes

1. Bertolt Brecht, *Große kommentierte Berliner und Frankfurter Ausgabe, Band 26: Journale 1 [1913–1941: Tagebücher 1913–1922; Journale 1938–1941]* (Frankfurt-am-Main: Suhrkamp Verlag, 1994), 295; cited in Stephen Parker, *Bertolt Brecht: A Literary Life* (London: Bloomsbury, 2015), 251, trans. and italics per Parker. Given what we now know about trunk-makers, we might think Brecht was risking his professional career by storing his manuscripts in this way.

2. Maurice Merleau-Ponty, "'Western' Marxism," in *Adventures of the Dialectic*, trans. Joseph Bien (Evanston, IL: Northwestern University Press, 1973), 30–58.

3. Perry Anderson, *Considerations on Western Marxism* (London: Verso, 1979); Georg Lukács, *History and Class Consciousness: Studies in Marxist Dialectics*, trans. Rodney Livingstone (Cambridge, MA: MIT Press, 1972).

4. Some of the key debates are collected in Theodor Adorno, Walter Benjamin, Ernst Bloch, Bertolt Brecht, and Georg Lukács, with an Afterword by Fredric Jameson, *Aesthetics and Politics* (London: Verso, 1980).

5. Numerous other writers and thinkers might be added to this roster. A recent book by Domenico Losurdo adds Alain Badiou, Slavoj Žižek, and the collaborative authors Michael Hardt and Antonio Negri, as well as, somewhat bafflingly, Giorgio Agamben (who does at least work in the light of Benjamin) and Michel Foucault. See Domenico Losurdo, *Il marxismo occidentale: Come nacque, come morì, come può rinascere* (Bari and Rome: Laterza, 2017). A number of English names might (more) plausibly be identified with this tradition, including, of course, Perry Anderson himself, as well as the historians whose account of English capitalism and class formation I have drawn on in previous chapters, such as Eric Hobsbawm and E. P. Thompson, and the cultural theorist Raymond Williams.

6. Stuart Jefferies, *Grand Hotel Abyss: The Lives of the Frankfurt School* (London: Verso, 2016); Michael Löwy, *Georg Lukács: From Romanticism to Bolshevism*, trans. Patrick Camiller (London: Verso, 1979), 16, 9.

7. Löwy, *Georg Lukács*, 67.

8. In addition to Cedric Robinson's *Black Marxism*, there are many significant points

of reference for the critique of Marxism for its tendency toward a universalizing Eurocentrism. I shall note just two of them here. Dipesh Chakrabarty, for example, identifies in the "transition narratives," such as the one offered earlier in the present book, a tendency to understand "development," "modernity" and so on as universal processes, in relation to which the history of India, for instance, is read in terms of "failure" or "lack," because the process of development is understood to be "incomplete." See Dipesh Chakrabarty, *Provincializing Europe: Postcolonial Thought and Historical Difference* (Princeton and Oxford: Princeton University Press, 2008), 30–31 A similarly sympathetic and fruitful though critical engagement with Marx, from an indigenous perspective, may be found in Glen Sean Coulthard, *Red Skin, White Masks: Rejecting the Colonial Politics of Recognition* (Minneapolis and London: University of Minnesota Press, 2014). See esp. 6–15.

9. Saidiya V. Hartman, "The Position of the Unthought: An Interview with Saidiya V. Hartman," by Frank Wilderson III, *Qui Parle* 13, no. 2 (2003): 183–201. Hartman's use of this term is at 186.

10. Frank Wilderson III, "Gramsci's Black Marx: Whither the Slave in Civil Society," *Social Identities* 9, no. 2 (2003): 225–40, at 229.

11. Ibid., 226.

12. Ibid., 229–30.

13. Karl Marx, *Capital: A Critique of Political Economy, Volume 1*, trans. Ben Fowkes (Harmondsworth, UK: Penguin Books, 2004), 279.

14. Susan Buck-Morss, "Hegel and Haiti," *Critical Inquiry* 26, no. 4 (2000): 821–65, at 822.

15. Cited in Parker, *Bertolt Brecht*, 227.

16. Ibid.

17. Cited in Patty Lee Parmalee, *Brecht's America* (Columbus: Ohio State University Press, for Miami [OH] University, 1981), 12. As Parmalee points out (16–17), Brecht had in fact already been reading Upton Sinclair's Chicago novel, *The Jungle*, which would be an important source for *In the Jungle of Cities*, so Brecht's "epochal" discovery is hardly his own alone.

18. Conrad's novel begins with the narrator describing the story being told on a boat afloat on the Thames in London, a story introduced by its teller—the novel's protagonist, Marlow—thus: "'And this also,' said Marlow suddenly, 'has been one of the dark places of the earth.'" Joseph Conrad, *Heart of Darkness* (New York: Penguin Books, 2017), 5.

19. For a discussion of this absence—not just from Brecht's work, but also, with the exception of Krenek's *Johnny spielt auf,* from German theatre and musical production at the time, despite a contemporary interest in jazz—see Joy H. Calico, *Brecht at the Opera* (Berkeley and Los Angeles: University of California Press, 2008), 78–79.

20. In addition to his well-known works for theatre with "American" settings—*In the Jungle of Cities, Mahagonny, Happy End, The Flight across the Ocean* (aka *The Lindbergh Flight*), *The Resistible Rise of Arturo Ui, Saint Joan of the Stockyards*—there are numerous fragments indicating that Brecht was preoccupied with "American" projects for several years in the mid- to late 1920s. The best source for analysis of this material, and of the sources upon which Brecht drew, both directly and indirectly, is Parmalee's *Brecht's America.*

21. Bertolt Brecht, "Ane Smith Relates the Conquest of America," in *Collected Poems*, trans. Tom Kuhn and David Constantine (New York: Liveright Publishing, 2018), 155. More information about these fragments in the Brecht archive is offered by Patty Lee

Parmalee in *Brecht's America*, 95–101. The poem seems to stand for a storytelling process that the text of the opera says took three months (see Parmalee, *Brecht's America*, 96).

22. For reflections on Brecht's childhood immersion in play based on his reading of May, see Stephen Parker, *Bertolt Brecht*, 23–24.

23. Parmalee, *Brecht in America*, 132.

24. Bertolt Brecht, "Anmerkungen zur *Dreigroschenoper*," *Schriften zum Theater*, 7 vols. (Frankfurt-am-Main: Suhrkamp Verlag, 1963–4), 2: at 91.

25. Bertolt Brecht, "Notes on *The Threepenny Opera*," in *Brecht on Theatre*, 3rd, rev. ed., ed. Marc Silberman, Steve Giles, and Tom Kuhn (London: Methuen, 2014), 71–80, at 72. Brecht made an earlier version of the key point of this train of thought in "There Is No Big City Theatre," in which he wrote that "I believe that if they served alcohol in any of the established Berlin theatres—but not in mine—it would make it completely impossible to stage a serious play. In fact I would maintain that a single man smoking a cigar in the stalls during a Shakespeare performance could bring about the collapse of art in the West. He might as well light a bomb as his cigar. I would be very much in favour of allowing the audience to smoke during our performances. Primarily for the actors' sake. In my opinion it is entirely impossible for an actor to try to fool a man smoking in the stalls with an unnatural, spasmodic, and outdated kind of theatre." I am indebted to Holger Syme for the proposal that "kramphaft," translated here as "spasmodic," might better be rendered as "uptight."

26. Sean O'Hagan, "A Radical Returns," *The Guardian*, April 3, 2005, online at https://www.theguardian.com/artanddesign/2005/apr/03/art.art1 (accessed February 8, 2019).

27. Fernando Ortiz, *Cuban Counterpoint: Tobacco and Sugar*, trans. Harriet de Onís (Durham, NC: Duke University Press, 1995), 200, 206–7.

28. Marcy Norton, *Sacred Gifts, Profane Pleasures: A History of Tobacco and Chocolate in the Atlantic World* (Ithaca, NY: Cornell University Press, 2008).

29. Alfred Sohn-Rethel, *Intellectual and Manual Labour: A Critique of Epistemology*, trans. Martin Sohn-Rethel (London: Macmillan, 1978).

30. See Eleanor Skimin, "Reproducing the White Bourgeois: The Sitting Room Drama of Marina Abramović," *TDR/The Drama Review* 62, no. 1 (2018): 79–97, for a very fruitful exploration of the relations among class, race, and sitting down in theatre and performance.

31. "Notes on the Opera [*Rise and Fall of the City of Mahagonny*]," in *Brecht on Theatre*, 61–71, at 66.

32. Baruch Spinoza, "Letter 17," in Spinoza, *The Letters*, trans. Samuel Shirley (Indianapolis and Cambridge: Hackett, 1995), 125–26.

33. My notes on Spinoza's Brazilian had been made somewhat sketchily, and were in the same file as notes that appeared to come from my reading of Susan Buck-Morss's essay "Hegel and Haiti," cited above. They mentioned that the "mangy Brazilian" (as I'd written) was a "second rebus." On returning to Buck-Morss's essay, I found nothing about either Spinoza or Brazilians, but was able to track the figure down via Warren Montag's book to Spinoza's *Letters*. Later I realized that my initial supposition had been more or less but not quite correct, inasmuch as she does make a brief mention of Spinoza's "mangy Brazilian" in the book she published extending her earlier article: Susan Buck-Morss, *Hegel, Haiti and Universal History* (Pittsburgh: University of Pittsburgh Press, 2009), 84–85.

34. Stanley Cavell, "The Avoidance of Love: A Reading of *King Lear*," in *Must We Mean What We Say? A Book of Essays*, updated edition (Cambridge: Cambridge University Press, 2015), 246–325.

35. This theatrical epistemology bears some resemblance to the "phenomenophilia" discussed by Rei Terada, by which she describes the perceptual practices of poets and thinkers who, in different ways, turn their attention away from those things that the world seems to insist upon: "The phenomenophile's suspensions and imagined suspensions of fact perception imply critical insight, as though they were proto-assertions of something that could be coming to be and does not yet have the liabilities of anything that is." Rei Terada, *Looking Away: Phenomenality and Dissatisfaction, Kant to Adorno* (Cambridge, MA: Harvard University Press, 2009), 33.

Epilogue

The Theatre Professors Persist

Theatre professors persist, however, in going to the theatre. Mindful of Brecht's caution that spectators—even though they are "scientific" these days—are still in the habit of leaving their brains behind in the cloakroom with their coats, they make sure, wherever possible, that they bring all the way to their seats in the stalls, along with their brains, a recognition of the historicity of their subjectivity. Although there will be no smoking—at least, in the bourgeois theatres they usually attend—to entrance them into a recollection of what this history has entailed, they will do their best to hang on to this hard-earned wisdom and hold themselves apart from their own subjectivity. They will keep a close eye on themselves. They will scrutinize their spectatorship, pay attention to the shape of their attention. They will be vigilant.

But such vigilance will never be more than a subjective act of resistance to the objective determinations of class and everything else that history has thrown together in the formation of theatre professors. They might hope, then, for some assistance from the theatre itself. What might a theatre maker do to blow the necessary smoke into the eyes of the theatre professors? Or if that turns out not to be enough—because the power of the apparatus so massively overwrites whatever you try to put on in it—might some systematic transformation of the theatre itself be required instead? This is, arguably, what Brecht himself was attempting, within and against capitalism in the 1920s and 1930s, and as a participant in a systematic effort to transform society in a noncapitalist direction in the postwar DDR. It is a familiar idea that part of the point of Brecht's theatre was to represent the world as historically contingent, and thus susceptible to (revolutionary) change. It is perhaps less frequently noted that part of the point of this point was that the spectator, too, is the product of specific historical conditions, and thus equally suscep-tible to alteration. Such alteration will arise not, of course, by means of the salutary or educational effects of the theatre (although that is not ruled out as part of the package) but, rather, as a result of the changes in historical real-ity wrought in the attempt to build a socialist alternative.

The vigilance of the professors involves, therefore, a recognition that things (including professors) could be different (though they aren't), and that whatever may have been said about spectatorship as a universal human condition (in an age of pervasive mass media, for instance), there still exist subjects who, while they may live in the society of the spectacle, do so not, or at least not always, as spectators. Of course, the representative institutions and media (government, education, television, etc.) of contemporary capi-talism have been crafted in the image and the interests of the bourgeois spec-tator, often working to bind or seduce all sorts of nonbourgeois others into at least partial assent to their spectatorial logics (with all the attendant con-sequences for subject formation). But those who have both suffered and en-joyed historical experiences other than the one whose history is traced in the present book, and whose identity is therefore less bound up with looking at (the lives of) others, may hold out some hope, even to theatre professors, that it is possible to encounter the world otherwise. The problem, from the per-spective of the theatre professors, might be how to persuade these others to come with them to the theatre (with cheap tickets or appropriate education or, ideally, a social-democratic combination of the two). Even if this is achieved, what if the seductive powers of the spectatorial logics these other subjects encounter there, at the theatre, prove powerful enough to undo their other ways of seeing things?

In any case, the idea that there might be such spectators—whatever truth it may contain—is, of course, a bourgeois fantasy, a specialist application of the trope of the "Noble Savage," which, as Hayden White has argued, func-tioned in its eighteenth-century heyday as a "fetish" by which the rising bour-geoisie could capture for themselves the "nobility" that the aristocracy had heretofore claimed to be their own "natural" attribute. By attributing nobil-ity to the "savages" of the Americas, bourgeois writers showed that it could not be regarded as the exclusive property of any single class, but something attributable, instead, to all humanity—but only, White writes, "in principle." For as soon as the nobility of the bourgeoisie had been established, the very same bourgeoisie then "immediately turned to the task of dehumanizing those classes below them in the same way that, in the seventeenth and eighteenth centuries, Europeans in general had done to the natives of the New World."[1] It is interesting, in light of White's interpretation, to consider a version of the fantasy that is not a million miles away from its articulation by Addison in the form of the Trunk-Maker. The author in this case is Theodor Adorno, writing about the social and spatial organization of the theatre:

Where today we have the gallery—uncertainly curtailed by the nearby wall, and somehow vaguely extended, as if the vertical order of the circles had lost its validity—the sky used to peer in on the theatre and the play of the drifting clouds dreamily made contact with the human theatre beneath. Those who sat there were the spokesmen of the clouds in the trial of the stage action taking place below; the legitimacy of that action could be weakened or broken by their objections. It was here that Ibykus' cranes were summoned as witnesses, and here that the chorus of the Furies received their answer. The dome has long since closed over the theatre and now reflects the sounds coming from the stage, barring a view of the sky. But those who sit nearest to it, for a small sum of money, and at the furthest remove from the stage, know that the roof is not firmly fixed above them and wait to see whether it won't burst open one day and bring about that reunification of stage and reality which is reflected for us in an image composed equally of memory and hope. Today, when the stage is bound by the text and the audience by bourgeois conventions, the gallery is the only part of the theatre which is open to true improvisation. It has entrenched itself at the outermost end of the auditorium and from the wood of the folding seats it builds its barricades.

The natural history of the gallery only reveals itself fully in the South. You have to have experienced the wild excitement of the bullfight, the foam on the waves of enthusiasm which splash up from the gallery towards the open horizon. I found traces if this in a music hall in Marseilles. There, right up above, at home nowhere else, surrounded by a thick fug of smoke, with girls, caps and drink, the harbour people had settled from the long evening voyage; faces confiscated from elsewhere and which would have looked better on any stage than in the auditorium. As they shouted, clapped and joined in the performance with encouraging remarks, over the heads of respectable citizens, it

186 • Scenes from Bourgeois Life

was as if the masquerade on the stage and the mummers in the gallery were conspiring to join forces against those in between, either by invading the stage from above or through a liberation of the entire auditorium by a stage full of eccentrics.[2]

Adorno composed this fantasia by combining a number of familiar tropes. The gallery itself, of course, which is the topic of this section of his text, almost invariably figures in theatre history and associated fictions as that part of the theatre in which a nonbourgeois class may be found enjoying a more exuberant and authentic experience than those in the stalls below. The enjoyment is expressed in their shouting, their clapping, and their joining in, all of which, happily, violate the decorous conventions of the bourgeoisie. The "fug" of their smoke suggests (in concert with his contemporary, Brecht) an audience whose judgment is valid precisely to the degree that it is also clouded (and closer, by definition, almost) to the sky, which the bourgeois theatre has domed over. The theatre they are enjoying (and which, the reader must presume, both is and is not the same performance as that savored by the bourgeoisie) is closer, in Adorno's account, to the bullfight's life-and-death confrontation between human and animal than it is to the well-regulated bourgeois theatre championed by Gotthold Ephraim Lessing and enjoyed (or not) by Adorno and his friends. The bullfight (a Southern European entertainment) still preserves, perhaps, something of Greek tragedy's mythical proximity to animal sacrifice, and the fantasy as a whole clearly owes much to the idea that, however upholstered and interior the bourgeois theatre of today may be, its origins (and thus its truth) is to be found in Greek theatres open to the blazing skies of the Mediterranean South. For this characteristic Hellenism is obviously also here a question of a Northern European's (German, English) fantasy about the South: not just the cradle of European civilization (and barbarity) but also the location for an easy life, great to visit despite (or rather because) of its proximity to so-called primitive pleasures (like bullfighting) not normally available in the North. Marseille plays its own special part in the specification of this particular fantasy: its "harbour people" might very well contain the kind of people who show up in port cities in the Mediterranean, arriving by sea (with or without trunks) from locations even further south, beyond the edge of Europe. It was in Marseille, too, that Adorno's friend Walter Benjamin's experiments with hashish took the bourgeois Berliner to an intoxicating experience at the very (social) edge of Europe: "a very advanced post, this harbor tavern . . . no bourgeois sat there."[3] That Adorno, Benjamin, and Brecht were all entertaining their own versions of this intoxicating anti-bourgeois Southern fantasy at around the same time suggests something of its appeal to the bourgeois intellectual Left of the time.[4]

If Addison's Trunk-Maker asks its readers to consider whether or not the bourgeois theatre can be appreciated (or not) by a "large black Man whom no body knows" (and whether it matters whether or not it can), Adorno's fantasy invites a similar set of questions. Might the appreciation of a non-bourgeois (smoky, Southern) audience for the theatre indicate the possibility of a (restored or future) theatre that would transcend the class divisions of bourgeois life? Adorno's text suggests a participatory theatre that is simultaneously the restoration of the theatre as it should be (and as it was before the bourgeoisie) and the transcendence of bourgeois norms in a future reconciliation of those who have been separated both by class and by the spectatorial organization of the theatre. In other words, it is a fantasy about the nature of theatre, one that stands in for and obscures other possible histories (such as the one suggested in the present book) in which the "natural" history of theatre is precisely a history of class (and racial) separation. It is a fantasy that allows its participants the luxury of avoiding the disturbing possibility that Trunk-Makers, once admitted in sufficient numbers, with their smokes and their drinks, to the bourgeois theatre, might turn out not to like it at all, and would end up using their sticks to knock it down, once and for all.

The love of Greece (the South, the Mediterranean) expressed by professors like Adorno is not without touristic aspects (even if the original Grand Tour, in which the future legislators of bourgeois Europe acquired their first-hand acquaintance with classical antiquity, rarely ventured beyond Naples). As Milo Rau and his colleagues found during their research visit to the Eastern Mediterranean as part of preparations for *Compassion*, today's tourism operates in shockingly close proximity to what has been called—recently, and misleadingly—Europe's "migrant crisis."[5] When he drowned, three-year-old Alan Kurdi, images of whose dead body circulated globally as a *memento mori* for global spectators of the "crisis," was traveling between Bodrum and Kos, both of which are popular destinations for tourists. So is the island of Lesvos, which received, according to the UN High Commission for Refugees, 57 percent of all refugee arrivals in Greece by sea in the "crisis" year of 2015.[6] Their presence on the island—for some spectators—momentarily col-

lapsed the distance that European economic and security policy had established between bourgeois consumption and the conditions of its production,
generating an unsettling mixture of anxiety and humanitarian warmth, as
demonstrated in this 2015 post to a TripAdvisor forum:

> We spent 2 weeks on the island [Lesvos] in June and were struck by
> the tragedy of people fleeing home and leaving all they know. The
> piles of life jackets on northern beaches make haunting holiday pho-
> tographs. When we were able to give food and water to families the
> gratitude and smiles, and the thank yous given in English, actually
> added a whole new level to an already wonderful break. Don't hesitate
> to travel to this and other front line refugee islands and in return don't
> hesitate to contact our representatives and demand that this country
> does more to help the impoverished Southern European countries
> deal with this problem.[7]

A theatre professor might be tempted to heap scorn on such responses
and might feel no need to explain why. There would be precious little
moral or political basis for doing so, however, as this tourist's expression of
feeling in response to "the tragedy" is no more or less than the communication of the spectatorial predicament that theatre professors have historically been disposed to cultivate, in themselves and in others (even as they
have learned and taught others to frame their responses in terms less vulnerable to political critique). To be able to move beyond this combination
of pity and critique, a theatre professor might want to think about packing
it in altogether and joining either an activist NGO, such as Sea-Watch, or
a revolutionary political organization.[8] But instead, the theatre professor
persists in going to the theatre.

Thomas Bellinck may feel that he is part of the same problem. He is not,
precisely, a theatre professor, but he is the next best thing. As he announces
at the beginning of his 2019 production, *Simple as ABC #3: The Wild Hunt*,
Bellinck is a "theatre director." Described as an "audio performance," this
work for theatre opens on a scene of spectatorship.[9] A man (who will turn
out to be Bellinck) sits with his back to the audience on one of those benches
to be found in front of paintings in museums. Rather than a painting, he appears to be contemplating an empty black screen hanging center stage. The
mise-en-scène also includes a display vitrine, into which Bellinck will soon

place his European Union passport; a two-faced classical bust that will turn out to represent Aristotle; a sculpture of a muzzled hunting dog; and a large oil painting, hanging at Bellinck's left as he gazes upstage. This all occupies the forestage. Further back, and partly obscured by a translucent scrim, the rest of the stage is visible, but appears to be in a state of preparation: it looks almost as though it is affording an accidental glimpse of what is necessary to make the production visible, but which should itself be invisible.

The theatre professor will eventually learn that the painting is Peter Nicolai Arbo's *The Wild Hunt of Odin* (1872). It shows an airborne phalanx of armed horsemen and horsewomen in the clouds above a twilit landscape and is understood to depict a European myth about a supernatural hunt of living humans. This, Bellinck explains, also describes a contemporary reality; for today, he says, humans are indeed hunted by other humans: dehumanized "migrants" and "refugees" are chased down and killed by armed agents of European states. Noting the ubiquity of "museums of hunting" in European cities (he has in mind what we more frequently call Museums of Natural History), he reveals that his project with this latest piece is to invite his mainly Afghan and Iraqi collaborators to imagine and describe paintings that could be included in a museum dedicated to the hunting of humans. The performance, then, after Bellinck's introductory remarks (which include a discussion of Aristotle's theorization of drama in relation to his political conceptions of human hierarchy), consists primarily in the recorded voices of these collaborators describing their imaginary paintings, and capturing thereby, for the audience—to whom, crucially, they are not, nor indeed, in many cases, cannot be, present—scenes and stories from the lives of people forced to abandon their homes. Transcriptions of their descriptions appear on the black screen.

This is not a merely expedient use of subtitles for translation to allow those spectators who understand neither Arabic nor Farsi to understand what is said. It is integral to the form of the work. Where spectators might expect to see, they must read, and thus start to consider the conditions under which it might be possible to see the scenes described; to think about how theatre manages the distance between those who speak, those who look, those who see, and those who are seen (or unseen). Here, people who cannot be seen, because they are not here, describe scenes that are not to be seen, other than in the imaginations of the people who *are* here, listening and reading. All the production's choices about what is seen and heard—which might be characterized together as its ekphrastic condition—gets in the way of at least some of theatre's spectatorial gratification, inviting (or nudging, perhaps) the audience to give up on spectatorship a little: to expect neither "haunting holiday photographs" nor the presence of Others appearing before them to give accounts of themselves.

Bellinck's *Wild Hunt*, then, is trying to work against one of the modern theatre's most familiar ethical and affective structures, in which the suffering of distant Others is presented, prolonged, and eventually ended in such a way that spectators may be able to convince themselves that, in witnessing this suffering, they have somehow contributed to bringing it to an end. This ethical pseudoactivity helps them forget their actual relation to the suffering displayed. Consider the structure in perhaps its purest and therefore most obviously toxic form: Thomas Bellamy's play, first performed under the title *The Friends* on August 5, 1789, at the Theatre Royal Haymarket in London (just weeks after the storming of the Bastille), and performed for the second and final time five days later at the same theatre under the title *The Benevolent Planters*.[10] The action, such as it is, is simple to the point of redundancy. The play begins as Jamaica plantation and slave owners, Goodwin and Heartfree, agree that, on the occasion of the island's annual "Jubilee," they will free Oran and Selima, a man and a woman they have enslaved, who had been lovers in Africa before they were enslaved. Rather than simply do so—which would of course altogether remove the need for the play—they arrange instead for Oran to participate in and win an archery competition (in which the victor will be granted his freedom), and for Selima to entertain them (and the audience at the Theatre Royal) with a song that expresses her sadness at her enslavement and her separation from Oran. This less than minimal plot is therefore simply a pretext for the construction of the ethical and affective situation in which spectators can simultaneously enjoy the suffering of others, admire their own and the planters' benevolence, and satisfy themselves that, in the light of this benevolence, there is no need for any structural change such as the abolition of slavery. Benevolence solicits blackface representations of sporting and musical labor, which solicits in turn a comfortable political complacency. Or, benevolence begets benevolence by way of the labor of the enslaved in the entertainment industry.

Thomas Bellinck (like Milo Rau, at least in *Compassion*) is trying to deal with the problem of working with a form and an institution in which this structure—even if it rarely appears in such pure and deadly form—still exerts a powerful attraction, for theatre makers and audiences alike. His predicament might be described like this: I want to contribute to some public thinking about the political problem of the "migrant crisis," but I work in theatre. The theatre tradition in which I work (in contemporary Europe) is particularly ill-suited to doing this because it lends itself so well to the presentation of suffering for the gratification of others. Do I therefore abandon theatre in order to make my political contribution—in other words, give up both the form and the public space my knowledge and expertise afford me? Or do I risk my political contribution being fatally compromised by the medium in which I am trying to make it? How, in the end, am I to avoid rewarding myself and the audience for our benevolence? Bellinck's solution, for now at least, is an action staged within his production. After a sequence in which, like the audience, he simply listens and looks as the audio-recorded ekphrases play, the theatre director, having done what he can—just enough, perhaps—to blow a little smoke into a few eyes, leaves the stage. The voices continue to do their work. The theatre professor sits in the dark, and then leaves. Later he, too, will wonder what to do.

Notes

1. Hayden White, "The Noble Savage Theme as Fetish," in *Tropics of Discourse: Essays in Cultural Criticism* (Baltimore and London: Johns Hopkins University Press, 1978), 183–96, at 194.

2. Theodor Adorno, "The Natural History of the Theatre," in *Quasi una Fantasia: Essays on Modern Music*, trans. Rodney Livingstone (London and New York: Verso, 1998), 65–78, at 67–68.

3. Walter Benjamin, "Hashish in Marseille," in *Reflections: Essays, Aphorisms, Autobiographical Writing*, ed. Peter Demetz (New York and London: Harcourt Brace Jovanovich, 1978), 137–45, at 139.

4. Cf. Bertolt Brecht, "Notes on the Opera [*Rise and Fall of the City of Mahagonny*]," in *Brecht on Theatre*, 3rd, rev. ed., ed. Marc Silberman, Steve Giles, and Tom Kuhn (London: Methuen, 2014), 61–71. All three writings appeared within three years: Adorno's "Natural History of the Theatre" (1931–33), Brecht's "Notes on the Opera" (1931), Benjamin's "Hashish in Marseille" (1932). Benjamin's "experiment" took place on June 29, 1931; he had been visiting Brecht in the nearby seaside village of Le Lavandou. See Stephen Parker, *Bertolt Brecht: A Literary Life* (London: Bloomsbury, 2015), 288–90. That summer, according to Stefan Müller-Doohm, Adorno led a seminar on aesthetics devoted to Benjamin's *Origins of the German Tragic Drama*, and "Natural History of the Theatre" is deliberately written in the style Benjamin used for *Origins*. Stefan Müller-Doohm, *Adorno: An Intellectual Biography*, trans. Rodney Livingstone (Cambridge: Polity Press, 2005), 145, 149.

5. Critics of this widely used term point out that it has at least two damaging consequences. The first is that the word "migrant" tends to help entrench a moralizing but

untenable (and immoral) distinction between refugees (who are understood to have left their homes as a result of war or other direct threats to their personal security) and migrants (who have supposedly left their homes in search of better chances to secure their livelihoods). For many critics this distinction is meaningless, not least because it fails to see that the economic "push and pull" factors are themselves the effect of an underlying economic violence to which the prosperity of the bourgeoisie has historically subjected millions of nonbourgeois subjects, especially (but not only) those living beyond the borders of the capitalist "core." The second is that the word "crisis" suggests that the events of 2015—in which the flows of people across the Mediterranean became a visible political issue for millions of European citizens and for their political leaders—were in some way exceptional, rather than part of an ongoing normality, produced and sustained by the economic and security policies of the capitalist "core," most notably by the states of the European Union. See, for example, Céline Cantat, "Rethinking Mobilities: Solidarity and Migrant Struggles beyond Narratives of Crisis," *Intersections: East European Journal of Society and Politics* 2, no. 4 (2016): 11–32; Michael Collyer and Russell King, "Narrating Europe's Migration and Refugee 'Crisis,'" *Human Geography: A New Radical Journal* 9, no. 2 (2016): 1–12.

6. United Nations High Commissioner for Refugees (UNHCR), "Lesvos Island— Greece, Factsheet," November 12, 2015; online at https://www.unhcr.org/uk/protection/operations/5645ddbc6/greece-factsheet-lesvos-island.html (accessed July 12, 2019).

7. Trip Advisor, post by antoninewall, "13. Re: Lesvos Greece—Refugee Crisis," August 10, 2015; online at https://www.tripadvisor.co.uk/ShowTopic-g189479-i1459-k8744537-o10-Lesvos_Greece_Refugee_Crisis-Lesbos_Northeast_Aegean_Islands.html#68622989 (accessed July 12, 2019). In the preceding paragraph of this forum posting, the author makes precisely the distinction between "refugee" and "migrant" that is the object of the critiques alluded to above, but without, it should be noted, any explicit moral hierarchy being established between them: "They are divided into young single men looking for a better life and families with young children fleeing a war."

8. "Sea-Watch e.V. is a non-profit organization ["eingetragener Verein"] that conducts civil search and rescue operations in the Central Med. In the presence of the humanitarian crisis, Sea-Watch provides emergency relief capacities, demands and pushes for rescue operations by the European institutions and stands up publicly for legal escape routes." Sea-Watch e.V., "Civil Sea Rescue of People in Flight"; online at https://sea-watch.org/en/ (accessed August 31, 2019). Sea-Watch's operations are the subject of recent video work by Forensic Oceanography, some of which was presented in the 2019 edition of Kunstenfestivaldesarts (KFDA) in Brussels, in a four-part video installation entitled *Liquid Violence*. Forensic Oceanography is part of Forensic Architecture: "a research agency, based at Goldsmiths, University of London. We undertake advanced spatial and media investigations into cases of human rights violations, with and on behalf of communities affected by political violence, human rights organisations, international prosecutors, environmental justice groups, and media organisations"; online at https://forensic-architecture.org/about/agency (accessed August 31, 2019). *Liquid Violence* was presented in the same edition of KFDA as Thomas Bellinck's *Simple as ABC #3: The Wild Hunt*, discussed below, as well as Milo Rau's *Orestes in Mosul*, a staging of Euripides' play created by NTGent (Netherlands Theater, Ghent) "with a mixed ensemble of European and Iraqi actors. The process includes research and activities in Mosul, where the Jihadi

caliphate of ISIS was declared in 2014"; NTGent, "Orestes in Mosul— Milo Rau," on-line at https://www.ntgent.be/en/productions/orestes-in-mosul (accessed July 11 2019). Rau is now artistic director of NTGent. Bellinck, who also works as a researcher in Ghent, will present *Simple as ABC #3: The Wild Hunt* at NTGent in January 2020. Bellinck and Rau, along with Olivia Rutazibwa, discussed their thinking about the "borders of Europe" in an interview with Wouter Hillaert, partially reprinted in the KFDA program, originally published in full as Wouter Hillaert, "De enige manier om Europa op te bouwen is het af te breken" [The only way to build Europe is to break it down], *Rekto:Verso 83* (2019), and online at https://www.rektoverso.be/artikel/de-enige-manier-om-europa-op-te-bouwen-is-het-af-te-breken (accessed August 18, 2019).

9. Thomas Bellinck / ROBIN, *Simple as ABC #3: The Wild Hunt*, online at https://www.kfda.be/en/program/simple-as-abc-3-the-wild-hunt (accessed August 31, 2019).

10. Thomas Bellamy, *The Benevolent Planters* (London: J. Debrett, 1789). The manuscript, originally entitled "Slavery But a Name," is item LA 839 in the John Larpent Plays collection at the Huntington Library, San Marino, California, which is where the theatre professor first encountered it.

Bibliography

Joseph Addison and Richard Steele. *The Spectator*. Edited by Donald F. Bond. 5 vols. Oxford: Clarendon Press, 1965.

Theodor Adorno, *Beethoven: The Philosophy of Music*. Translated by Edmund Jephcott. Cambridge: Polity Press, 1998.

Theodor Adorno. "The Natural History of the Theatre." In *Quasi una Fantasia: Essays on Modern Music*, translated by Rodney Livingstone, 65–78. London and New York: Verso, 1998.

Theodor Adorno, Walter Benjamin, Ernst Bloch, Bertolt Brecht, and Georg Lukács, with an Afterword by Fredric Jameson. *Aesthetics and Politics*. London: Verso, 1980.

Jean-Christophe Agnew. *Worlds Apart: The Market and the Theater in Anglo-American Thought, 1550–1750*. Cambridge: Cambridge University Press, 1986.

Louis Althusser. *Lenin and Philosophy and Other Essays*. Translated by Ben Brewster. New York: Monthly Review Press, 2001.

Perry Anderson. *Considerations on Western Marxism*. London: Verso, 1979.

Perry Anderson. "Origins of the Present Crisis." *New Left Review* 23, no. 1 (1964): 26–53.

Anon. *Great Newes from the Barbadoes; or, A True and Faithful Account of the Grand Conspiracy of the Negroes against the English, and the Happy Discovery of the Same*. London, 1676.

Matthew Arnold, ed., *The Six Chief Lives from Johnson's "Lives of the Poets."* London: Macmillan and Co., 1886.

T[revor] H[enry] Aston and C[harles] H. E. Philpin, eds. *The Brenner Debate: Agrarian Class Structure and Economic Development in Pre-industrial Europe*. Cambridge: Cambridge University Press, 1987.

Christopher B. Balme. *The Theatrical Public Sphere*. Cambridge: Cambridge University Press, 2014.

Francis Barker. *The Tremulous Private Body: Essays in Subjection*. London: Methuen, 1984.

Emily C. Bartels. "Too Many Blackamoors: Deportation, Discrimination, and Elizabeth I." *Studies in English Literature, 1500–1900* 46, no. 2 (2006): 305–22.

Ian Baucom. *Specters of the Atlantic: Finance Capital, Slavery, and the Philosophy of History*. Durham, NC: Duke University Press, 2005.

Martin Belam. "Glasgow University to Make Amends over Slavery Profits of Past." *The Guardian*, September 17, 2018. Online at https://www.theguardian.com/stage/2018/sep/09/bristol-old-vic-slave-trade-theatre-reopens-25m-facelift (accessed September 28, 2018).

Ian A. Bell. *Literature and Crime in Augustan England.* London and New York: Routledge, 1991.

Thomas Bellamy. *The Benevolent Planters.* London: J. Debrett, 1789.

Catherine Belsey. *The Subject of Tragedy: Identity and Difference in Renaissance Drama.* London: Methuen, 1985.

Walter Benjamin. "Hashish in Marseille." In *Reflections: Essays, Aphorisms, Autobiographical Writing,* edited by Peter Demetz, 137–45. New York and London: Harcourt Brace Jovanovich, 1978.

Lauren Berlant. *The Female Complaint: The Unfinished Business of Sentimentality in American Culture.* Durham, NC: Duke University Press, 2008.

Lauren Berlant. *The Queen of America Goes to Washington City.* Durham, NC: Duke University Press, 1997.

Walter Benjamin, "Paris, Capital of the Nineteenth Century," in *The Arcades Project.* Translated by Howard Eiland and Kevin McLaughlin. Cambridge, MA and London: The Belknap Press of Harvard University Press, 1999.

Robin Bernstein. *Racial Innocence: Performing American Childhood and Race from Slavery to Civil Rights.* New York: NYU Press, 2011.

"Births, Marriages, Deaths, Preferments, Promotions, and Bankrupts," *Universal Magazine of Knowledge and Pleasure.* Monthly periodical. London: John Hinton, 1750.

Richmond P. Bond. *Queen Anne's American Kings.* Oxford: Oxford University Press, 1952.

Edward Kamau Brathwaite. "Caliban, Ariel, and Unprospero in the Conflict of Creolization: A Study of the Slave Revolt in Jamaica in 1831–32." *Annals of the New York Academy of Sciences* 292, no. 1 (1977): 41–62.

Bertolt Brecht. *Brecht on Theatre.* Third, revised ed. Edited by Marc Silberman, Steve Giles, and Tom Kuhn. London: Methuen, 2014.

Bertolt Brecht. *Collected Poems.* Translated and edited by Tom Kuhn and David Constantine. New York: Liveright Publishing, 2018.

Bertolt Brecht, *Große kommentierte Berliner und Frankfurter Ausgabe, Band 26: Journale 1. [1913–1941: Tagebücher 1913–1922; Journale 1938–1941].* Frankfurt-am-Main: Suhrkamp Verlag, 1994.

Bertolt Brecht. *Schriften zum Theater.* 7 vols. Frankfurt-am-Main: Suhrkamp Verlag, 1963–4.

Robert Brenner. "Agrarian Class Structure and Economic Development in Pre-industrial Europe." *Past & Present* 70, no. 1 (1976): 30–75.

Robert Brenner. "The Origins of Capitalist Development: A Critique of Neo-Smithian Marxism." *New Left Review* 104, no. 1 (1977): 25–92.

John Brewer. *The Pleasures of the Imagination: English Culture in the Eighteenth Century.* New York: Farrar, Straus and Giroux, 1997.

John Brewer and Roy Porter, eds. *Consumption and the World of Goods.* Abingdon, UK: Routledge, 1993.

Daphne A. Brooks. *Bodies in Dissent: Spectacular Performances of Race and Freedom, 1850–1910.* Durham, NC: Duke University Press, 2006.

Paul Brown. "'This Thing of Darkness I Acknowledge Mine': *The Tempest* and the Discourse of Colonialism." In *Political Shakespeare: Essays in Cultural Materialism,* edited by Jonathan Dollimore and Alan Sinfield, 48–71. Manchester: Manchester University Press, 1985.

Susan Buck-Morss. "Hegel and Haiti." *Critical Inquiry* 26, no. 4 (2000): 821–65.

Susan Buck-Morss. *Hegel, Haiti, and Universal History.* Pittsburgh: University of Pittsburgh Press, 2009.

Judith Butler. *Gender Trouble: Feminism and the Subversion of Identity.* New York and London: Routledge, 1990.

George Gordon Byron. *The Life, Letters and Journals of Lord Byron.* Edited by Thomas Moore. London: John Murray, [1830] 1932.

Craig Calhoun, ed. *Habermas and the Public Sphere.* Cambridge, MA: MIT Press, 1992.

Joy H. Calico. *Brecht at the Opera.* Berkeley and Los Angeles: University of California Press, 2008.

Céline Cantat. "Rethinking Mobilities: Solidarity and Migrant Struggles beyond Narratives of Crisis." *Intersections: East European Journal of Society and Politics* 2, no. 4 (2016): 11–32.

Cesare Casarino and Antonio Negri. *In Praise of the Common: A Conversation of Philosophy and Politics.* Minneapolis: University of Minnesota Press, 2008.

Stanley Cavell. "The Avoidance of Love: A Reading of *King Lear*." In *Must We Mean What We Say? A Book of Essays,* 246–325. Updated edition. Cambridge: Cambridge University Press, 2015.

Dipesh Chakrabarty. *Provincializing Europe: Postcolonial Thought and Historical Difference.* Princeton and Oxford: Princeton University Press, 2008.

Kathleen Chater. *Untold Histories: Black People in England and Wales during the Period of the British Slave Trade, c. 1660–1807.* Manchester: Manchester University Press, 2009.

Michael Collyer and Russell King. "Narrating Europe's Migration and Refugee 'Crisis.'" *Human Geography: A New Radical Journal* 9, no. 2 (2016): 1–12.

Joseph Conrad. *Heart of Darkness.* New York: Penguin Books, 2012.

Glen Sean Coulthard. *Red Skin, White Masks: Rejecting the Colonial Politics of Recognition.* Minneapolis: University of Minnesota Press, 2014.

Brian Cowan. "Mr. Spectator and the Coffeehouse Public Sphere." *Eighteenth-Century Studies* 37, no. 3 (2004): 345–66.

David Dabydeen. *Hogarth's Blacks: Images of Blacks in Eighteenth Century English Art.* Manchester: Manchester University Press, 1987.

David Brion Davis. *The Problem of Slavery in the Age of Revolution, 1770–1823.* Oxford: Oxford University Press, 1999.

Lennard J. Davis. *Factual Fictions: The Origins of the English Novel.* Philadelphia: University of Pennsylvania Press, 1997.

Jacques Derrida. "Declarations of Independence." *New Political Science* 7, no. 1 (1986): 7–15.

Philip J. Deloria. *Playing Indian.* New Haven: Yale University Press, 1998.

Elizabeth Maddock Dillon. *The Gender of Freedom: Fictions of Liberalism and the Literary Public Sphere.* Stanford, CA: Stanford University Press, 2004.

Maurice Dobb. *Studies in the Development of Capitalism.* New York: International Publishers, 1947.

Jonathan Dollimore. *Radical Tragedy: Religion, Ideology and Power in the Drama of Shakespeare and His Contemporaries.* Brighton: Harvester, 1984.

Jonathan Dollimore and Alan Sinfield, eds. *Political Shakespeare: Essays in Cultural Materialism.* Manchester: Manchester University Press, 1985.

Terry Eagleton. *The Function of Criticism: From "The Spectator" to Post-structuralism.* London and New York: Verso, 1996.

Terry Eagleton. *The Ideology of the Aesthetic.* Oxford and Cambridge, MA: Blackwell.

Terry Eagleton. "The Subject of Literature." *Cultural Critique* 2 (1985–86): 95–104.

Peter Earle. *The Making of the English Middle Class: Business, Society, and Family Life in London, 1660–1730.* Berkeley and Los Angeles: University of California Press, 1989.

Barbara Ehrenreich and John Ehrenreich. "The Professional-Managerial Class." In *Between Labor and Capital,* edited by Pat Walker, 5–45. Boston: South End Press, 1979.

Dena J. Epstein. *Sinful Tunes and Spirituals: Black Folk Music to the Civil War.* Urbana and Chicago: University of Illinois Press, 1977.

Olaudah Equiano. *The Interesting Narrative of the Life of Olaudah Equiano, or Gustavus Vassa, the African.* 9th ed. London, 1794.

Peter Erickson and Kim F. Hall. "'A New Scholarly Song': Rereading Early Modern Race." *Shakespeare Quarterly* 67, no. 1 (2016): 1–13.

Frantz Fanon. *The Wretched of the Earth.* New York: Grove Press, 1964.

Silvia Federici. *Caliban and the Witch: Women, the Body and Primitive Accumulation.* New York: Autonomedia, 2004.

Henry Fielding. *The History of Tom Jones, a Foundling.* London: Vintage Books, 2007.

Henry Fielding. ["Uses to Which Learning Is Put."] *Covent Garden Journal,* January 21, 1752. Reprinted in Alexander Drawcansir [Henry Fielding]. *The Covent Garden Journal,* vol. 1, ed. Gerard Edward Jensen, 167–72. New Haven: Yale University Press, 1915. Also in *The Great Age of the English Essay: An Anthology.* Edited by Denise Gigante, 169–74. New Haven: Yale University Press, 2008.

Nicholas Foster. *A Briefe Relation of the Late Horrid Rebellion Acted in the Island Barbadas, in the West-Indies.* London, 1650.

Marcie Frank. *Gender, Theatre and the Origins of Criticism: From Dryden to Manley.* Cambridge: Cambridge University Press, 2002.

Nancy Fraser. "Rethinking the Public Sphere: A Contribution to the Critique of Actually Existing Democracy." *Social Text* 25–26 (1990): 56–80.

Michael Fried. *Art and Objecthood: Essays and Reviews.* Chicago and London: University of Chicago Press, 1998.

Peter Fryer, *Staying Power: Black People in Britain since 1504.* Atlantic Highlands, NJ: Humanities Press, 1984.

Catherine Gallagher. "The Rise of Fictionality." In *The Novel I: History, Geography and Culture,* edited by Franco Moretti, 336–63. Princeton: Princeton University Press, 2006.

C. H. George. "The Making of the English Bourgeoisie 1500–1750." *Science & Society* 35, no. 4 (1971): 385–414.

Gretchen Gerzina. *Black London: Life before Emancipation.* New Brunswick, NJ: Rutgers University Press, 1995.

Denise Gigante. "Sometimes a Stick Is Just a Stick: The Essay as (Organic) Form." *European Romantic Review* 21, no. 5 (2010): 553–65.

Simon Gikandi. *Slavery and the Culture of Taste.* Princeton and Oxford: Princeton University Press, 2011.

Paul Gilroy. *The Black Atlantic: Modernity and Double Consciousness.* Cambridge, MA: Harvard University Press, 1993.

Willi Goetschel. "Spinoza's Dream." *Cambridge Journal of Postcolonial Literary Inquiry* 3, no. 1 (2016): 39–54.

Stephen Greenblatt. *Renaissance Self-Fashioning: From More to Shakespeare*. Chicago: University of Chicago Press, 1980.

Neil Guthrie. "'No Truth or Very Little in the Whole Story'?: A Reassessment of the Mohock Scare of 1712." *Eighteenth-Century Life* 20, no. 2 (1996): 33–56.

Jürgen Habermas. *The Structural Transformation of the Public Sphere: An Inquiry into a Category of Bourgeois Society*. Translated by Thomas Burger (with Frederick Lawrence). Cambridge, MA: MIT Press, 1991.

Imtiaz Habib. *Black Lives in the English Archives, 1500–1677: Imprints of the Invisible*. London and New York: Routledge, 2016.

Kim F. Hall. "Reading What Isn't There: 'Black' Studies in Early Modern England." *Stanford Humanities Review* 3, no. 1 (1993): 23–33.

Jerome Handler. "Slave Revolts and Rebellions in Seventeenth-Century Barbados." *Nieuwe West-Indische Gids / New West Indian Guide* 56, no. 1–2 (1982): 5–42.

Michael Hardt and Antonio Negri. *Multitude: War and Democracy in the Age of Empire*. New York: Penguin, 2004.

Michael Hardt and Antonio Negri. *Commonwealth*. Cambridge, MA: Harvard University Press, 2009.

Saidiya V. Hartman. "The Position of the Unthought: An Interview with Saidiya V. Hartman." By Frank Wilderson III. *Qui Parle* 13, no. 2 (2003): 183–201.

Saidiya V. Hartman. *Scenes of Subjection: Terror, Slavery, and Self-Making in Nineteenth-Century America*. Oxford and New York: Oxford University Press, 1997.

David Harvey. *The Limits to Capital*. Oxford: Blackwell, 1982.

Michael Hays. *The Public and Performance: Essays in the History of French and German Theater 1871–1900*. Ann Arbor: UMI Research Press, 1981.

Ambrose Heal. *The Signboards of Old London Shops: A Review of the Shop Signs Employed by the London Tradesmen during the XVIIth and XVIIIth Centuries*. London: B. T. Batsford, 1947.

Henry Heller. *The Birth of Capitalism: A 21st-Century Perspective*. London: Pluto Press, 2011.

Geraldine Heng. "The Invention of Race in the European Middle Ages I: Race Studies, Modernity, and the Middle Ages." *Literature Compass* 8, no. 5 (2011): 315–31

Geraldine Heng. "The Invention of Race in the European Middle Ages II: Locations of Medieval Race." *Literature Compass* 8, no. 5 (2011): 332–50.

Dieter Hildebrandt, *Pianoforte: A Social History of the Piano*. Translated by Harriet Goodman. London: Hutchison, 1988.

Wouter Hillaert. "De enige manier om Europa op te bouwen is het af te breken." *Rekto:Verso 83* (2019). Online at https://www.rektoverso.be/artikel/de-enige-manier-om-europa-op-te-bouwen-is-het-af-te-breken (accessed July 11, 2019).

Rodney Hilton, ed. *The Transition from Feudalism to Capitalism*. London: Verso, 1978.

G. Hinchliffe. "Impressment of Seamen during the War of the Spanish Succession." *Mariner's Mirror* 53, no. 2 (1967): 137–42.

Eric Hinderaker. "The 'Four Indian Kings' and the Imaginative Construction of the First British Empire." *William and Mary Quarterly* 53, no. 3 (1996): 487–526.

Charles Hirschman. "The Origins and Decline of the Concept of Race." *Population and Development Review* 30, no. 3 (2004): 385–415.

Eric Hobsbawm. "The Crisis of the 17th Century II." *Past & Present* 6, no. 1 (1954): 44–65.

Eric Hobsbawm. "The General Crisis of the European Economy in the 17th Century." *Past & Present* 5, no. 1 (1954): 33–53.

Eric Hobsbawm. "The Seventeenth Century in the Development of Capitalism." *Science & Society* 24, no. 2 (1960): 97–112.

Stephen Howe, ed. *The New Imperial Histories Reader*. London: Routledge, 2010.

Phillippa Hubbard. "Trade Cards in 18th-Century Consumer Culture: Circulation, and Exchange in Commercial and Collecting Spaces." *Material Culture Review* 74–75 (2012): 30–46.

Nicholas Hudson. "'From Nation to Race': The Origin of Racial Classification in Eighteenth-Century Thought." *Eighteenth-Century Studies* 29, no. 3 (1996): 247–64.

Peter Hulme. *Colonial Encounters: Europe and the Native Caribbean, 1492–1797*. London: Methuen, 1986.

Fredric Jameson. *The Political Unconscious: Narrative as a Socially Symbolic Act*. Ithaca, NY: Cornell University Press, 1981.

Stuart Jeffries. *Grand Hotel Abyss: The Lives of the Frankfurt School*. London: Verso, 2016.

Samuel Johnson. *Lives of the Most Eminent English Poets, with Critical Observations on Their Works. A New Edition, Corrected*. 4 vols. London: C. Bathurst et al., 1783.

Owen Jones. "We're Not All Middle Class Now: Owen Jones on Class in Cameron's Britain." *New Statesman*, May 29, 2014. Online at https://www.newstatesman.com/culture/2014/05/we-re-not-all-middle-class-now-owen-jones-class-cameron-s-britain (accessed March 4, 2018, 2019).

Miranda Kaufmann. "Caspar van Senden, Sir Thomas Sherley and the 'Blackamoor' Project." *Historical Research* 81, no. 212 (2008): 366–71.

Lawrence E. Klein. "Addisonian Afterlives: Joseph Addison in Eighteenth-Century Culture." *Journal for Eighteenth-Century Studies* 35, no. 1 (2012): 101–18.

Jürgen Kocka. "The Middle Classes in Europe." *Journal of Modern History* 67, no. 4 (1995): 783–806.

Lisa Lampert. "Race, Periodicity and the (Neo-) Middle Ages." *Modern Languages Quarterly* 65, no. 3 (2004): 391–421.

Richard Ligon. *A True and Exact History of the Island of Barbadoes*. London, 1657.

Peter Linebaugh and Marcus Rediker. *The Many-Headed Hydra: Sailors, Slaves, Commoners, and the Hidden History of the Revolutionary Atlantic*. London and New York: Verso, 2012.

John Locke, *Two Treatises of Government*, edited by Peter Laslett, Cambridge: Cambridge University Press, 1960.

Ania Loomba. *Gender, Race, Renaissance Drama*. Manchester: Manchester University Press, 1989.

Domenico Losurdo. *Il marxismo occidentale: Come nacque, come morì, come può rinascere*. Bari and Rome: Laterza, 2017.

Michael Löwy. *Georg Lukács: From Romanticism to Bolshevism*. Translated by Patrick Camiller. London: New Left Books, 1979.

Georg Lukács. *History and Class Consciousness: Studies in Marxist Dialectics*. Translated by Rodney Livingstone. Cambridge, MA: MIT Press, 1972.

George Lukács and Lee Baxandall. "The Sociology of Modern Drama." *Tulane Drama Review* 9, no. 4 (1965): 146–70.

Thomas Babington Macaulay. *The Life and Writings of Addison*. London: Longman, Brown, Green and Longmans, 1852.

Erin Mackie. *Rakes, Highwaymen and Pirates: The Making of the Modern Gentleman in the Eighteenth Century*. Baltimore: Johns Hopkins University Press, 2009.

C. B. Macpherson. *The Political Theory of Possessive Individualism: Hobbes to Locke*. Oxford: Clarendon, 1962.

Karl Marx. *Capital: A Critique of Political Economy, Volume 1*. Translated by Ben Fowkes. Harmondsworth, UK: Penguin Books, 2004.

Karl Marx. *The Eighteenth Brumaire of Louis Bonaparte*. New York: International Publishers, 1963.

Karl Marx. "Theses on Feuerbach." In Karl Marx and Friedrich Engels, *The German Ideology: Part One, with Selections from Parts Two and Three*, edited by C. J. Arthur, 121–23. London: Lawrence and Wishart, 1970.

Karl Marx and Friedrich Engels. *The Communist Manifesto*. Translated by Samuel Moore. Harmondsworth, UK: Penguin Books, 1967.

Deirdre McCloskey, *Bourgeois Equality: How Ideas, Not Capital or Institutions, Enriched the World*. Chicago: University of Chicago Press, 2016.

Deirdre McCloskey. *The Bourgeois Virtues: Ethics for an Age of Commerce*. Chicago: University of Chicago Press, 2006.

Neil McKendrick. "Sir John Plumb" (obituary). *The Guardian*, October 22, 2001.

Neil McKendrick, John Brewer, and J. H. Plumb, *The Birth of a Consumer Society: The Commercialization of Eighteenth-Century England*. London: Hutchinson, 1982.

Herman Melville. *Correspondence*. Edited by Lynn Horth. Evanston, IL: Northwestern University Press, and Chicago: Newberry Library, 1993.

Maurice Merleau-Ponty. *Adventures of the Dialectic*. Transated by Joseph Bien. Evanston, IL: Northwestern University Press, 1973.

Nicholas Mirzoeff, *The Right to Look: A Counterhistory of Visuality*. Durham, NC: Duke University Press, 2011.

Catherine Molineux. *Faces of Perfect Ebony: Encountering Atlantic Slavery in Imperial Britain*. Cambridge, MA: Harvard University Press, 2012.

Warren Montag. *Bodies, Masses, Power: Spinoza and His Contemporaries*. London and New York: Verso, 1999.

Rosalind C. Morris. "*Ursprüngliche Akkumulation:* The Secret of an Originary Mistranslation." *Boundary 2* 43, no. 3 (2016): 29–77.

Fred Moten. *In the Break: The Aesthetics of the Black Radical Tradition*. Minneapolis: University of Minnesota Press, 2003.

Stephen Mullen and Simon Newman. *Slavery, Abolition and the University of Glasgow*. Glasgow: University of Glasgow, History of Slavery Steering Committee, 2018. Online at https://www.gla.ac.uk/media/media_607547_en.pdf (accessed September 28, 2018).

Stefan Müller-Doohm. *Adorno: An Intellectual Biography*. Translated by Rodney Livingstone. Cambridge: Polity Press, 2005.

Antonio Negri. *Savage Anomaly: The Power of Spinoza's Metaphysics and Politics*. Translated by Michael Hardt. Minneapolis and Oxford: University of Minnesota Press, 1991.

Carrie Noland. *Agency and Embodiment: Performing Gestures/Producing Culture*. Cambridge, MA: Harvard University Press, 2009.

Marcy Norton. *Sacred Gifts, Profane Pleasures: A History of Tobacco and Chocolate in the Atlantic World*. Ithaca, NY: Cornell University Press, 2008.

Felicity A. Nussbaum. *The Limits of the Human: Fictions of Anomaly, Race, and Gender in the Long Eighteenth Century*. Cambridge: Cambridge University Press, 2003.

Felicity A. Nussbaum. "The Theatre of Empire: Racial Counterfeit, Racial Realism." In *A New Imperial History: Culture, Identity and Modernity in Britain and the Empire, 1660–1840*, edited by Kathleen Wilson, 71–90. Cambridge: Cambridge University Press, 2004.

Sean O'Hagan. "A Radical Returns." *The Guardian*, April 3, 2005. Online at https://www.theguardian.com/artanddesign/2005/apr/03/art.art1 (accessed August 30, 2019).

Daniel O'Quinn. *Staging Governance: Theatrical Imperialism in London, 1770–1800*. Baltimore: Johns Hopkins University Press, 2005.

Fernando Ortiz. *Cuban Counterpoint: Tobacco and Sugar*. Translated by Harriet de Onís. Durham, NC: Duke University Press, 1995.

Stephen Parker. *Bertolt Brecht: A Literary Life*. London: Bloomsbury, 2015.

Patty Lee Parmalee. *Brecht's America*. Columbus: Ohio State University Press, for Miami [OH] University, 1981.

Carole Pateman. *The Sexual Contract*. Cambridge: Polity Press, 1988.

Orlando Patterson. *Slavery and Social Death*. Cambridge, MA: Harvard University Press, 1982.

Ronald Paulson, ed. *Hogarth's Graphic Works*. Third, revised edition. London: The Print Room, 1989.

Plato, *The Republic*. Translated by Desmond Lee. Second, revised edition. London: Penguin Books, 1987.

J. H. Plumb. *The Growth of Political Stability in England, 1675–1725*. London: Macmillan, 1967.

J. H. Plumb. *In the Light of History*. London: Allen Lane, 1972.

Anthony Pollock. "Neutering Addison and Steele: Aesthetic Failure and the Spectatorial Public Sphere." *ELH* 74, no. 3 (2007): 707–34.

Jacques Rancière. *The Emancipated Spectator*. Translated by Gregory Elliott. London and New York: Verso, 2009.

Richard Cullen Rath. *How Early America Sounded*. Ithaca, NY and London: Cornell University Press, 2003.

Roberto Fernandez Retamar, Lynn Garafola, David Arthur McMurray, and Robert Márquez. "Caliban: Notes towards a Discussion of Our Culture in America." *Massachusetts Review* 15, no. 1–2 (1974): 7–72.

Robbie Richardson, *The Savage and Modern Self: North American Indians in Eighteenth-Century British Literature and Culture*. Toronto: University of Toronto Press, 2018.

Nicholas Ridout. *Stage Fright, Animals and Other Theatrical Problems*. Cambridge: Cambridge University Press, 2006.

Joseph Roach. *Cities of the Dead: Circum-Atlantic Performance*. New York: Columbia University Press, 1996.

Joseph Roach. "Theatre History and the Ideology of the Aesthetic." *Theatre Journal* 41, no. 2 (1989): 155–68.

Cedric J. Robinson. *Black Marxism: The Making of the Black Radical Tradition*. Chapel Hill: University of North Carolina Press, 2000.

Nicholas Rogers. "Money, Land and Lineage: The Big Bourgeoisie of Hanoverian London." *Social History* 4, no. 3 (1979): 437–54.

Marvin Rosen. "The Dictatorship of the Bourgeoisie: England, 1688–1721." *Science & Society* 45, no. 1 (1981): 24–51.

Ignatius Sancho. *Letters of the Late Ignatius Sancho, an African. To Which Are Prefixed, Memoirs of His Life.* London: J. Nichols, for C. Dilly, 1784.

Salvatore Settis. *The Future of the "Classical."* Translated by Allan Cameron. Cambridge: Polity Press, 2006.

Jared Sexton. "The Social Life of Social Death: On Afro-Pessimism and Black Optimism." *InTensions* 5 (2011): 1–47. Online at http://www.yorku.ca/intent/issue5/articles/jaredsexton.php (accessed August 18, 2019).

Audra Simpson. *Mohawk Interruptus: Political Life across the Borders of Settler States.* Durham, NC: Duke University Press, 2014.

Alan Sinfield. "Give an account of Shakespeare and Education, showing why you think they are effective and what you have appreciated about them. Support your comments with precise references." In *Political Shakespeare: Essays in Cultural Materialism,* edited by Jonathan Dollimore and Alan Sinfield, 158–81. Manchester: Manchester University Press, 1985.

Eleanor Skimin. "Reproducing the White Bourgeois: The Sitting Room Drama of Marina Abramović." *TDR/The Drama Review* 62, no. 1 (2018): 79–97.

Hans Sloane. *A Voyage to the Islands Madera, Barbados, Nieves, S. Christophers and Jamaica.* London: J.Newbery, 1707.

Christopher Smart. *The Horatian Canons of Friendship.* London, 1750.

Adam Smith. *An Inquiry into the Nature and Causes of the Wealth of Nations.* 2 vols. Edited by Edwin Cannan. Chicago: University of Chicago Press, 1977.

Peter Smithers. *The Life of Joseph Addison.* Second edition. Oxford: Clarendon, 1968.

Alfred Sohn-Rethel. *Intellectual and Manual Labour: A Critique of Epistemology.* Translated by Martin Sohn-Rethel. London: Macmillan, 1978.

Hortense J. Spillers. *Black, White and in Color: Essays on American Literature and Culture.* Chicago: University of Chicago Press, 2003.

Baruch Spinoza. *The Letters.* Translated by Samuel Shirley. Indianapolis and Cambridge: Hackett, 1995.

Daniel Statt. "The Case of the Mohocks: Rake Violence in Augustan London." *Social History* 20, no. 2 (1995): 179–99.

Richard Steele and Joseph Addison. *The Spectator.* Edited by Donald F. Bond. 5 vols. Oxford: Clarendon Press, 1987.

Lawrence Stone. "The Bourgeois Revolution of Seventeenth-Century England Revisited." *Past & Present* 109, no. 1 (1985): 44–54.

Paul M. Sweezy and Maurice Dobb. "The Transition from Feudalism to Capitalism." *Science & Society* 14, no. 2 (1950): 134–67.

Rei Terada. *Looking Away: Phenomenality and Dissatisfaction, Kant to Adorno.* Cambridge, MA: Harvard University Press, 2009.

E. P. Thompson. "Eighteenth-Century English Society: Class Struggle without Class?" *Social History* 3, no. 2 (1978): 133–65.

E. P. Thompson. *The Making of the English Working Class.* London: Victor Gollancz, 1963.

E. P. Thompson. "Patrician Society, Plebeian Culture." *Journal of Social History* 7, no. 4 (1974): 382–405.

E. P. Thompson. "The Peculiarities of the English." *Socialist Register* 2, 1965): 311–62.

Vanessa Thorpe. "New Life for Historic Theatre as It Faces Up to 'Slave Trade' Past." *The Observer*, September 9, 2018. Online at https://www.theguardian.com/stage/2018/sep/09/bristol-old-vic-slave-trade-theatre-reopens-25m-facelift (accessed September 28, 2018).

Coll Thrush. *Indigenous London: Native Travelers at the Heart of Empire*. New Haven: Yale University Press, 2016.

Kyla Wazana Tompkins. *Racial Indigestion: Eating Bodies in the Nineteenth Century*. New York: NYU Press, 2012.

Zacharias Conrad von Uffenbach. *London in 1710: From the Travels of Zacharias Conrad von Uffenbach*. Translated and edited by W. H. Quarrell and Margaret Mare. London: Faber and Faber, 1934.

Bryan Wagner. *Disturbing the Peace: Black Culture and the Police Power after Slavery*. Cambridge, MA: Harvard University Press, 2009.

Dror Wahrman. *Imagining the Middle Class: The Political Representation of Class in Britain, c. 1780–1840*. Cambridge: Cambridge University Press, 1995.

Dror Wahrman. *The Making of the Modern Self: Identity and Culture in Eighteenth-Century England*. New Haven: Yale University Press, 2004.

Immanuel Wallerstein. "The Bourgeois(ie) as Concept and Reality." *New Left Review* 167, no. 1 (1988): 91–106.

Michael Warner. *Publics and Counterpublics*. New York: Zone Books, 2002.

Jace Weaver. *Red Atlantic: American Indigenes and the Making of the Modern World, 1000–1927*. Chapel Hill: University of North Carolina Press, 2014.

Max Weber. *The Protestant Ethic and the Spirit of Capitalism*. Translated by Talcott Parsons. Mineola, NY: Dover Publications, 2003.

Emily Weissbourd. "'Those in Their Possession': Race, Slavery, and Queen Elizabeth's 'Edicts of Expulsion.'" *Huntington Library Quarterly* 78, no. 1 (2015): 1–19.

Roxann Wheeler. *The Complexion of Race: Categories of Difference in Eighteenth-Century British Culture*. Philadelphia: University of Pennsylvania Press, 2000.

Hayden White. "The Noble Savage Theme as Fetish." In *Tropics of Discourse: Essays in Cultural Criticism*. Baltimore and London: Johns Hopkins University Press, 1978.

Jonathan White. "A World of Goods? The 'Consumption Turn' and Eighteenth-Century British History." *Cultural and Social History* 3, no. 1 (2006): 93–104.

Frank Wilderson III. "Gramsci's Black Marx: Whither the Slave in Civil Society?" *Social Identities* 9, no. 2 (2003): 225–40.

Raymond Williams. *The Country and the City*. New York: Oxford University Press, 1973.

Raymond Williams. *The Sociology of Culture*. New York: Schocken Books, 1982.

Kathleen Wilson, ed. *A New Imperial History: Culture, Identity and Modernity in Britain and the Empire, 1660–1840*. Cambridge: Cambridge University Press, 2004.

Kathleen Wilson. "The Performance of Freedom: Maroons and the Colonial Order in Eighteenth-Century Jamaica and the Atlantic Sound." *William and Mary Quarterly* 66, no. 1 (2009): 45–86.

Ellen Meiksins Wood. *The Origin of Capitalism: A Longer View*. London and New York: Verso, 2002.

Ellen Meiksins Wood. *The Pristine Culture of Capitalism: A Historical Essay on Old Regimes and Modern States*. London and New York: Verso, 1991.

Ellen Meiksins Wood and Neal Wood. *Class Ideology and Ancient Political Theory: Socrates, Plato, and Aristotle in Social Context*. Oxford: Blackwell, 1978.

Neal Wood. *John Locke and Agrarian Capitalism*. Berkeley and Los Angeles: University of California Press, 1984.

Neal Wood. *The Politics of John Locke's Philosophy: A Social Study of "An Essay Concerning Human Understanding."* Berkeley and Los Angeles: University of California Press, 1983.

Judith Woods. "We're All Middle Class Now, Darling." *The Telegraph,* January 22, 2010.

Anne Wootton. "Campbell Introduces First-Years to Slavery and Justice Committee." *Brown Daily Herald,* October 23, 2006. Online at http://www.browndailyherald.com/2006/10/23/campbell-introduces-firstyears-to-slavery-and-justice-committee/ (accessed September 28, 2018).

Anne Wootton. "In Colonial Rhode Island, Slavery Played Pivotal Role." *Brown Daily Herald,* October 17, 2006. Online at http://www.browndailyherald.com/2006/10/17/in-colonial-rhode-island-slavery-played-pivotal-role/ (accessed September 28, 2018).

Anne Wootton. "Slavery & Justice Report to Be Released Today." *Brown Daily Herald,* October 23, 2006. Online at http://www.browndailyherald.com/2006/10/23/slavery-justice-report-to-be-released-today/ (accessed September 28, 2018).

Index

Foucault, Michel, 71
Frank, Marcie, 83
Fraser, Nancy, 81
Fried, Michael, 11

Gay, John, 126, 134, 148
gender, 41, 45, 46, 69, 86–88, 154
Gikandi, Simon, 122
"Glorious Revolution," 23–26, 75
Gramsci, Antonio, 151, 152

Habermas, Jürgen, 79–81, 83–84
Habib, Imtiaz. 117, 119
Harrington, James, 41
Hartman, Saidiya, 70, 155
Harvey, David, 34, 43
Hays, Michael, 69–70, 71
Hegel, Georg Friedrich Wilhelm, 48,
    156–57
Hobbes, Thomas, 41, 139
Hogarth, William, 105–108, 122
Horkheimer, Max, 151
Hubbard, Phillippa, 105

Ibsen, Henrik, 3, 12, 32
ideology, 33, 69–73
"Indians" and "Indian Kings," 77, 126–37,
    162
Ireland (Northern), 13

Jamaica, 39, 76, 87, 120, 121, 122, 190
Johnson, Boris, 4
Johnson, Samuel, 66–67, 111
Jonson, Ben, 89

Kant, Immanuel, 41, 48
Kocka, Jürgen, 78

labor, laborers, 28, 33, 35, 37–39, 42, 44,
    46, 52, 53, 65, 76, 80, 86, 87, 104, 115,
    117, 119, 122, 125, 129, 137, 155–57, 173,
    190
Lardi, Ursina, 14–20
leisure, 44, 61, 64, 65, 76, 91, 94, 101, 121,
    125,131, 156, 158, 168, 173, 174
Ligon, Richard, 76–77, 122
literature, 44, 62, 68–73, 85, 106–9

Locke, John, 41–45, 59, 65, 139
London(ers), 3, 5, 8, 13, 40, 58–60, 62, 64,
    76–78, 81, 82, 85, 104, 105, 107, 108,
    110–14, 116, 117, 119, 120–22, 124–27,
    129–32, 134–37, 139, 155, 190
Lukács, György, 70, 151–53, 167, 168
    History and Class Consciousness, 48–51,
    150

Macaulay, Thomas Babington, 2, 3, 66–68
Macpherson, C.B., 41, 44
Marcuse, Herbert, 151
Marx, Eleanor, 3
Marx, Karl, 3, 31–37, 42, 43, 44, 45, 52, 75,
    91, 93, 156, 157, 178
    Capital, 25, 36, 35–37, 49, 51
Marx, Karl and Friedrich Engels, *Commu-
    nist Manifesto*, 25–30
Marxism, 45, 50, 150–57, 158, 162–64
Marxism (Western), 150–57
media, 8–11, 13, 18, 20, 48, 60, 61, 90, 94,
    105, 116, 126, 127, 132, 133, 185
Melville, Herman, 108
Merleau-Ponty, Maurice, 151–52
middle class, 27, 31, 77–78
Middleton, Thomas, 89
migrant / immigrant, 16, 18, 116, 161, 187–
    89
"Mohocks," 77, 126–27, 132–34, 135–37
money, 31, 35, 43, 44, 51, 60, 88, 172, 185
Montag, Warren, 138–40
Morris, Rosalind, 33–34

Negri, Antonio, 138–139
newspaper(s), 4, 5, 76, 78–80, 82, 86
Noland, Carrie, 72–73, 89
Norton, Marcy, 171

O'Neill, Eugene, 4
onstage, 6, 9–12, 15, 17–19, 53, 70, 128, 148

parents, 15, 24, 38, 149
Parmalee, Patty Lee, 162–63
Pateman, Carole *The Sexual Contract*, 45,
    46, 47, 86, 87
Patterson, Orlando, 124
photograph, 16–18, 188, 190